D1483076

Special Education: Past, Present and Future

Special Education:
Past, Present and Future

Edited by Peter Evans and Ved Varma

The Falmer Press
(A Member of the Taylor & Francis Group)
London · New York · Philadelphia

UK The Falmer Press, Rankine Road, Basingstoke, Hampshire RG24 0PR

USA The Falmer Press, Taylor & Francis Inc., 1900 Frost Road, Suite 101, Bristol PA 19007

First published 1990

British Library Cataloguing in Publication Data
Special education: past, present and future.
1. Great Britain, Special education
I. Evans, Peter, II. Varma, Ved P. (Ved Prakash),
371.9′0941
ISBN 1-85000-464-1
ISBN 1-85000-465-X pbk

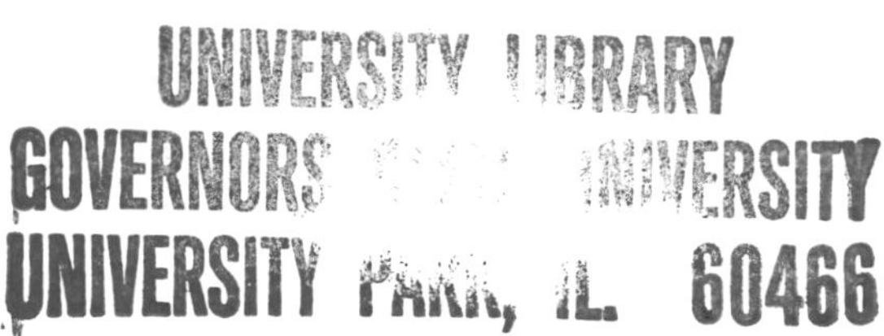

Jacket design by Caroline Archer

Typeset in 10½/13 point Bembo by
Bramley Typesetting Limited, 12 Campbell Court, Bramley, Basingstoke, Hants.

Printed and bound in Great Britain by
Redwood Press Limited, Melksham, Wiltshire

Contents

Foreword

Special Education: Past, Present and Future is a *festschrift* for Maurice Chazan and Phillip Williams, both of whom, as witnessed by the first two chapters of this book, have made a substantial contribution to the field of special education. All too often such individuals remain known only through their publications; while a work such as this one cannot redress that imbalance in any significant way, it can help to provide some insight into the creative energy that goes on behind the scenes that develops our understanding of a field such as special education and influences educational practices and government policy.

While this book was being planned, substantial changes were taking place in education law. It seemed an appropriate time to take stock of the situation and some of the implications of these changes for special education within an historical perspective. The chapters by Wedell, Norwich, Galloway and Fish provide perspectives on some of the administrative aspects of special education. The remainder of the book addresses specific categories of disability. It may be argued that this approach reflects an outmoded view approaching special educational needs. Perhaps a word or two is in order on this point.

It is our view that some children who experience difficulties in learning have them as a result of individually acquired biological problems. Children with sensory and physical disabilities immediately spring to mind. This does not apply to all children requiring special education provision who come to the attention of the authorities, but it does apply to many. It is also true that, as the situation exists at present, many of these children require special teaching methods and equipment that have been developed in various countries and which have proved to be effective in helping children gain full access to the curriculum. It seems to us that it does no good at all to deny these points; in fact to do so may well be counter-productive.

What we need to do is build on this knowledge and to share it more liberally and effectively. We all have to learn to be much more sensitive to children's multiple learning needs. To do this we must know as much as possible about the various approaches that have been tried and the resulting problems that have been encountered across the whole range of learning difficulty.

What we must *not* do is assume that a greater 'awareness' of the problems that many children can experience will necessarily lead to effective solutions in our schools. Awareness will certainly help, but it is not *the* single answer. It is necessary to acquire the skills to teach children with special educational needs. This is not easy, especially as many of the teaching skills involved are rarefied indeed.

We have learned that many children's learning needs are more extensive than can be reflected in a single label, and that educational placement decisions must not stem from oversimplified assumptions or from administrative convenience only. We must not throw out the baby with the bath water. Much good work has been done. We must now integrate that knowledge and those skills within ourselves. Before this is achieved we cannot hope to have effective integrative practice.

It is with these thoughts in mind that this book has been compiled.

Peter Evans
Ved Varma

Christmas 1989

Chapter 1

An Appreciation of the Work of Professor Maurice Chazan

Alice Laing

It is difficult to write an appreciation of Maurice Chazan's work without sounding overly effusive. His contribution to Special Education has been wide-ranging and profound and his lasting influence on his colleagues and his students reflects his power as a professional. All his work for those with special educational needs shows his personal integrity and determination. Nothing has ever been skimped.

A double Honours degree in classics is not perhaps the conventional mode of entry into Special Education. George Seth, then lecturing in Child Development on the teacher training course in Cardiff, was the first of a number of outstanding academics and practitioners who caused this change of direction into the field of Educational Psychology. Others were Valentine, Schonell and Wall, who were involved in the MA course in Education at Birmingham University which he undertook part-time while teaching in Birmingham. A full-time training year as an educational psychologist followed, a rather unique training inasmuch as it took place in the Department of Psychological Medicine of Guy's Hospital, London; this course was supported by the National Association of Mental Health (now MIND). However, as already indicated, Maurice Chazan is certainly thorough and, although appointed to an educational psychologist's post in Liverpool in 1950, he proceeded over the next few years to take a University of London external BA in Psychology.

This somewhat circuitous route led to his appointment in 1960 as lecturer in the Department of Education at University College of Swansea, where he became a senior lecturer in 1964, a reader in 1971 and was appointed to a personal chair in Education in 1976, retiring in 1985. Lest this bare listing of progress up the academic ladder may seem to imply a cosseted existence devoted to research, it has to be said that teaching always featured largely throughout his time in Swansea and on several occasions he undertook the leadership of the Department, the last occasion being during the seven years prior to his retirement when administration and organization were very difficult indeed. What is remarkable is how much research and writing he contrived to carry out despite the heavy demands on his time which his commitment to the Department entailed. His colleagues in Swansea certainly appreciate what he has done for them.

It is appropriate, however, that in a publication of this kind most attention should be given to the contribution which Maurice Chazan has made – and is still making – to the field of Special Education. Clearly, research has been a major interest throughout, particularly in three areas: emotional and behavioural difficulties; compensatory education; and special education needs in the early years. All have in common a concern with practical implications for the teachers and parents involved and all have led to publications of lasting merit.

Emotional and behavioural difficulties in children and adolescents have been a major interest with him since 1950, beginning with a joint medical and psychological study of children with congenital heart disease carried out at Guy's Hospital (1951), moving on to the adjustment problems of a group of grammar school pupils in Liverpool (1959) and coming to centre on the behavioural implications of learning difficulties in children and the learning implications of emotional difficulties (1962a; 1965; 1966; 1968a; 1978a; 1982a: 1985). This series of publications and other very useful research reviews on trends in post-war theory and practice with regard to maladjustment (1963; 1974a), on the effectiveness of remedial teaching of reading (1967a) and on maladjustment and reading difficulties (1969a), reveal the breadth of his concern. His writings cover school phobia (1962b), inconsequential behaviour (1968b), autism (1973a) and aggression (1986a). Every stage and type of educational provision has been considered: the early years (1978b; 1979a; 1980; 1982b; 1983a); infant schools (1971a; 1974b; 1984; 1987a); junior schools (1972; 1987b); secondary schools (1959; 1966); and special schools (1964a and b; 1967b).

There is throughout Maurice Chazan's work an emphasis on the early identification and assessment of special educational needs and on programme planning subsequent to these activities (1976a). In noting and charting pupils' behaviour difficulties, he has considered what teachers (1961; 1974c), parents (1973b; 1978c) and educational psychologists (1970a; 1974d; 1976b; 1978d; 1979b; 1988) can contribute, both separately and working together. He has always argued for an holistic approach to understanding individual development, as he has always been acutely aware of the interactional complexity which leads children to behave as they do. In the same way, he has always seen assessment without the attendant development of programmes to help the situation as a wasted opportunity. Several publications are, therefore, specifically aimed to help teachers develop such programmes, on their own as far as is appropriate and in conjunction with other professionals (1973c; 1983b and c).

The handbook intended to help teachers of young children cope with behaviour difficulties in the classroom (1983b) is a good example of Maurice Chazan's work in this area of interest. It is a joint publication with several authors contributing and it is largely because of his editing skills that differences in style and approach have been smoothed out. The book itself deals, in the first section, with recognizing and understanding behaviour difficulties, all the necessary schedules to help teachers being presented in the Appendices. Parents and other professionals are clearly involved right from the start. The second section aims to help teachers decide on what action to take. The approach is not prescriptive but rather presents the information necessary for the teachers themselves to make up their own minds: '. . . our main aim has been to provide nursery staff with material that will be of practical use and will encourage them to think positively and constructively about ways of handling children with behaviour problems'. This has always been Maurice Chazan's philosophy and it has kept him from pursuing any one approach to tackling emotional and behaviour difficulties at the expense of others. Eclecticism is not always a bad policy; it is highly appropriate to the flexible and responsive approach which children with behaviour difficulties need.

Compensatory education was very much under scrutiny in the 1960s and 1970s and a large-scale research project, funded by the DES, was centred in Swansea under the direction of Maurice Chazan and Phillip Williams. Their work aimed to examine the nature and effect of disadvantage in children at the infant school stage (1968c; 1969b; 1971b and c; 1973d and e; 1978e; 1979c and d). Maurice Chazan was particularly interested in how a disadvantaged home background might affect children's response to schooling, with regard to both attainment and behaviour. Thus, he became particularly concerned with children's pre-school environment (1970b; 1971d), their language development (1976c; 1982c) and the extent to which their behaviour changed over the early years at school (1978f).

As well as the publications already noted, two major volumes (1976d; 1977) present the findings in the areas for which Maurice Chazan assumed responsibility. The sheer bulk of the information presented in these makes it difficult to summarize the findings here but, throughout, the same philosophy of concern for children's strengths as well as their weaknesses, of regard for parents and how help might best be offered to them, of practical advice to teachers and of the involvement of other professionals to the benefit of children's educational progress can be found. His argument is of the persistence of behaviour problems over the infant school years, 42.5 per cent of children rated as 'poorly adjusted' on fairly strict criteria on entry to the infant school still showing behaviour problems two years later (1974b). The implications of these findings led him both to devising the handbook for nursery staff already mentioned and to research in the area of the pre-school which is the third major aspect of his work to be discussed here.

As is already obvious, the 1970s were particularly productive years both for research and for publications. International recognition led, amongst other commitments, to publications on work in cognate areas abroad (1973f; 1978g). At home, one research project appraising how satisfactory and acceptable to parents was the provision made nationally for identifying, and advising on, special needs in the very early years led to specific recommendations being made on these points in the Warnock Report (DES, 1978). A second project (1980) investigated where young children with special educational needs were to be found immediately prior to formal school entry — in mainstream nursery schools/classes, special units, playgroups or at home. It has to be said that the current situation seems little different in many respects from what was found then. Considerable goodwill towards young children with special needs does not necessarily crystallize into practical opportunities for integrated education. Furthermore, it was disappointing to find in 1980 that some of the shortfall between what might have been and what actually was being offered had been pointed out in 1961 (Caplan). It is doubtful, indeed, whether any real progress has been made since the 1970s in coordinating services for parents, in providing pre-school placements on the basis of need rather than of availability or local policy, and in supporting the staff working with young children who require special provision. The last chapter of the 1980 publication was headed 'The changing outlook' and made a number of suggestions which can be set alongside other current research findings.

> No one can deny that there is a very strong case indeed for making parents active participants with other professionals in the early development of their handicapped child (1980).
>
> Many LEAS are reluctant to spell out (to parents) their duties over assessing and providing for special needs: only 46 per cent refer to the duty to secure provision; only 26 per cent refer to the need to keep provision under review; only 11 per cent refer to the duty to integrate children with special needs into ordinary schools (Rogers, 1986).
> Parents need, first of all, to understand the nature of the handicap . . . Parents need to be guided towards an educative role so that opportunities for the child to progress in his development are not missed (1980).
>
> Parents value those who are seen as actively helping their child with

> educational difficulties, but the relationship between assessment and help is only vaguely comprehended (Sandow *et al.*, 1987).

Apart from a reluctance to use 'handicapped' and 'his', changes would seem to have been minimal in these respects since 1980.

Maurice Chazan's contribution to child development has not been confined solely to the area of special education. He has edited books on reading readiness (1970c) and early education (1973g), looked at the evaluation of pre-school programmes (1975) and is co-author of a general text on aspects of development in children between the ages of five and eight years (1987a), a book again aimed specifically at helping practising teachers. His interests, however, remain focused on emotional development, language acquisition and the role of the educational psychologist, as well as of the parents, in helping children's development.

His professionalism is reflected in his involvement over many years with the training of educational psychologists. He not only wrote on developments in such training in 1971e, and in 1974d along with Philip Williams, Terence Moore and Jack Wright, but he was also concerned with the setting up by the British Psychological Society, post-Summerfield, of a diploma in Educational Psychology for which he was an examiner for a period. In this respect, too, many trainee psychologists in Swansea have benefited greatly from both his academic knowledge and his practical understanding of children as he has always contributed to the training course there. He also established the advanced training courses for teachers involved in special educational provision, which have been over the years an important element in the Department at Swansea (1962c; 1968d).

Anyone with Maurice Chazan's expertise is inevitably going to find himself on many committees. Over the years, he has been on the Educational Research Board of the Social Science Research Council, the United Kingdom National Commission for UNESCO Education Advisory Committee, various DES advisory committees and the Special Education Panel of the CNAA. Currently, he serves on the BPS Fellowships Committee and has recently been appointed to the All Wales Advisory Panel on the Development of Services for People with Mental Handicaps. He has considerable international standing, having spent time in America, Norway, Italy and Australia lecturing on special education and early education. He was a member of a Council of Europe working party on the evaluation of pre-school education; currently, he serves on the Board of Directors of the International Council of Psychologists and is a member of the International Study Group on Special Education. Nearer home, he remains a staunch supporter of what is now the National Council for Special Education, having in the past led its research committee for several years.

No one can deny the extent and the quality of his contribution to special education. Those who do not know him well may find his obvious scholarship and competence somewhat formidable on first acquaintance. Those who are fortunate enough to know him better, soon come to appreciate the sense of fun and the capacity for genuine friendship which he possesses. People are always asking for news of him, a sure sign of something more than respect, although respect there is in plenty.

His contribution has not stopped with his retirement. A small-scale but interesting research study has looked at teachers' strategies in coping with emotional and behavioural difficulties in the classroom at the point of transition from the infant to the junior school stage (1986b; 1987b), a study firmly based on the teachers' own views and showing sensitivity towards their situation as well as indicating growth points for developing alternative strategies if these are required. He has also recently completed research in a rather different aspect of special education — a survey, for the Welsh Office, of leavers from schools in Wales for pupils with severe learning difficulties, focusing on provision and placement. He is still signing contracts for the next book — and the next!

He once told me that his first commercially successful venture into writing was when he was awarded a prize of one pre-decimalization penny for a story written in the infant school. Someone had a good eye for emerging talent — *ex parvo multum*!

References

1. Maurice Chazan's work

'The intellectual and emotional development of children with congenital heart disease' (with others), *Guy's Hospital Reports*, 100, 4, pp. 331–42, 1951.

'Maladjusted children in grammar schools', *Brit. J. Educ. Psychol.*, 29, pp. 198–206, 1959.

'The importance of "seven-plus" in the prevention and treatment of educational backwardness', *Forward Trends*, 6, 1, pp. 27–30, 1961.

'The relationship between maladjustment and backwardness', *Educational Review*, 15, 1, pp. 54–62, 1962a.

'School Phobia', *Brit. J. Educ. Psychol.*, 32, pp. 209–17, 1962b.

'The training of teachers of backward children', *Forward Trends*, International Conference Edition, pp. 65–70, 1962c.

'Maladjusted pupils: trends in post-war theory and practice', *Educ. Res.*, VI, pp. 29–41, 1963.

An enquiry into maladjustment among children in special school for the educationally subnormal, Report of 27th Biennial Conference of the Association for Special Education, pp. 37–43, 1964a.

'The incidence and nature of maladjustment among children in schools for the educationally subnormal', *Brit. J. Educ. Psychol.*, 34, pp. 292–304, 1964b.

'Factors associated with maladjustment in educationally subnormal children', *Brit. J. Educ. Psychol.*, 35, pp. 277–85, 1965.

'Teaching maladjusted children', *Univ. Coll. of Swansea Faculty of Educational Journal*, pp. 23–5, 1966.

'The effects of remedial teaching in reading: a review of research', *Rem. Educ.*, 2, 1, pp. 4–12, Spring, 1967a.

'Recent developments in the understanding and teaching of educationally subnormal children in England and Wales', *Amer. J. Ment. Defic.*, 72, 2, pp. 244–52, 1967b.

'Children's emotional development' in Butcher, H.J. (Ed.) *Educational Research in Britain*, University of London Press, 1968a.

'Inconsequential behaviour in schoolchildren', *Brit. J. Educ. Psychol.*, 38, pp. 5–7, 1968b.

Compensatory education: defining the problem, in Occasional Publication No. 1, Schools Council Research Project in Compensatory Education, 1968c.

'Follow-up study of mature students', *Univ. Coll. of Swansea Faculty of Education Journal*, pp. 27–9, 1968d.

'Maladjustment and reading difficulties: recent research and experiment', *Rem. Educ.*, 4, 3, pp. 119–23, 1969a.

'The deprived and the disadvantaged' (with Philip Williams), *Dialogue*, 2, 12, February, 1969b.

'The assessment of maladjustment', in Mittler, P.J. (Ed.) *The Psychological Assessment of Mental and Physical Handicaps*, Methuen, 1970a.

'Compensatory Programmes and Early Childhood Education in the USA', in Cox, T. and Wait, C.A. (Eds) *Teaching Disadvantaged Children in the Infant School*, Schools Council Research Project in Compensatory Education, 1970b.

Reading Readiness (editor), Univ. Coll. of Swansea Faculty of Education, 1970c.

'Behaviour problems in the infant school' (with Susan Jackson), *Journal of Child Psychology and Psychiatry*, 12, pp. 191–210, 1971a.

Compensatory Education and the New Media (editor with G. Downes), Swansea, Schools Council Research Project in Compensatory Education, 1971b.

Compensatory programmes for disadvantaged children, Report of 1st National Conference of the Joint Council for the Education of Handicapped Children, pp. 76–81, 1971c.

Just Before School (with Alice F. Laing and Susan Jackson), Oxford, Basil Blackwell (for Schools Council), 1971d.

'The role of the educational psychologist in the promotion of community mental health', *Community Development Journal*, 6, 3, pp. 173–82, Autumn, 1971e.

Aspects of Primary Education (editor), Cardiff, University of Wales Press, 1972 (Charles Gittins Memorial Volume).

'Autism, communication disorders and subnormality', in Laing, A.F. (Ed.) *Educating Mentally Handicapped Children*, Univ. Coll. of Swansea Faculty of Education, 1973a.

The needs of handicapped children attending day special schools: practical and psychological help for parents, Report of 31st National Conference, Association for Special Education, pp. 190–95, 1973b.

'Strategies for helping poorly adjusted children in the infant school', *Therapeutic Education*, 1, 2, pp. 5–13, Autumn, 1973c.

Compensatory Education (editor), London, Butterworths, 1973d.

'Disadvantage and nursery schooling', *Special Education*, 62, 3, pp. 19–33, 1973e.

'Special education for maladjusted children and adolescents in Norway', *Journal of*

Child Psychology and Psychiatry, 14, pp. 57–69, 1973f.
Education in the Early Years (editor), Univ. Coll. of Swansea Faculty of Education, 1973g.
'The treatment of maladjusted pupils: research and experiment 1960–1969', in Pringle, M.K. and Varma, V.P. (Eds) *Advances in Educational Psychology*, Vol. 2, University of London Press, 1974a.
'Behaviour problems in the infant school: changes over two years' (with Susan Jackson), *Journal of Child Psychology and Psychiatry*, 15, 1, pp. 33–46, 1974b.
'Maladjustment in the primary school: the role of the teacher in its identification', *Education 3–13*, 2, 1, pp. 32–6, 1974c.
The Practice of Educational Psychology (with Philip Williams, Terence Moore and Jack Wright), London, Longman, 1974d.
(i) 'The evaluation of pre-school education: research in the United Kingdom' and (ii) 'The use of tests in the evaluation of pre-school educational programmes', in *Problems in the Evaluation of Pre-School Education*, Strasbourg, Council of Europe, 1975.
'The early identification of children with adjustment problems', in Wedell, K. and Raybould, E.C. (Eds) *The Early Identification of Educationally 'at risk' Children*, Educ. Review Occ. Pubs. No. 6, Univ. of Birmingham, 1976a.
Educational Psychologists and School Counsellors: Role Relationships. Occ. Papers of Division of Educ. and Child Psychology of B.P.S., 11, Autumn, pp. 498–537, 1976b.
'Language programmes for disadvantaged pupils' (with Theo Cox), in Williams, P. and Varma, V.P. (Eds) *Piaget, Psychology and Education*, Hodder & Stoughton, 1976c.
Studies of Infant School Children, Vol. I — Deprivation and School Progress (with others), Basil Blackwell (for Schools Council), 1976d.
Studies of Infant School Children, Vol. II — Deprivation and Development (with others), Basil Blackwell (for Schools Council), 1977.
'School-based treatment of maladjusted children', *Therapeutic Education*, 6, 1, 1978a.
'Educational handicap' in Fontana, D. (Ed.) *The Education of the Young Child* (with A.F. Laing), Open Books, 1978b.
Education and preparation for parenthood, Unit 24 in Carver, V. (Ed.), Open University, 1978c.
'The Expanding Role of the Psychologist in the Education Service' (inaugural lecture), Univ. College of Swansea, 1978d.
Deprivation and the Infant School (editor, with P. Williams), Basil Blackwell (for Schools Council), 1978e.
'Behaviour problems in infant school children in deprived areas' (with Susan Threfall), in Anthony E.J., Koupernik, C. and Chiland, C. (Eds) *The Child in His Family: Vulnerable Children*, Vol. 4, John Wiley, 1978f.
International Research in Early Childhood Education (editor), NFER, 1978g.
'The education of handicapped underfives' (with A.F. Laing), *Education for Development*, 5, 3, 28–34, 1979a.
'Identification, Assessment and Treatment: the Role of the Educational Psychologist', in Laing, A.F. (Ed.) *Young Children with Special Needs*, University College of Swansea Department of Education, 1979b.
'Towards a comprehensive strategy for disadvantaged under fives', *Early Child Development and Care*, 6, 1/2, pp. 7–23, 1979c.
'Compensatory education in the infant school', in Hermelin, R. (Ed.) *Teaching the Handicapped Child*, College of Special Education, 1979d.

Some of Our Children: the early education of children with special needs (with others), London, Open Books, 1980.

'The integration of under-fives with special needs: problems and possibilities' (with A.F. Laing), in Heaslip, P. (Ed.) *The Challenge of the Future: professional issues in Early Childhood Education*, Dept. of Education, Bristol, 1981.

'Disadvantage, behaviour problems and reading difficulties', *J. Assoc. Education Psychologists*, 5, 10, pp. 3–6, 1982a.

Children with Special Needs: the early years (with A.F. Laing), Milton Keynes, Open University Press, 1982b.

'Language and learning: Intervention and the child at home', in Davies, A. (Ed.) *Language and Learning at School and Home*, London, Heinemann 1982c.

'The identification of "at risk" pre-school children: attitudes and practices in England and Wales', *International Psychologist*, 24, 3, pp. 21–4, 1983a.

Helping Young Children with Behaviour Difficulties (with others), London, Croom Helm, 1983b.

'The management of behaviour problems in young children', *Early Child Development and Care* (with others), 11, 304, pp. 227–44, 1983c.

'Young Children with Special Educational Needs', in Fontana, D. (Ed.) *The Education of the Young Child* (2nd edition, revised and updated, see 1978b above), Basil Blackwell, 1984.

'Behavioral Aspects of Educational Difficulties', in Duane, D.D. and Leong, C.K. (Eds) *Understanding Learning Disabilities*, Plenum Publishing Corporation, 1985.

'The management of aggressive behaviour in young children' (with A.F. Laing), in Tattum, D.P. (Ed.) *Management of Disruptive Pupil Behaviour in Schools*, London, John Wiley, 1986a.

'Teachers' strategies in coping with behaviour difficulties in young children' (with A.F. Laing), *J. Assoc. for Malad. Children* (Maladjustment and Therapeutic Education), 3, 3, pp. 11–20, 1986b.

Teaching Five to Eight Year-Olds (with others), Blackwell, 1987a.

Teachers' Strategies in Coping with Behaviour Difficulties in First Year Junior School Children (with A.F. Laing), Birmingham, Assoc. Workers for Maladjusted Children, 1987b.

'The Research Face', in Wright, H.J. and Radford, J. (Eds) *The Several Faces of Educational Psychology*, Leicester, British Psychological Society (Group of Teachers of Psychology, Wessex and Wight Branch), 1988.

2. *Other References*

CAPLAN, G. (1961) *An Approach to Community Mental Health*, London, Tavistock Publications.

DEPARTMENT OF EDUCATION AND SCIENCE (1978) *Special Education Needs* (The Warnock Report), London, HMSO.

ROGERS, R. (1986) *Caught in the Act*, London, CSIE and the Spastics Society.

SANDOW, S., STAFFORD, D. and STAFFORD, P. (1987) *An Agreed Understanding?*, Windsor, NFER-Nelson.

Chapter 2

An Appreciation of the Work of Professor Phillip Williams

David Mitchell

When I accepted the invitation to write this tribute to Phillip Williams, I resolved that, as far as possible, it should give expression to his own analytic skills and personality. In what follows I will therefore be quoting generously from an interview I conducted with Phillip during the Christmas period of 1987.

Phillip's professional career reflects the unique blend of a man who was educated and trained in the natural sciences, psychology and education; a bicultural person who is at home in both English and Welsh societies — but with a special affinity for the latter; an academic who has left people and institutions the better for having worked with him as a teacher, researcher and administrator; and an educational psychologist who has had a significant role in influencing educational psychology and special education in post-war Britain.

The Student

Phillip's 11-plus education commenced at Pontypridd Boys' Grammar School. From the Leys School he then received a state bursary to attend St John's College, Cambridge, where he took an MA in natural sciences. From Cambridge he proceeded to London where he studied for a teacher's diploma at the London Institute of Education, a B.Sc. in psychology at Birkbeck College while he was teaching, and trained as an educational psychologist at the Tavistock Clinic. Later, he gained his Ph.D. as an external student with Philip Vernon as his tutor.

The Educational Psychologist

The next phase of Phillip's career centred on his work in educational psychology. From 1953 to 1961, Phillip worked as an educational psychologist, first in Southampton and subsequently in Glamorgan. His skills as a practitioner were then recognized by the University College of Swansea where from 1961 to 1970, he coordinated the training of educational psychologists. At Swansea, Phillip and his colleagues pioneered a model of training which was particularly concerned with providing entry into the profession for graduates in psychology who needed training and experience as teachers. These experiences, together with his activities as secretary of one of the British Psychological Society's divisions of educational and clinical psychologists, led to Phillip's appointment to the influential Summerfield Committee which, in 1968, reported to the Secretary of State for Education and Science on issues to do with the recruitment and training of educational psychologists in England and Wales.

Looking back on this period, Phillip attributes the concern for expanding educational psychology to a growing recognition that the medical model was having an undue influence on special education and that 'educational principles were neglected, so there was an unexplored, unchartered territory which had to be developed'. It was increasingly being recognized, he recounts, that educational psychologists would play a critical role in any changes. As he notes:

> In the twenty years after the 1944 Education Act, special education in this country was really an emergency service. It just dealt with children with the greatest need and dealt with them in what was virtually the only way possible then, which was to set up separate schools and units. By the mid 1960s, the demand for special education grew and people realized that educational psychologists had a much greater role to play, both as professionals and, in many cases, as contributors to developments in the training of teachers.

The Distance Educator

Phillip's potential to contribute to the broader field of education, together with his innovatory approach to solving problems, gained further recognition when, in 1970, the Open University appointed him to one of the foundation chairs of educational studies and, subsequently, to the post of Dean of the Faculty of Education. He describes this period as 'a tremendously exhilarating experience . . . the most effective, the most memorable, part of my career'. In this phase of his career, the professional energies of Phillip and his colleagues were largely devoted to the pioneering efforts of getting the institution going, at times in the face of a Tory government that was suspicious, but which eventually came to accept the philosophy of the Open University.

He evaluates the impact of the Open University on special education very positively, noting, firstly, that largely because of its being a 'home-based' university, it probably had enrolled more students with special needs than any other British university — and perhaps more than all other UK universities combined. Secondly, it taught a pioneering undergraduate course on special needs, initially in the social work and rehabilitation fields, though strongly multi-disciplinary in conception. Thirdly, he felt that the subsequent development of a course on special needs in education was influential. Though controversial, 'partly because of the radical line it took, it nevertheless had a stimulating and positive effect on many people in the field'.

Phillip's work at the Open University culminated in his appointment to the Warnock Committee which, in 1978, reported to the Secretary of State for Education and Science on the education of handicapped children and young people. He considers that several factors gave rise to this committee, the main one being pressure on the part of interested groups, particularly parents. This thrust from the periphery to the centre, he feels, contrasted with the development of PL 94–142 in the United States where there were strong political moves on behalf of handicapped children.

Parents' concerns at that time were primarily related to the issue of integration: 'instead of seeing a march onwards to more and more special schools and more and more special units, many parents felt that there was a strong case to be made for providing special education in ordinary schools.' Phillip notes that this pressure for integration was to some extent counterbalanced by the views of what was then a strong lobby in the heads and staff of special schools 'who were not only firm believers in the advantages of separate education for some children, but were also understandably concerned about their future in a world of integration'.

Several matters to do with the relationship between the recommendations of the Warnock Committee and the 1981 Education Act are of concern to Phillip. Chief of these were the failure of government to follow up on the committee's emphatic recommendations on teacher education, pre-school education, and provisions for the 16- to 19-year-olds. These deficiencies, together with the fact that it took three years from Warnock to get the Act onto the statute books and another two years for it to become implemented, led Phillip to describe the 1981 Act as a 'reluctant Act'. In addition to errors of omission, practice following the Act has departed quite significantly from what Phillip considered to be the Warnock Committee's intentions on statementing: 'It was never intended to be the kind of bureaucratic exercise it has become . . . [It] was meant to be an informal rather than a rigidly formal activity.' Part of the problem, he feels, lies in the excessive attempts to accommodate to the rights of parents to be consulted at different stages and to go through appeal processes. While not wishing to deny these rights, he feels that there should be more room for flexibility in their interpretation.

He is concerned, too, at the way in which integration has been implemented in the schools, both in relation to the Warnock recommendations and to the 1981 Act. While he recognizes that Warnock never recommended integration for all children, he nevertheless feels that 'in relation to the majority of children with special needs . . . [integration] has gone too slowly'.

The Welshman

In 1978, Phillip returned to Wales, taking up his position of Professor of Education and Head of the School of Education at the University College of North Wales, Bangor. He took early retirement from that position in 1983 and since then has held the appointment of emeritus professor. Apart from his administrative and teaching duties, during this phase of his career Phillip has been engaged in a range of research and publishing activities. Two of these reflect his long-standing interests in the intersection between special education and children's cultural backgrounds, which had been given earlier expression in the Schools Council compensatory education project which he co-directed in the 1960s: a project on developing language tests and teaching materials for slow learners in the Welsh language (e.g. Williams, 1985) and a book on special education and minority communities (Williams, 1984).

On the theme of adapting education to the cultural backgrounds of children, Phillip observes that

> If you speak two languages, you've got the keys to two cultures and you see each of those two cultures in a much richer way . . . There is no country in the world that does not have an ethnic minority but the problem is that the majority often do not realize what are the issues that worry and concern, and sometimes anger, the minorities.

Of contemporary developments in education, the 'Education Reform Act' attracts major criticism from Phillip Williams on several grounds, particularly in relation to its effects on special education. He feels that one of the main purposes of the Act is to improve competition between schools by measuring standards in the basic subjects. He predicts that many schools will be reluctant to have their average performances reduced by admitting numbers of children with learning difficulties. The alternative is to excuse these children from the national assessment of school standards – a modern version of the old 'Standard O' principle, providing an equally insidious way of stigmatizing children, and one which equally deserves to be abandoned. If, sadly, this alternative is to be followed, there will have to be a principle for determining which low-attaining children are to be excused; presumably 'the statement' will be the basis for this. This will lead to 'a rush on the part of schools to get their children with learning difficulties statemented . . . which will impose an enormous strain on the special education system'. The only good which might emerge, he feels, could be a consequent simplification of the statementing procedure – the right result for the wrong reasons. Related to this is the principle of schools opting out of local authority control, which he envisages as setting the clock back to a divided education system:

> Opting out will mean that the schools with influential parents with high standards will see this as an opportunity for initiative, for developing as competitors to the independent schools. They will want that freedom, they will take it, they will attract more children, they will arrange matters so that the brightest children will be attracted, and there is a danger that we will be left with schools in the local authorities which will have to cater for a preponderance of less able children.

He is critical, too, of the values that seem to underlie the Act. He sees these as revolving around 'making teachers work harder and producing better standards by driving children on' – the stick for the many and the carrot for the few. This is quite contradictory to the values of special education, he feels, which are 'the values of compassion, not competition: rewards should not be inexorably linked to high performance; the individual struggles with himself, as much as competing with others.'

Phillip also feels that the notion of the core curriculum will introduce an element of rigidity into schools at the very time when they are becoming more accommodating to children with special educational needs: 'How on earth does the core curriculum fit the kinds of skills one wants to see in children, for example, with severe learning difficulties, or emotional or behavioural problems? Social skills aren't mentioned; life skills aren't mentioned.' A further example of inflexibility is provided in the proposals for national assessment of children at the ages of 7, 11, 14 and 16. Although in favour of moderating national standards, he believes that sampling is a far more effective procedure than a national examination for all children. While always an advocate of the importance of diagnosing children's learning difficulties, Phillip argues that

> You need different approaches for different schools. It is nonsense to use the same tests to assess standards in, for example, a school

in an affluent London suburb, a school in rural bilingual Wales, and a school in multi-ethnic Bradford. The objectives of the schools will be different, as will their curricula.

The Scholar

No overview of Phillip Williams's career would do justice to his signal contributions to educational psychology and special education without reference to his scholarship. His publications include books on children's responses to special schooling (Williams and Gruber, 1967), educational psychology (Chazan, Moore and Williams, 1974), behaviour problems in schools (Williams, 1974), reading (Davies and Williams, 1975), educational disadvantage (Chazan and Williams, 1978; Williams, 1984) and a glossary of special education (Williams, 1988), as well as a series of some twenty books on children with special needs published by Open University Press which he has coedited with Peter Young. His contributions at the international level are reflected in visiting appointments to universities in Wisconsin (1965), Calgary (1969 and 1975) and Monash (1976), as well as in British Council-sponsored lecture tours to India, the Middle East, South America, Australia and New Zealand. The esteem in which he is held by his professional and academic peers has led to Phillip being appointed to a great range of bodies: as well as the Summerfield and Warnock committees, he has served on the Psychology Committee of the Social Science Research Council, the Schools Council Committee for Wales (as Chairman), the Education sub-committee of the University Grants Committee, the Schools Broadcasting Council for Wales, and the Wales Advisory Board for Higher Education.

In his retirement he continues to teach and to write, in particular developing an advanced version of his glossary of special education with the aid of a Leverhulme Emeritus Fellowship. He spends much of his spare time walking his beloved Welsh mountains with his wife, Glenys, and his current ambition is to develop the first vineyard in Anglesey.

Finally, what are the beliefs and values that give coherence to Phillip Williams's career? When I asked this question of him, he thought for a while and then observed that in choosing a career there is a view that one has to decide between trying to do good and seeking out the truth and that, in spite of his research activities, it has been the first of these principles which has been the governing theme. Those who know Phillip well would gently disagree. They would argue that he continues, as he has always done, both to do good *and* to seek out the truth, wherever he may be and whatever his current field of enquiry — and always in a quiet, dignified and unassuming manner.

References

CHAZAN, M., MOORE, T., WILLIAMS, P. and WRIGHT, J. (1974) *The Practice of Educational Psychology,* London, Longman.

CHAZAN, M. and WILLIAMS, P. (1978) *Deprivation and the Infant School*, Oxford, Blackwell.

DAVIES, P. and WILLLIAMS, P. (1975) *Aspects of Early Reading Growth*, Oxford, Blackwell.

WILLIAMS, P. (Ed.) (1974) *Behaviour Problems in School*, London, Hodder & Stoughton.

WILLIAMS, P. (Ed.) (1984) *Special Education in Minority Communities*, Milton Keynes, Open University Press.

WILLIAMS, P. (Ed.) (1988) *Glossary of Special Education*, Open University Press.

WILLIAMS, P. and GRUBER, E. (1967) *Response to Special Schooling*, London, Longman.

WILLIAMS, P. *et al.* (1985) *Profion Bangor*, Llandyssul, Gwasg Gomer.

Chapter 3

Children with Special Educational Needs: Past, Present and Future

Klaus Wedell

Tracing the development of the education of children with special needs in this country could, until recently, have been done with optimism. The understanding of the nature of children's needs has increased, although it has also opened up an awareness of how much further there is to go. The effectiveness of educational approaches is improving, and in certain areas (not only of education) preventive measures are showing results. Most important of all, perhaps, the attitudes of society in general are changing, and there is a greater recognition of the rights of those with special needs as members of society and a commitment to improve their educational opportunity further. However, the effects of the recent financial constraints, and the provisions of the 1988 Education Act and its associated Circulars, have cast a pall of doubt over those concerned with the education of those with special needs as to whether the advances which have been achieved can be maintained, let alone furthered.

Historically, one can divide the developments in the education of those with special educational needs into four periods: the period before the 1944 Education Act, the lead up to the publication of the Warnock Report in 1978, the ten years after this, and the present period following the 1988 Education Act (Education Reform Act). In this chapter, I will focus mainly on the last two periods, since the earlier ones have already been well chronicled by others (e.g. Chap. 2 of the Warnock Report, DES, 1978; Chap. 1, Society of Education Officers, 1986).

The development of educational provision in England for children with what we now call special educational needs, has followed a pattern similar to that in other countries. Initially, provision was made through charitable support. Then, as education was made more generally available through legislation, provision started to be made by official authorities. When education became compulsory for all children across a wider age range, special educational provision was also systematized as a specific form of provision.

In more recent years, the views about the rights of those with special educational needs, and the advances in the understanding of needs and the approaches to education, have led to a realization that a more differentiated response to individual needs is required in all education, and that special education forms a part of education in general.

1. Before the 1944 Education Act

The earliest provision was set up for those whose disabilities most obviously constituted a specific handicap – those with visual and with hearing impairment. Through charitable initiative, the first school for the blind was opened in 1791, and for the deaf in the early part of the 1760s. Provision for those with physical handicap was started in 1865, and for those with mental handicap in 1847. The functions of these establishments were aimed more at training than at education, in the attempt to engage those concerned in some form of employment either inside or outside the institution. Provision of this kind began to become more widespread in the subsequent years. The Education Act of 1870 extended elementary education, and school boards started to set up special classes initially for those with sensory or physical handicaps. The Royal Commission on the Blind and Deaf (1886) recommended that education should be compulsory for those with these disabilities, and the Education Act of 1893 endorsed this. In 1896 a Committee on 'Defective and Epileptic' children was set up which recommended that all 'defective' children should be given access to education. However, the ensuing legislation (Education Act 1899) only empowered school boards to make provision. Obligatory provision was finally introduced for 'defective' children in 1914, and for physically handicapped and epileptic children in 1918. The 1921 Education Act confirmed the statutory provision for these children, but as separated in special schools and classes.

Provision so far had been directed at those with sensory and physical disabilities and those with mental handicaps. Provision for those with emotional and behaviour problems was also started through voluntary agencies and hospitals, in the form of clinics and homes. The first full-time child guidance clinic run by an education authority was set up in Glasgow in 1937. So, by the end of the 1930s, there was broadly a recognition of the presently accepted range of special educational needs.

2. From the 1944 Act to the Warnock Report

The 1944 Education Act was produced in the anticipation that after the end of the war, there would be a concern to extend the educational opportunities for all. Special education was to be recognized as part of Local Education Authorities' (LEAs') planned provision. There was even an awareness that this implied an aim to integrate. The Warnock Report quotes Mr Chuter Ede, the Parliamentary Secretary, as saying:

> I do not want to . . . make it appear that the normal way to deal with a child who suffers from any of these disabilities is to be put into a special school where he will be segregated. Whilst we desire to see adequate provision of special schools we also desire to see as many children as possible retained in the normal stream of school life.

The Act recognized that up to 17 per cent of the school population might require special educational help, and that the less severely handicapped would in any case have to be provided for in ordinary schools. However, this recognition in principle of the range of children's needs could not be followed up in practice, because the constraints in finance and qualified personnel had the consequence that only the more severely handicapped children were assessed. In any case, the large class sizes in ordinary schools made it difficult to carry out a positive integration policy.

The Act referred to those requiring special education as having 'disabilities of body or mind', and so clearly indicated that special education was concerned solely with problems 'within the child'. This view of special needs was reflected in the terminology used in the ensuing 1945 Handicapped Pupils Regulations to refer to the eleven categories of handicap: deaf, partially deaf, blind, partially sighted, physically handicapped, delicate, diabetic, epileptic, educationally subnormal, maladjusted, and those with speech defects. In order to be allocated provision, children had to be diagnosed by doctors in the School Health Service as falling within one of these categories. The continued use of medical personnel for assessment was largely inevitable since, the number of educational psychologists was still far too small to take on this task.

The 1944 Act also specified that some children were to be regarded as too handicapped to benefit from education and so would be given into the care of the health service. These children were to be termed 'ineducable'.

The categorization of children with special educational needs was reflected in a rapid increase in the number of special schools, although LEAs differed in the rate at which they allocated funds to set these up. The demands for assessment, and the rise of the rôle of psychological testing, particularly in relation to the '11+' examination, led to an increased demand for educational psychologists. Remedial teaching was also started, initially as a result of the distinction which was made between children who were termed 'backward' and those termed 'retarded'. These developments, and the need to staff the special schools and classes, led to a demand for the training of specialist teachers in addition to the teachers of the hearing and visually impaired, for whom training was already mandatory. The first Chair in Special Education was finally set up at Birmingham University, and Mr Ronald Gulliford was appointed to it.

In the period following the Second World War an increasing amount of research was directed at children with special educational needs, particularly in the United States. One line of research was aimed at a greater differentiation of children's needs, particularly of those regarded as mentally handicapped. For example, it was found that children with cerebral palsy had abilities which had previously been masked by their incapacity to respond. This led to the development of more specialized educational methods, through which these children were then able to make significant progress. As a result, it became increasingly evident that assessment should be directed at identifying children's educational needs, in order that they could be given appropriate educational help. It came to be recognized that this could not be achieved through the classification of children into handicap categories, which had no direct educational implications. Needless to say, parents became increasingly concerned that their children's educational needs should be met, and in the period following the war many parents' organizations were started, which then exerted pressure for improved educational provision. In the first instance, these organizations often set up their own provision, and so, in a sense, started a second cycle of development in special education.

Another major line of research investigated the effect of social deprivation on children's early cognitive, and consequent educational, progress. This research also originated mainly in the USA, and demonstrated that early deprivation had a significant effect. As a result, it became apparent that children's educational progress reflected not only factors within the child, but also factors within the child's environment. This led to a major early education programme in the USA called the Headstart Programme. Some years later a similar smaller scale programme was started in this country, in what were termed 'Educational Priority Areas'.

A third development during this period was the growing concern for the rights of the minorities. Equal educational opportunities were seen as essential to realizing these rights, through participation in the general system of education. Integrated education was regarded as necessary to enable an individual to become an accepted member of society, and also as an end in itself. These views led to a strong demand that those with special educational needs should be educated in ordinary schools. As was mentioned above, these views were already being expresssed when the 1944 Act was debated in Parliament.

Not surprisingly, an early concern was that those who had been termed 'ineducable' should be admitted to the education system. This was achieved with the passage of the 1970 Education (Handicapped Children) Act, which brought children who were in the responsibility of the health service under the educational responsibility of LEAs. The Act took effect in 1971, and gave the children access to special education in hospitals or in special schools and classes. While this legislative change was undoubtedly a major step forward, it did not change the view of special education as separated from the mainstream of education.

At this time, also, the Hester Adrian Research Centre, which was to be devoted to research on mental handicap, was set up at Manchester University. The centre began to make a major contribution to the education of those with severe learning difficulties under its Director, Peter Mittler, whose chair was later established there.

All these developments led to pressure from a commission to look into the education of children with special educational needs. After a number of setbacks, a committee of enquiry was established under the chairmanship of an Oxford University lecturer, Mrs Mary Warnock (who was subsequently made a Baroness). The committee started its work in 1974, and completed its report in 1978.

Before considering the findings of the report, it is necessary to mention some developments which occurred while the committee was still at work. In 1975, after a period of consultation and investigation, the important Circular 2/75 (DES, 1975) was issued dealing with the identification and assessment of children with special educational needs. This Circular was issued in response to developments in professional practice, and prompted the idea of early identification, and of the importance of focusing the assessment of children on their educational needs. The Circular affirmed that assessment was a progressive process from initial identification of need to subsequent clarification of educational requirements. It specified that the procedure for assessing a child for special educational provision should involve a teacher, an educational psychologist and a doctor, and that the decision about the nature of provision should be made by an educational professional (an experienced educational psychologist or education adviser). However, to be legally enforceable, the necessary form still had to be signed by a doctor as prescribed in the 1944 Act.

Aspects of integration were also being promoted in an Act of 1970 and an Act of 1976, but the Secretary of State decided in 1977 to postpone any implementation until the Warnock Committee's recommendations were known. By the time this occurred, pressures for change had thus already become very strong.

3. From the Warnock Report to the 1988 Education Act

There is no doubt that the Warnock Committee report has come to be regarded as a major formulation of ideas about the nature of special educational needs and about good practice prevailing at the time it was published. The Committee made 224 recommendations, but for the purposes of this chapter, it is more useful to consider the ideas about special education put forward in the report.

The Committee affirmed that there were no grounds for postulating a clear dividing line between those who were handicapped and those who were not. The handicap resulting from a disability had to be seen as relative to the constraints and resources of the environment, and to the aspirations of the individual and the demands of society. The categories of handicap did not have educational significance, since no direct implications about an individual's educational needs could be derived from them. Moreover, children's needs were usually more or less complex, and so rarely fitted neatly into a single category.

The Committee therefore proposed that the use of categories should cease, and that one should instead talk about children's 'special educational needs', a term used in 1970 by Professor Gulliford as the title of a book. These needs might take a variety of forms, and occur across a range of severity. The Committee put forward the idea of a continuum of need, and, on the basis of epidemiological studies, concluded that up to 20 per cent of children might have a special educational need at some time in their schooling. Children with special educational needs could therefore not be regarded as a distinct population, and the general aims of education applied as much to them as to other children. Clearly the extent to which a given child might progress towards those aims might vary, as might the means necessary to support the child's progress. Special education should therefore not be seen as a separate form of education.

By stressing that the aims of education were the same for all children, and that the concept of handicap was relative, the Committee laid the basis for promoting the integration of children with special educational needs into ordinary schools, subject to the requirement to meet these needs. The continuum of special educational needs had to be matched with a continuum of provision. The message is well summarized in the following quotation: 'Special education is about meeting individual needs and involves as much integration as possible and as much special help as necessary' (Society of Education Officers, 1986).

The Committee also stressed the importance of early recognition of, and help for, children's special educational needs. In this connection, and also generally, the Committee pointed to the important role of parents in the education of their children. Parents' rights to participate in decisions about their children's education were strongly affirmed. For these rights to be realized, the Committee pointed out that parents had to have access to relevant information about their children. The concern among professionals about confidentiality had to be subject to this requirement. Parents also needed information about what special educational provision was available and how access to it could be obtained. The Committee recommended that the parents of children with special educational needs should be allocated a 'named person', who could help them with this process.

The inadequacy of special educational provision after school leaving age was noted by the Committee, and they recommended that this should be tackled as a matter of urgency. They also noted that a major effort was needed to extend and improve the initial and further training of teachers, both classroom teachers in ordinary schools, and teachers involved in the various aspects of special education.

Following the publication of the Warnock Report, the government of the day instituted a wide ranging consultation, and LEAs were required to make a response by February 1979. This consultation exercise itself made an impact on LEA and other services, since they were led to examine the adequacy of their practices, and to focus their attention on the need to make appropriate provision. However, the economic climate was not favourable, and when the government (which had changed by then), came to issue a White Paper in response to the Report, many of the Committee's recommendations were accepted, but no additional resources were offered. It was claimed that school numbers were falling, and the necessary resources could be found out of the consequent scope for savings. England thus became the only developed country to attempt special educational reform without an allocation of additional funds to carry it out.

Following the White Paper, legislation was prepared, and a new Education Act was passed in 1981 which, however, was not put into effect until 1983. The Act incorporated a fascinating formulation of the Warnock Committee's concept of special educational needs: 'A child has special educational needs if he has a learning difficulty which calls for special educational provision to be made for him.' This definition must take a prize for circularity, but in fact represents a very shrewd assessment of the nature of the decision it represents. Special educational provision is defined as: 'provision which is additional to or . . . different from . . . provision made generally . . .' The formulation thus recognizes the relativity of the definition of special educational need which formed the basis of the Warnock Committee's conception. A child's difficulty in learning represents a teacher's difficulty in teaching, and so leads to a 'call' for special educational help. That help is by definition 'special' in the situation where it is called for, because otherwise the prevailing resources, the 'generally made provision', would have been judged adequate to help the child. 'Learning difficulty' refers solely to the fact that a child has difficulty in learning, and does not specify a cause. A later section of the Act brings in some ideas of causation, when reference is made to disabilities which may hinder a child from making progress. This formulation again leaves open to interpretation how one might decide that a child's progress is hindered. The entire concept of special educational need is grounded in the recognition that need is relative. One part of the formulation in the Act sounds as though it might bring in an external criterion for establishing learning difficulty: 'A child has a learning difficulty if he has a significantly greater difficulty in learning than the majority of children of his age.' Since there is no definition of 'significant', the formulation clearly does not take one much further.

I have dwelt at some length on the issue of the definition of special educational need in the Act, because later on I will be reporting findings that it is still not fully understood. It seems that people find it difficult to accept the fact that the definition is relative, presumably because that is in fact the way that decisions are made.

The remaining early sections of the 1981 Act set out the important principle that ordinary schools should ensure that children's special educational needs are identified and met. The Act then goes on to specify the procedure to be followed if children's needs cannot be met, and this in fact takes up the main remaining portion of the Act. The result has been that the Act is often wrongly seen as being predominantly concerned with this procedure which involves drawing up a 'statement' for a child.

The Act refers to children who require special educational provision, and then states that, for some of these children, the LEA may decide that it needs to determine the provision to be made. The Act lays down that an LEA makes this decision on the basis of a multi-professional assessment of the child, and in practice, the decision turns on whether the LEA judges it appropriate to make provision for an individual child, which it does not make potentially accessible to all children. The 'statement' is the document which is drawn up to record the assessment information, and the provision prescribed by the LEA. Circular 1/83 (DES, 1983) which was written to explain how the Act should be implemented, formulated that this decision on the part of the LEA would occur if the 'generally available' provision for extra help was not found to be adequate to meet the child's needs.

Unfortunately, in a subsequent judicial review, the judge ruled that the term 'generally available' was not included in the Act, and so could not be applied. In practice, the term special educational provision is used to refer to the 20 per cent of children whom the Warnock Committee regarded as having special educational needs, and the statement procedure was intended to be used for the 2 per cent of children for whom a statement was maintained. However, the Act very clearly states that children for whom statements are maintained should be educated in ordinary schools, unless the parents do not agree to this, or unless three other conditions are not met. These conditions are that such a placement makes it impossible to meet the child's needs, or it hinders other children's needs being met, or if it is not compatible with the efficient use of resources. These conditions have often been regarded as providing an LEA with excuses for not making integrated provision, but it is important that they are seen as challenges to improve the provision it makes in ordinary schools.

The Act and the Circular set out a number of other requirements in line with some of the recommendations of the Warnock Report. The involvement of parents is stressed, particularly in decisions about provision. Parents are given recourse to a tribunal, if they cannot reach agreement with the LEA about the provision to be made for their child. However, the tribunal is only given power to make recommendations to the LEA, and not to force a change in its decision. There is more of an attempt to convey the spirit of the Warnock Report in Circular 1/83, and it is worth noting that the DES exceptionally commissioned a small research project to inform itself about the workings of the previous procedures as a preparation for writing the Circular (Wedell, Welton and Vorhaus, 1982). However, the Act and the Circular undoubtedly come short of incorporating all of the main recommendations of the Warnock Report. One of the main omissions is the recommendation about providing a 'named person' to help parents.

The DES commissioned three research projects to monitor the implementation of the Act. One of the projects was intended to study the way in which the statement procedure was implemented, and another looked at the way LEAs provided support for children with special educational needs in the ordinary school, and at the way in which special schools developed outreach support. The third project studied various forms of teacher in-service training for special educational needs. The following are some of the findings emerging from these studies.

A questionnaire survey to LEAs was carried out in one of the studies (Goacher *et al*, 1988), to find out what were the main changes which had occurred since the Act came into force in April 1983. Commitment to integration was cited by 37 per cent of LEAs as the main reason for changes in their pattern of provision, and 76 per cent of LEAs reported increased proportions of children with statements in ordinary schools. More LEAs reported decreases than increases in the number of children in residential and day special schools, except with regard to children with emotional and behaviour problems. Since this survey only enquired about changes, the data quoted have to be set in the context of the patterns of provision existing in the LEAs in April 1983. It is likely that the consultation about the Warnock Report already started many LEAs on the way to improving their provision. More recently, Swann (1988) has analyzed figures for admissions to special schools, and found that 69 per cent of English LEAs reduced their level of integration in the period between 1982 and 1987. As a proportion of the school population as a whole, admission figures fell between 1982 and 1983, but then started to rise again to 1985. It is difficult therefore to know whether or not there has been a trend towards more integration. What is quite clear, is that there are very great differences in practice between LEAs. Some of these differences are related to their circumstances, and some may reflect differences in policy. For example, more shire than metropolitan LEAs had higher proportions of children with statements in ordinary schools. However, more shire counties had higher proportions of children with statements. This could be interpreted as indicating the greater difficulty in making special educational provision generally available in rural areas, so that more children have to be given access to it by means of statements.

These differences in statement rates support the view that the relative definition of 'special educational need' in the Act was appropriate. However, this was still not accepted by some LEAs, who, for example, decided that statements should only be given to children who were placed in special schools, or never gave them to children under school age. It is clear that the full implications of the decision to maintain a statement had not been generally grasped. This was also found to be the case by the Parliamentary Select Committee on Education, Science and the Arts, which enquired into the implementation of the 1981 Act in 1987 (House of Commons, 1987).

The statement procedure itself came under much criticism, since it seemed to require an inordinate amount of time and personnel. Research findings showed that the statement procedure was, on average, completed in twenty-one weeks, but that there was a very wide range of duration. The causes for this were very varied, but the consequence was that there was often a delay in children obtaining access to help.

Parents were more involved in decisions about special educational provision for their children, because the procedure required that they were shown the statement in draft form. On the other hand, this did not necessarily mean that they had participated in the making of the decisions. Various studies (e.g. Rogers, 1986) found that parents had insufficient information about the procedure as such, and also did not know what the range of provision available for their children was. The specification of a child's needs in a statement was also sometimes so general or vague, that it was difficult to know whether a recommended form of provision actually matched a child's needs. This uncertainty on the part of parents was exacerbated if the parents were not familiar with English (ILEA, 1985).

It seems likely that the Warnock Report and the 1981 Act made their major impact on provision for children with special educational needs in the ordinary school, the so-called '18 per cent'. These are, of course, the children who had been catered for (or not) in ordinary schools all along, and the proportion of whom might be well above the notional '18 per cent'. Research (Goacher, Evans, Welton and Wedell, 1988) showed that considerably more LEAs increased their various support services for children and teachers in ordinary schools. The nature of the support also changed. Awareness of the extent of need for support soon led to a realization that efforts had to be made to give teachers in ordinary classes more knowledge about helping children with special educational needs. As Gipps, Gross and Goldstein (1986) showed, advisory, 'remedial' and other support services changed their focus from direct work with children, to indirect work through their teachers. The same study also showed that such a change had to be very carefully prepared, if it was not to be resented by teachers, or made ineffective in other ways.

There is not space here to describe all the other developments in support for children with special educational needs. One must at least mention the involvement of parents in the education of pre-school children through a massive extension of the Portage approach as a result of an earmarked government grant to LEAs. Similarly, a government grant established SEMERCs (Special Education Microprocessor Resource Centres). They have made a major contribution to the use of microprocessor technology in special needs education. Across the range of children with learning difficulties there has been an increase in objectives-oriented approaches to teaching, based on curriculum development.

These changes in approaches to support had implications for teacher training. The Warnock Committee had already drawn attention to this. The Committee had called for 'special needs awareness' courses for teachers in ordinary school, for an element of special education in all initial training, and for an increase in opportunities for specialist training. At the time of the Report, for example, it was estimated that only 22 per cent of all teachers in special schools in England and Wales had an additional qualification in special education. In the period following the Report there was an increase in specialist training courses, and the Advisory Council for the Supply and Education of Teachers (ACSET), in a report to the DES just before the Council was abolished, made extensive recommendations about special education teacher training, including the inclusion of an element in initial teacher training. The latter has since been included in the specifications for the recognition of teacher training courses.

In 1983, the government earmarked a proportion of LEAs' funding for the training of what came to be called 'special educational needs coordinators' in ordinary schools. The funding was for one-term courses to give teachers who would have designated responsibilities a basic knowledge and competence to offer first-line help to children, support to other teachers, and to liaise with outside support services. A considerable number of these courses were set up, but even so, the supply did not meet the demand The idea of a designated teacher was helpful, but often the teachers in fact were not able to make the intended contribution in their schools because their position did not allow them sufficient influence (Cowne and Norwich, 1986).

A major change in the funding of in-service teacher training took place in 1986. The government devolved to LEAs the planning of in-service provision, requiring them to bid for funds to carry it out. These funds were found by a corresponding retention of the normal LEA expenditure grant. The government retained some influence in the determination of training, through the proportion of the required finance it offered to provide. It designated certain areas of training as national priorities, for which 70 per cent of the cost was allocated, in contrast to 50 per cent support allocated for the LEAs' own choices. The consequence of this arrangement at a time when LEAs' financial resources were becoming very constrained, was that secondment for full-time courses of special educational needs training was very much reduced, particularly in those areas of training which were not accorded national priority. This, in turn, led to the closing of some courses in Polytechnics and Universities.

Findings from the research on the implementation of the 1981 Act showed that, although LEAs had not received additional funding to meet the requirements of the Act, they had in fact met the additional costs largely through allocating a greater proportion of their resources to this area of education. Some savings were made through changes in the use of special schools, particularly through a reduction in the number of children sent to schools outside the LEA. However, as was pointed out above, some of the main increases in provision occurred in support of children whose needs had not previously been targetted in the ordinary schools. The research had found a general commitment to raising the level of special needs support, and to giving this area of education greater priority than previously. The Parliamentary Select Committee, in its report, stressed that the development of special needs services had to be planned, coordinated and carried out at the level of the LEA, since it was too complex an operation to be managed at the level of the school. However, in recent years, the increasing constraints on LEA finance has made it very difficult for LEAs to protect special needs services from the cuts which they have had to make in other areas, and reductions in services and support are being reported. So, at the end of the period covered in this section of this chapter, there are signs that the very considerable boost in efforts to implement the recommendations of the Warnock Report and the demands of the 1981 Acts are beginning to be impeded.

I have confined myself in the above account, to describing developments in the education services. Space does not allow an account of the related development of support for children with special educational needs in the health and social services. However, research on the implementation of the 1981 Act has emphasized the need for much greater coordination of the statutory and voluntary services if the full potential of the services is to be realized.

4. The 1988 Education Act and the Future

When he introduced the 1988 Education Bill (the 'Education Reform Bill'), the Secretary of State for Education said that the purpose of the Bill was to provide 'a better education, relevant to the late twentieth century and beyond, for all our children, whatever their ability, wherever they live, whatever type of school their parents choose for them' (DES, 1987). Those concerned with the education of children with special educational needs, therefore, were very hopeful that the Act would build on the principles of the Warnock Report and the 1981 Act. Unfortunately, in its original version the Bill only made sparse reference to special educational needs. Several amendments were added as the result of the concern which was expressed about this. However, even in its final form, the Act is not formulated in the spirit of the developments in special education which have been achieved over the ten years between the publication of the Warnock Report and the enactment of the 1988 Act. It has to be added that in many respects the Act does not reflect advances in education in general.

One of the government's expressed purposes in establishing a National Curriculum was to ensure that all pupils were offered the essential components of education. The point was stressed that children were entitled to this, and that the Act would ensure this. The aims of education, as formulated in the first section of the Act, are expressed in a broad way, but as the former Senior Chief HMI Sheila Brown is reported to have pointed out, there is a gap between the content of the proposed National Curriculum and these aims. The wording of the Act recognizes that the National Curriculum does not cover the content of the whole curriculum. However, as the whole detail of the Act is concerned with the National Curriculum, there is justifiable anxiety that the remaining part of the curriculum will not receive the necessary attention and emphasis. This is particularly relevant to the education of children with special educational needs at all levels. As a group of special educators stated in a memorandum: 'What appears to be missing . . . is the breadth of curriculum objectives in terms of personal and social accomplishments . . . which employers and parents now expect . . .' (Fish, Mongon, Evans and Wedell, 1987).

The Act describes the National Curriculum in section 2, as consisting of courses of study and arrangements for assessment. It is therefore inferred that children with special educational needs may not be able to follow these courses or undertake the assessments in the form or at the time at which they may be prescribed, depending on the nature of their needs. Since access to the National Curriculum is regarded as an entitlement for all children, the Act has to make provision for the National Curriculum to be modified or 'disapplied' for children whose needs preclude them from receiving the Curriculum in its prescribed form. The Act has sections dealing with this with respect to children who have statements, and to children for whom headteachers may want to modify or disapply the Curriculum temporally. The Act also makes provision for Orders to be made, for the Curriculum to be modified or disapplied in certain 'cases and circumstances', rather than to pupils as individuals. This provision is not only directed at children with special educational needs.

While one can understand that a rigid specification of a curriculum may imply that a given pupil cannot follow it in the way it is prescribed, the whole development of making the curriculum accessible to pupils with special educational needs over recent years has been aimed at avoiding this. Teachers have been encouraged to identify the essential elements of curricular content, and to develop ways of presenting it to pupils with a wide variety of learning needs. Current research on children with moderate learning difficulties, for example, has shown how these approaches are being successfully applied (Ireson, Evans, Redmond and Wedell, 1988). Teachers are not only developing ways in which content can be modified to allow for different styles of presentation and response, but are responding to individual pupils' learning needs in flexible ways as required at any particular point in the pupil's learning. Interestingly, it was found in the research that in schools which had attempted to structure the progression of their curricular content, it was easier for teachers to know how to extend the curriculum to pupils with special educational needs. In other words, the structuring of the curriculum being attempted by the Curriculum Working Parties could in fact be of help to teachers in this respect, if only they were allowed to apply it appropriately.

Developments in special needs education over recent years have, as has been stated earlier, been directed at recognizing the continuum of special needs. The usual range of a teacher's response to the variety of pupils in a class therefore merges into the more 'special' approaches required for pupils with more severe needs. Both the curriculum Working Groups which have so far reported, make strong pleas that the courses of study which they have designed, should be made accessible to pupils with different forms of special needs.

The Act and the subsequent Circulars in their draft or final forms show a confusion about the process of assessment itself. Assessment is only specified for the core and foundation subjects of the National Curriculum. The main confusion seems to derive from the failure to understand the relationship between different forms of assessment and the various purposes for which assessment may be carried out. The report of the Task Group on Assessment and Testing attempted to clarify these issues. The group proposed that assessment should be based on the progression of the curriculum, and asserted that assessment should be 'the servant, not the master' of the curriculum. The group also made the distinction, which was not evident from the wording of the Act and several of the Circulars, between the purposes of assessment of the individual pupil and the assessment of groups. For those teaching children with special educational needs, on-going curriculum-based assessment is essential to ensure that pupils are getting the help they need. However, the Act proposes four assessment stages at 7, 11, 14, and 16, and some of the Circulars in their draft form suggest that these assessments will form the basis of teachers' decisions about children's needs. This confusion about the function of assessment has not yet been resolved.

Assessment is also to be used to provide aggregate information about the achievement levels of pupils in schools. This information is to be used by LEAs and the government to monitor the effectiveness of schools, and is also to be made available to parents. The draft Circulars dealing with this proposal suggest that pupils who do not receive the whole National Curriculum should be excluded from this aggregation. Although, in principle, this group could include 'high flyers' as well as low achievers, it seems more likely to involve the latter. However, in either case, it is unlikely to be unknown to the pupils concerned, and one wonders how this will affect their views of themselves. Once again, it seems that the mechanism of implementing the Act is counteracting the general educational aims set out in its first section. The purpose of obtaining data on the achievement of all the pupils in a school should surely be to identify any needs for increasing the school's capacity to be a resource of its pupils, and to indicate how this should be achieved.

In the previous section of this chapter, the major developments in support at school level and at LEA level were described. One may therefore ask whether the 1988 Act is likely to further these developments in the organizational provisions it proposes. It has to be said at the outset, that given a strong commitment to maintaining the move towards the support of children with special educational needs, there is little in the organizational provisions of the Act which need stand in the way of further progress. The delegation of financial management to the school could certainly even enhance the flexibility with which it responds to the special educational needs of pupils, and collaborates with the LEA to make integrated specialized provision for pupils with more severe special needs. Open enrolment could ensure that a school realized an aim to meet the needs of pupils living in its community, and built up flexible pupil interchange with its local special schools. Schools in a locality could combine into clusters to maximize their resources to ensure the effectiveness of their support (Wedell, 1987). Schools which consider opting out of LEA control can make sure that the views of parents of pupils with special educational needs are canvassed before decisions are taken, and can weigh up carefully how services to these pupils are to be provided. They can also formulate clear policies on how they will be able to extend their support for the further integration of children with special educational needs.

Unfortunately, the provisions of the Act cannot be seen to facilitate or even to encourage such commitment, and since the resources available to education are severely constrained, it will certainly be particularly difficult to maintain the commitment even where it exists at present. The arrival of the 1988 Act has exposed the balance of forces between central and local government, parents and professional educators. It is impossible to predict whether the momentum of commitment to furthering the education of children with special educational needs, which has been achieved over the years since the Warnock Report, will be sufficient to influence future policy and practice. The Act does not offer any assurance on account of the gap between its avowed aims and its provisions (Wedell, 1988). Will the LEAs in their reduced power and the teaching profession be able to take a lead? Baroness Warnock has been quoted as saying that it cannot be left to parents to ensure the right to a proper education for all children. However, the organizations of parents of children with special educational needs have been in this situation before, and will hopefully not be disheartened now.

References

DEPARTMENT OF EDUCATION AND SCIENCE (1975) *The discovery of children requiring special education and the assessment of their needs* (Circular 2/75), Dept. of Education and Science.

DEPARTMENT OF EDUCATION AND SCIENCE (1978) *Special educational needs (The Warnock Report)*, HMSO.

DEPARTMENT OF EDUCATION AND SCIENCE (1983) *Assessments and statements of special educational needs* (Circular 1/83), Dept. of Education and Science.

FISH, J., MONGON, D., EVANS, P.L.C. and WEDELL, K. (1987) *The National Curriculum Consultation: a memorandum*, available from the author.

GIPPS, C., GROSS, H., GOLDSTEIN, H. (1986) *Warnock's 18%*, Lewes, Falmer Press.

GOACHER, B., EVANS, J., WELTON, J. and WEDELL, K. (1988) *Policy and provision for special educational needs*, Cassell.

HOUSE OF COMMONS (1987) *Special educational needs: implementation of the Education Act 1981* (Third report from the Education, Science and Arts Committee, Session 1986/7), HMSO.

INNER LONDON EDUCATION AUTHORITY (1985) *Equal opportunities for all?* (The Fish Report), Inner London Education Authority.

IRESON, J., EVANS, P., REDMOND, P. and WEDELL, K. (in press) 'Developing the curriculum for children with learning difficulties: towards a grounded model', *British Educational Research Journal.*

ROGERS, R. (1986) *Caught in the Act*, CSIE and the Spastics Society.

SOCIETY OF EDUCATION OFFICERS (1986) *Special education*, Councils and Education Press.

SWANN, W. (1988) 'Integration? Look twice at statistics', *British Journal of Special Education*, **15**, 3 p. 102.

WEDELL, K., WELTON, J. and VORHAUS, G. (1982) 'Challenges in the 1981 Act', *Special Education: Forward Trends*, **9**, 2 pp. 6–8.

WEDELL, K., (1986) 'Effective clusters', *Times Educational Supplement* 19.9.86.

WEDELL, K. (1988) 'The new Act: a special need for vigilance', *British Journal of Special Education*, **15**, 3 pp. 98–101.

Chapter 4

Decision-making about Special Educational Needs

Brahm Norwich

Introduction

The aim of this chapter is to consider some of the key conceptual and practical problems which arise in making decisions about whether a child has special educational needs (SEN). It will be argued that although the 1988 Education Reform Act will involve basic changes in education practices through the operation of the National Curriculum and the Local Management of Schools (LMS), decision-making for special needs will continue to depend on the framework set up by the Education Act, 1981. Such decision-making takes place at Local Authority level in relation to the individual educational needs of particular children. The framework of statutory procedures, the role of the various participants in the process, and the obstacles which have emerged in this decision-making are well documented in the recent DES-funded study on the implementation of the 1981 Act, conducted at the London University Institute of Education in a three-year study by Goacher, Evans, Welton and Wedell (Goacher *et al.*, 1988). It is not my intention to cover this detailed ground here.

One of the conceptual frameworks used in this study identifies the basic set of principles of the 1981 Act as concerned with:

(1) the *nature* of special educational needs;
(2) the *rights* of those with special educational needs and their parents;
(3) the *effectiveness* of identifying, assessing and meeting special educational needs.

In trying to consider some of the issues which arise in making decisions about individual SEN, I will consider a particular interpretation of the findings concerned with the *nature* of special educational needs and how these issues affect the *effectiveness* of identifying, assessing and meeting such needs. This will lead to a model of some areas of decision-making and finally some discussion of possible implications which bear on the effectiveness of provision.

The Nature of Decisions about Special Education Needs

In the recent evaluation study of the implementation of the 1981 Education Act (Goacher *et al.*, 1988), the new definition of special educational needs was described as the 'heart of the matter'. Problems with this definition were associated with many of the practical difficulties: difficulties in communication between professionals, parents and education officers, in the sharing of a compatible understanding about special provision, in the recording of special educational needs and provision and in the delays and uncertainties of the statutory assessment procedure.

The current definition of special educational needs is widely considered to constitute a major change from the previous framework based on educational handicaps, the categorization approach. The new definition is seen as interactive in that it identifies the causes of difficulties in both environmental and child factors. It is also seen as relative in that special educational needs depend on what provision is generally available. The pre-Warnock Report framework is usually represented as attributing children's difficulties to factors 'within the child'. Under the 1944 Education Act, children were referred to as having 'disabilities of body or mind'. Assessment was concerned then with identifying particular disabilities, hence the categorization approach. The main arguments against this categorization or 'within child' approach were summarized in the Warnock Report. Concepts of handicap and disability were abandoned because they were considered to deal neither with the complexities of individual need, nor to convey anything of the type of educational help needed. The argument is that the concept of SEN is more positive as it is concerned with everything about the child, abilities and disabilities, as well as resources and constraints in the environment which bear on educational progress.

In view of the difficulties surrounding the concept of SEN it is useful to go over the arguments used in abandoning the categorization approach. My aim is to highlight the nature of the argument in order to point out the continuities between pre- and post-Warnock thinking and not to dwell only on the differences which are often overemphasized. In doing this, I will argue that there has been a false emphasis on categorization as the main difficulty with the 1944 handicap framework and a basic confusion over the role and significance of categorization. My aim is to reinterpret the significance of the concept of special educational needs in a way which will, it is hoped, cast some light on some of the difficulties experienced in this field of education provision.

According to Warnock there are basically four key points against the use of categories:

(1) children often suffer from more than one disability resulting in categorization difficulties which affect school provision;
(2) categories promote the idea that all children in the same category have similar educational needs;
(3) categories as the basis for special provision draw resources away from children not covered by the statutory categories;
(4) categories have the effect of labelling children and schools adversely and this persists beyond school and can stigmatize unnecessarily.

Most weight was given to points 3 and 4 above, after account had been taken of two points in favour of statutory categories:

(1) categories help to focus attention on the needs of different groups of children with difficulties;
(2) categories offer a valuable safeguard for the rights of handicapped children to an education suited to individual needs.

The argument for abandoning categories has resulted in practice in a change of terminology to less derogatory terms with less medical connotation – e.g. 'moderate learning difficulties' for 'educational subnormality'. Nevertheless, the term SEN is itself a category, as is the term 'learning difficulty', now a more general category than the categories of handicap.

There is a confusion in the Warnock perspective between categories of educational handicap and categories of child difficulty or disorder. There were two distinct meanings to the concept of handicap pre-Warnock:

(1) having a disability, disorder or difficulty which required educational methods other than those normally used in ordinary schools, viz., special educational treatment (cf. 1962 Regulations on Handicapped Pupils); and
(2) having a disability, disorder or difficulty sufficiently marked or prolonged to adversely affect life activities (cf. Isle of Wight, Court Report).

The first meaning is a narrower one as it refers to the impact of a difficulty such that special educational provision is required. Categories of education provision pre-1981 Act were defined in terms of these categories of educational handicap in the first meaning and not in terms of handicap defined in the second meaning, which is a more generalized one usually associated with an epidemiological perspective. A child could have a disorder or difficulty in the areas of literacy, cognition, emotion or behaviour, which would be categorized in terms of kinds of disorder/difficulty (meaning 2) but not have an educational handicap in the sense of requiring special education provision in the school system (meaning 1). For example, a child with a psychiatric disorder would not necessarily have been considered to require placement at a special school for maladjusted children. This is the gap between the 2 per cent and 18 per cent of children with special educational needs — 2 per cent by meaning 1 and 18 per cent by meaning 2.

It is interesting to note that in abandoning categories of handicap, the Warnock Report used the argument that there was no clear distinction between the more severe degrees (2 per cent in special schools) and the 18–20 per cent of children with difficulties said to have less severe difficulties in ordinary schools. Yet the basis for identifying this 18–20 per cent were the categorization schemes used in research such as The Isle of Wight Study (Rutter, Tizard, Whitmore, 1970) — handicap in the second meaning above. This indicates that in arguing for abandoning the distinction between the more severe (2 per cent) and the less severe instances of special educational need (18 per cent) a scheme of categorization was nonetheless being used.

What underlies the 'abandoning of categories' in special needs education is the move to separating the *delivery* of special education provision from the *location* of delivery in special schools. This is what mainstreaming or integration is about. In the 1944 Education Act handicap categories were tied to the statutory provision of special education which took place in special schools and units. The move to mainstreaming required the separation of categories of educational difficulties from the organization and location of special provision. What is currently the main issue is the nature of exceptional educational needs and the kinds and organization of provision to meet these needs. This was missed in Warnock's rejection of categories, as can be illustrated in analyzing the four Warnock arguments against categorization:

1. There is no reason in terms of a broader handicap category scheme (meaning 2) why a child cannot have more than one disability, disorder or difficulty. Categorization problems arise for the categories of special education provision (school and units) and by implication for education handicap (meaning 1). Unless there are special schools which provide for children with different combinations of difficulties there are problems with placements for some special children. This problem persists, however, under the 1981 Act framework in a different form; that of matching the kinds, combinations and locations of curricular modifications to the range and mixtures of special educational needs.
2. The problem that categories promote the idea that children described by a common general category have similar educational needs, so overlooking their individuality, applies to all categorization including that of children

with 'learning difficulties' or 'special educational needs'. The argument that a handicap category gives little indication of how best to help a child is a misleading one. Although this is clearly so if the assessment of the child only focuses on a general category of deficits (e.g. deafness, intellectual retardation), it does not follow that categorizing deficits does not play a critical role in the context of a rounded individual assessment of assets and deficits of the child and of the environment as they bear on educational development. In other words, assessing difficulties, disorders or disabilities in terms of some categorization scheme is a critical component of a comprehensive educational assessment. It is in the nature of general categorizations that they focus on similarities and differences between individuals and do not relate to the whole individuality of the person. Their value is not as an end in themselves but as a summary which can give broad indications of general kinds of provision needed. It is expecting too much of a categorization scheme to give detailed individual indications of what help is needed.

3. The argument that categorization draws resources away from children who need help (18 per cent) but who do not fit the statutory category (2 per cent), is not about categorization as such but about the form, extent and thresholds of the allocation of additional resources. The drawing away of resources depends on the extent of the additional scarce resources, there being a potential conflict of interest between children with less and more severe degrees of special educational need. This problem continues into the 1981 Act framework which still requires that some children's special educational provision is determined by the LEA, and who receive more resources than other children whose special educational provision is not determined by the LEA, but which are available in the ordinary school.

4. The problem of labelling and stigmatizing is associated with the use of statutory categories which have pejorative connotations. The use of statutory categories can accentuate negative prejudices and stereotypes of those with disabilities but statutory labelling is not the only source of stigma. There are also informal and interpersonal sources of prejudice. On the positive side, some system of positive action for those with disabilities depends on some administrative means for identifying those who are going to benefit, and this requires the use of categories. These problems continue into the 1981 Act framework with the use of the term SEN as a statutory category for the allocation of additional resources for some children.

This analysis leads to the view that the use of categories is an inherent part of the practical administrative arrangements for meeting special educational needs. What has changed with the 1981 Act is the terminology used and the way categories are used in the context of integration. The value of the move to thinking in terms of special educational needs is that it focuses on children as individuals in the particular context of their educational progress, without pre-judging the kind and location of provision to be made for them. This enables a comprehensive assessment of the children's functioning as the outcome of personal and environmental resources and deficits (Wedell, 1980). Such assessment goes well beyond identifying what disabilities or disorders are present, and despite current conceptions is quite compatible with the use of medical categories in so far as they have broad implications for educational progress.

A Redefined Interactive Concept of SEN

When the terms 'interactionist' and 'relative' are used it is usually to offer an alternative to the 'categorization' approach. There seem to be two main aspects to an interactionist-relativist approach. The first is that learning difficulties have multiple causation in particular educational contexts. SEN is thought to depend on interactions between personal resources (abilities, skills, motivations, dispositions) and deficits, with resources and constraints in the environment. In this position SENs are not necessarily taken as constant across different environmental conditions for a given deficit, on account of the different effects of these possible environmental factors. Similarly, SEN is not necessarily constant over time; there can be changes in either environmental or person factors. The second aspect of the relative-interactive nature of learning difficulties relates to a perceptual or phenomenological view that whether a child has a learning difficulty depends on the perspective of the perceiver. A child may be said to have SEN or learning difficulty in one class or school depending on the comparative performance of other children.

What underlies the move from a 'categorization within child' to an 'interactive relative' framework is a switch in theoretical model. Such theoretical models represent basic concepts and assumptions about the nature of human functioning, abilities and disabilities. The 'interactive relative' position involves a theoretical model in which educationally relevant causes are found mainly outside people, are considered in specific terms of what occurs in particular situations and are considered as alterable. Such a conceptual scheme can have the function of fostering a more hopeful and action oriented approach to disabilities and difficulties. This has contributed to its acceptance in a social climate of extending opportunities to disadvantaged groups including those with disabilities. Behind the appeal of this model are the assumptions that environmental factors are alterable and that attributions to personal disabilities are grounds for helplessness and hopelessness. Neither of these two assumptions is reasonable. Positive actions or interventions to prevent, cure, teach or rehabilitate are by definition environmental actions, but the object of the action may be the environment and/or the person. There are no grounds for believing that focusing action on environmental factors is any more effective than on 'within person' factors. Although working with the alterable in teaching is a practical approach, the concept of what is 'alterable' needs to be based on sophisticated causal assumptions and empirical evidence. It needs to be pointed out also that there may be little commitment to alter what can be altered. As regards the second assumption, there are undoubtedly painful adjustments to be made when difficulties and disabilities are identified, but this does not lead inevitably to helplessness and despair. Even in cases of severe disabilities, positive and hopeful attitudes can be maintained, despite the constant challenges and hardships of impairment.

These points indicate that there is a false opposition between a 'within person, categorization' model and an environmentalist version of an 'interactive relativist' model. There is a third way which combines the better features of both models. The following statements summarize such a synthesis:

1. Attributing a learning difficulty depends on explicit or implicit educational objectives, varying as the objectives vary in kind and level.
2. Learning difficulties are outcomes of the interaction of child and environmental causal factors.
3. These causal factors are sometimes found to be stable over time and consistent across learning situations; at other times they can change.
4. Describing a causal factor as stable does not necessarily imply that it will be unalterable in the future with the development of new methodologies and techniques.
5. The interaction of resources and deficits in the child and the environment can be compensatory or debilitating, depending on the strength and severity of the factors. There can be limits to the impact of resources on outcomes.
6. Child factors — both resources and deficits — influence the range of outcomes within which environmental factors can have an impact and are likely to be useful in informing the selection of educational objectives. These factors are not the only influence on the selection of educational objectives, which are set in terms of the common educational aims for all.
7. In an interactive model the outcomes of an interaction of causal factors — child and environmental — can influence or act directly as entry factors for subsequent learning.
8. The purpose of categorizing child and environmental factors is to enable some degree of general prediction or anticipation of future learning progress.

The purpose of arguing for a reconstructed interactionist model is to revive and endorse the positive and appropriate use of categories in the special needs field. This has to be distinguished from the negative use of categories:

(1) exaggerating the differences between children with ordinary and exceptional educational needs;
(2) treating all children who have a particular deficit as the same educationally;
(3) segregating, distancing and devaluing children as persons merely on account of having a deficit.

Categories of resources and deficits are useful in so far as they inform educational decision-making about the selection of relevant objectives, methods and learning activities. There will inevitably be areas of uncertainty about the likely outcomes of the interactions of resources and deficits within the child and between the child and the environment. These uncertainties relate mostly to threshold levels particularly at the moderate levels on the dimensions used in description. Where such uncertainties exist they need to be recognized openly and the resulting difficulties of prediction taken into account in making decisions about appropriate educational provision. Although there are likely to be fewer uncertainties at the more severe levels of deficit, using categories in description, explanation and prediction only gives general indications in so far as different individual cases show similar patterns of response. There remains the need for individual information to be taken into account to qualify these indications from the general case. In principle, ideas about the general case will be modified in the light of information from individual cases.

Practical Decision-making about Special Educational Needs

Problems in decision-making about SEN arise partly from confusions about the nature of special educational needs. A major confusion is the belief that a special educational needs perspective requires abandoning categories whether of disability, handicap, special educational needs or provision.

The 1981 Education Act has not abandoned categories but replaced specific categories of educational handicap (1944 Act) by the more general categories of learning difficulty or special educational need. The change can be represented visually (see Figure 4.1).

The main change in the 1981 Act scheme is to loosen the connection between special education provision (SEP) and special schools and units. This is done conceptually by widening the term's reference to include up to 18–20 per cent of children with less severe educational difficulties. As the figure indicates there is no middle level of description of the different kinds of SEN in the 1981 Act scheme though this does not imply that the definition of

Figure 4.1 Comparison between the 1944 and 1981 Education Acts' schema for representing categories of pupils with special educational needs

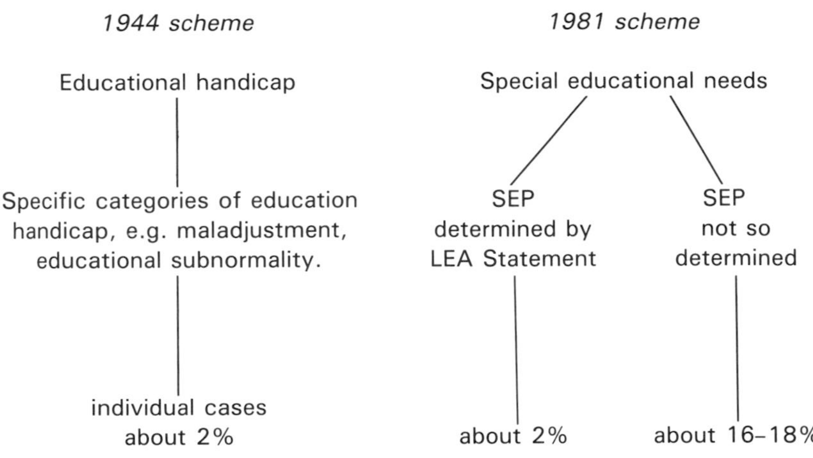

SEN is circular or tautological as commonly asserted. In Section 1(i) of the 1981 Act, a child is said to have SEN if he has a 'learning difficulty which calls for SEP to be made for him'. The term 'learning difficulty' is then defined in terms of:

(a) 'significantly greater difficulty in learning than the majority of children of his age'; or
(b) 'a disability which either prevents or hinders him from making use of educational facilities of a kind generally provided in schools, within the area of the local authority concerned, for children of his age'; or
(c) 'under the age of 5 years and is or would be if SEP were not made for him, likely to fall within paragraph (a) or (b) when over that age'.

This definition of SEN in terms of learning difficulty and then in terms of age norms and disability, though general and not helpful directly in setting specific thresholds or criteria for decision-making about SEN, is not circular. SEN is defined in terms other than just SEP. However, what counts as a disability, and the degree of learning difficulty which is significantly greater than the majority of children of his/her age has not been clarified in the Act nor in the Government Regulations or Circulars. In the 1981 Act there are now two general boundaries which separate (1) those who have SEN from those who do not and (2) those with SEN whose needs are met through 'generally available provision' in ordinary schools (Section 13, Circular 1/83) from those whose SEN are determined by the LEA (Section 5(1), Act).

In considering these two broad groups of children with SEN it is important to be clear about who makes decisions about them at which level in the education service. Decisions about children with SEN met within generally available provision are made directly by the teachers in ordinary schools, though no doubt these decisions are influenced by LEA policies, practices and resourcing for the 18 per cent. Decisions about children with SEN determined by the LEA are made through the statutory statementing procedures by professionals and officers with parental consultation. Circular 1/83 (Sections 13 to 16) outlines some of the broad criteria to be used in the decision-making. The new draft Circular to replace 1/83 in the light of the 1988 Act makes no changes in this respect. It is stated in Circular 1/83 that decisions about what constitutes 'additional or otherwise different provision' will vary from area to area depending on provision available in the LEA's schools. Nevertheless, the Circular does recommend some national uniformity in the criteria used:

> As a general rule the Secretary of State expects LEAs to afford the protection of a statement to all children who have severe or complex learning difficulties which require the provision of extra resources in ordinary schools, and in all cases where the child is placed in a special unit attached to an ordinary school, a special school, a non-maintained special school or an independent school approved for the purpose (Section 14).

SEN can be met according to the Circular from provision available in ordinary schools where:

> ordinary schools provide special educational provision from their own resources in the form of additional tuition and remedial provision, or in normal circumstances, where the child attends a reading centre or unit for disruptive pupils (Section 15).

It is evident that these guidelines depend on the meaning of the phrase 'ordinary schools provide special educational provision from their own resources'. The burden of the distinction between the two groups of SEN falls on the distinction between 'determined by the LEA' and 'ordinary schools provide from their own resources'. The guidance on when the LEA will determine SEP, and therefore make a statement of SEN is still not specific enough to deal with the cases of children who are integrated in ordinary schools and do not have 'severe or complex learning difficulties'. These cases are particularly important as they constitute a large proportion of the 2 per cent with SEN and who have been considered to need some protection of the additional resources allocated to them.

Another confusion which has arisen from the 1981 Act has been over the definition of the term special educational provision. The Act refers explicity to: 'educational provision which is additional to or otherwise different from the educational provision *made generally for children of his age* in schools maintained by the LEA concerned' (Section 1(3) (a)). The Circular uses the phrase 'generally available in ordinary schools in the area under normal arrangements' (Section 13). The use and interpretation of these phrases was at stake in the case of R. v. Hampshire Education Authority ex-parte J. (1985). The judge refused to accept the interpretation of SEP as what is additional or different from what was *available generally* in schools. The reasons for this refusal were that the term *available* is not used in the Act, only the Circular, and that the Act's definition of SEP is in terms of what is '*made generally* for children of his age'. The phrase 'made generally' was interpreted to mean 'provided for the general run of normal children, to the normal majority'. This interpretation avoids the paradox which arises from defining SEP in the locational terms of 'available generally'. If Special Educational Provision means provision which is not available generally in ordinary schools, then the more this provision is available in ordinary schools, the less SE provision there will be. This implication confounds the location of provision with what is provided in terms of modified objectives and methods. The preferred definition of SE provision, in terms of what is additional or different from provision for the general run of normal children, is therefore consistent with current ideas about describing SEP in terms of the different kinds of modifications made to the ordinary curriculum — modifications of access to the curriculum, to the climate for learning and to the level of curricular goals. These broad types of adaptations are not required for the general run of normal or ordinary children.

It follows that there is a distinction between the *type of education* called for and the *location of the provision*. The phrase '*made generally*' refers to the *type* of provision, whether it is provided for the 'general run of normal children' or not. The phrase *available generally* refers to the *location* of that provision, where it is available. There is a third factor implied in the 1981 Act framework which is concerned with the immediate *authorization* of the resources for SEP, whether from school, support services or LEA. There are therefore three areas for decision-making:

(1) type or provision needed:
    Is additional/different provision needed?
(2) location of provision:
    Where is it available?
    In ordinary school or special unit/school?
(3) authorization of provision:
    Who directly determines provision?
    Ordinary school or LEA?

Figure 4.2 Decision-making areas implied in the 1981 Act

	Decision alternatives			
Type	Generally made provision		Additional/different provision	
Location	In ordinary school	In centre, special unit or school	In ordinary school	In centre, special unit or school
Authorization by LEA	1 X	2 X	5 Statement of SEN present. Specialist support teaching in ord. school	6 Statement of SEN present. In special school or unit
Authorization by Ordinary School	3 ordinary provision	4 X	7 No Statement of SEN. Specialist support teaching in ord. school	8 No Statement of SEN. Off site centre

(X means — not possible as an outcome)

These decisions can be represented by Figure 4.2. For ease of explanation only, it is assumed that there are only two alternatives in each decision area, which is clearly an oversimplification.

By combining these decision alternatives eight possible outcomes arise. Three of these (1, 2 and 4) are not possible in practice as generally made provision occurring in ordinary school is the immediate responsibility of ordinary schools. Outcome 3 (ordinary provision) is distinct from outcomes 5 to 8 in the kind of provision which is thought to be required. Outcomes 6 and 8 are different from outcomes 5 and 7 in the location of the additional provision. Outcomes 5 and 6 are distinct from outcomes 7 and 8 in the immediate authorization of resources for the SEP.

Using this model it is possible to identify some of the main areas of difficulty in making decisions about SEN and SEP:

1. How will the phrase 'generally made provision' be interpreted; who will be counted in the 'normal majority' when it comes to decisions about the

nature and allocation of additional provision? Even with 'normality' taken as a question of degree, there is still the question of what degree of 'normality' calls for 'generally made provision'?

2. Having decided on the need for additional/different provision, where will this provision be available: in ordinary classes, some mix of in class and withdrawal, a mix of ordinary school or separate centre, unit or school? This is the issue of the degree to which special educational needs can be met in ordinary schools, the integration issue. If it is decided to make the special provision available in an ordinary school through, say, a mixture of setting up a resource centre and having in-class support, will such additional provision be considered as *determined* by the school or the LEA? This is a complex decision which depends on what is involved in LEAs determining SE provision. When a LEA determines provision this refers to a decision being made outside a particular school for a particular child about her/his SEN. It implies a set of criteria for deciding whether and what additional or different resources will be offered. Such a decision is taken in the procedures for issuing a Statement. If a LEA decides to offer additional/different resources without a Statement, as in the case of Oxfordshire LEA, this leaves the child without the statutory protection for this resource. This outcome is represented by outcome 7 in the Figure 4.2 model.

3. The third type of decision-making problem concerns the cases of young people mainly in secondary schools who attend off-site or on-site units on account of behaviour difficulties (disruption). Placement at these units is seen as necessary because the behaviour difficulties cannot be tolerated in ordinary schools and classes. The education provision received at these centres or units is different from what is generally made, it is located outside ordinary schools, is often resourced directly by the LEA, but not seen to call for the protection of a Statement. So instead of being an outcome 6 in the decision-making model (with a Statement in special unit or centre), they end up as outcome 8, with no Statement.

Conclusions

It has been argued that there are more continuities in the issues and difficulties which arise in this field between the pre- and post-1981 statutory framework than have often been recognized. We still need to use categories to summarize the similarities and differences between individual special educational needs and between the variety of curricular modifications for individual children. The previous problems identified by the Warnock Report persist in the 1981 Act framework and are not affected basically by the 1988 Act. Firstly, the problem of individuals not fitting categories continues in the difficulties of matching currently available provision to the complex special educational needs of some children. Secondly, referring to a child as having a learning difficulty, whether moderate or severe, can still lead some people to treat all children so described as having the same individual needs. Thirdly, when an LEA decides to determine an individual child's SEN and make additional provision, this process can still draw scarce resources away from those children with SEN whose needs are met through resources available in ordinary schools. On the other hand, the 1981 Act does represent a significant change from the 1944 framework, in terms of the move towards integration. This has involved a reconceptualization of special educational provision as available not only in special schools or units. This move represents the major conceptual change, not 'abandoning categories' of handicap.

What underlies the concern about categorization is the intention to avoid the damaging, discrediting and devaluing of those with difficulties and disorders. Unfortunately, this intention cannot be realized without some form of categorization. Categorization is required: (1) to identify those people who are going to receive additional or different education provision; and (2) to protect the additional resources used. Avoiding stigma is a delicate matter which is partly about *how* the additional resources are negotiated, allocated, used and protected. An identification process requires criteria and thresholds to differentiate between those who will and those who will not receive additional or different provision, even when the learning difficulties are a matter of degree. Yet, there are no simple procedures for 'discovering' criteria which would satisfy all parties concerned, parents, teachers, schools and LEAs. This gives rise to a major dilemma for which there is no final resolution. However, appeals to the relativity of special educational needs represent a response to only one aspect of the dilemma. What can be proposed is a working system for the setting and revising of specific criteria and thresholds.

It is recognized in the 1981 Act that account needs to be taken of conditions in LEA schools with the implication that these can vary from LEA to LEA. But, as Circular 1/83 and its draft revision implies, there are good reasons to have some degree of uniformity between different areas of the same country. The proposed working resolution is for there to be two levels of criteria setting — broad guidelines and criteria at a national level which are specific enough to facilitate the setting of even more specific procedures and criteria at LEA level. The national criteria will need to be more specific than those currently used by the DES. One of the possible reasons for the overgenerality of the current criteria in Section 14 of the Circular is the reluctance to make explicit use of more specific categories of special educational need. In view of the arguments made above, this reluctance could be questioned. Similarly, this central DES guidance could be more specific about the various kinds of special educational provision — clarifying what is different or additional in a 'modified' or 'developmental curriculum'. Within the current context of more central direction about a National Curriculum — i.e. generally made provision — there may be more inclination to make these specifications. However, it is crucial that these specifications are not so constraining that they prevent LEAs from elaborating their own versions of criteria and thresholds to meet local conditions. LEAs could be expected to publish formally their criteria, and review and update them with changing circumstances. Similarly, DES guidelines will need to be reviewed and updated in response to changing LEA and school conditions.

It is an essential part of this scheme that any set of criteria or thresholds will not be expected to deal with individual cases in a simple routine way. The primary emphasis will be on individual needs which are assessed in terms of an individual's functioning in context. Local criteria, based on national ones, will be used in the general summary descriptions which will be arrived at in making decisions about optimal provision. The relationship between an individual case and general criteria is not a mechanical one and in no sense is the individual to be seen as fully described in terms of general categories or descriptions. Regular action is needed to guard against the tendency to assume that a constructed category scheme has a fixed 'reality' which is independent of value judgments — about what constitutes a good common curriculum for all children, how much and for whom additional/different provision is desirable, and which degree of special educational need will be protected and by what form of protection. That there might be a working consensus about judgments should not be taken either as a justification for not reviewing and revising these judgments regularly.

The model of decision-making described above in terms of three areas could be useful in identifying where clarifications about the nature of the decisions need to be made. By using an analysis based on the distinction between the type of educational provision, the location of delivery and the determination of resources for the provision, some of the current difficulties could be dealt with more effectively. This model is not intended to lead to the specific decisions which need to be made. It could help to lay out some of the possibilities to be considered in deciding, for instance, which special educational provision to give added protection to by using the statementing procedure; what additional/different provision can be available in ordinary schools by allocating the special resources from the LEA to the ordinary school while still maintaining protection of the provision.

It was not my intention to consider these particular issues in detail, only to discuss the general framework within which such decisions could be made. It will be noticed that there have been few references to the Education Reform Act and its impact on decision-making in this field. This omission is no reflection on the wider importance of these changes to special needs education. My position has been that although Local Management of Schools (LMS) and the National Curriculum will have a major impact on special needs education, this impact will still operate within the framework of the 1981 Education Act. With the anxieties generated in the wake of the 1988 Act it is particularly important to keep sight of the central significance of the 1981 framework. This chapter has attempted to consider this framework in some depth. The hope is that this analysis will help to accommodate the provisions of the Reform Act in a positive way.

References

COURT, D. *Fit for the Future: The report of the Committee on Child Health Services*, London, HMSO.

DES (1962) *Handicapped Pupils and Special Schools, Regulations*, London, HMSO.

DES (1981) *Educational Act*, London, HMSO.

DES (1983) *Assessments and Statements of Special Educational Needs*, Circular 1/83, London, HMSO.

EVANS, J. (1987) *Decision-making for Special Needs*, University of London, Institute of Education.

GOACHER, B., EVANS, J., WELTON, J., WEDELL, K. (1988) *Policy and Provision for Special Educational Needs: Implementing the 1981 Education Act*, London, Cassell.

RUTTER, R., TIZARD, J., WHITMORE, K. (1970) *Education, Health and Behaviour*, London, Longman.

WARNOCK, M. (1978) *Special Educational Needs: Report of the Committee of Enquiry into the Education of Handicapped Children and Young People*, London, HMSO.

WEDELL, K. (1983) 'Assessing Special Educational Needs', *Secondary Education Journal*, 13, 15–16.

Chapter 5

Was the GERBIL a Marxist Mole?

David Galloway

Introduction

Before publishing the Education Reform Bill the government issued a series of 'consultation' documents. The consultation must have been wide-ranging since it elicited over 18,000 replies (Haviland, 1988). Few of these replies greeted the proposals with undiluted rapture. Professional opposition was massive. The government responded by guiding through Parliament a Bill, know derisively by its opponents as the GERBIL, which not only retained intact all the essential features of the consultation documents but which also introduced additional, equally contentious features such as the abolition of the ILEA. Initial reactions from educationalists were predictably critical (e.g. Lawton and Chitty, 1988).

The GERBIL has now grown up into an Act. Committees of the great and the good – greatness and goodness having been defined, presumably, by the Secretary of State and the Prime Minister – are busily beavering away at its implementation. It is beyond the scope of this chapter to consider whether beavers are more or less beneficial to their habitat, or destructive of it, than rodents. It is also beyond the scope of this chapter to consider whether the deluge of protest against all the Act's main clauses may have been the entirely predictable reaction of entrenched professional interest groups which saw their autonomy threatened (a reaction not unlike that with which some Communist Party interest groups in Russia are said to have greeted Gorbachev's reforms). I do, however, wish to analyze some of the Act's principal clauses in terms of their probable impact on children with special educational needs. Here, too, criticism has been consistently hostile.

Brennan (1987), for example, argued that the national curriculum would result in a narrowing of the curriculum on the grounds that 'pupils with learning problems may require ⅔, ¾ or even more time, to grasp the core subjects with consequent reduction in the time available for foundation study'. In passing, we might note that this is a somewhat curious argument. Implicitly it ignores the extraordinarily consistent evidence that many children with special needs, including those with moderate learning difficulties, make better educational progress in ordinary than in special classes. It also implies, in the face of explicit statements to the contrary, that schools will be able to regard the foundation subjects as voluntary parts of the national curriculum. Brennan, though, is not alone in his hostility. Peter (1988) also argued that the Bill would result in reduced curriculum choice, and criticized the absence of any explicit commitment to promote children's emotional development. The National Children's Bureau criticized the lack of commitment to personal and social education (Davie, 1987). Other aspects, notably provision for seeking grant maintained status, have aroused the concern of groups of parents with regard to children both in mainstream schools and in special schools (Fisher, 1987).

In this chapter I shall argue: (i) that dissatisfaction with the effectiveness of schools in educating their less able pupils crosses party political lines; (ii) that although the GERBIL is in fact the product of a reforming right wing government, an identical bill might equally well have been produced by a reforming government dominated by Marxists; (iii) that the national curriculum, national testing and provision for grant-maintained status may all be seen to have potential benefits for pupils with special educational needs. In all this I am assuming that there would be a *prima facie* case for regarding the GERBIL as a Marxist mole if it could be shown that its principal clauses: (i) were more likely to benefit traditional supporters of the left than of the right; (ii) were at least as consistent with an ideology of the left as of the right. Whether one welcomes or deplores the possibility of a Marxist mole producing a reform bill for Mrs Thatcher's government is a matter of political preference with which I am not concerned. I shall, however, argue that the Act's potential benefits for many children with special educational needs may be reduced as a result of pressure from professional groups supposedly acting in their interests.

Perceived Effectiveness of Education for Pupils with SEN: Consensus Between Left and Right?

Children with special needs in ordinary schools are a large and heterogeneous group. The Warnock Committee concluded that up to 20 per cent of pupils would need special educational treatment at some stage in their school careers (DES, 1978). In the same year the Scottish Education Department argued that up to 50 per cent of pupils might have some learning difficulty, and that teachers should accept responsibility for them. It is easy to point out that the way tests and behaviour screening instruments are constructed ensures that researchers, or government committees, can identify any proportion they care to select as having learning or adjustment difficulties. In this connection, figure of 15 or 20 per cent are arbitrary, reflecting a view that teachers might reasonably expect some form of additional support, over and above what is normally provided in a classroom, if they are to teach these children effectively.

Yet once we accept that as many as 20 per cent of children have special needs, let alone 50 per cent, we have to accept that evaluation of the education system's effectiveness with these pupils cannot be divorced either from educational or from political debate about its overall effectiveness. To be more specific, political debate about 'underachievement', educational disadvantage and the progress of lower ability pupils is referring to more or less the same large minority of children in ordinary schools that Warnock and the Scottish Education Department regarded as having learning difficulties. The conventional wisdom in the Conservative Party is encapsulated in quotations from Sir Keith Joseph (1983) and Rhodes Boyson (1988). In a much publicized speech to the Council of Local Education Authorities, Joseph explained the rationale for setting up a Lower Attaining Pupils Project: 'It is my job as Secretary of State to remind my partners in the Education service that the education of lower attaining 4th and 5th year secondary pupils is one of the most pressing problems with which we need jointly to come to grips.' Five years later, there was less talk of partnership, but Boyson (1988) felt able to conclude: 'We still do almost as well as competitor countries with the education of our top 20 per cent ability children. It is with the average and below average that we often do badly.'

From a totally different perspective, the ILEA (1984) endorsed enthusiastically a report which expressed deep concern about the effect of secondary schooling on the self-esteem of a large minority of pupils. Similarly, the work of authors such as Willis (1977) and Corrigan (1979) has to be seen as critical of the way in which schools perpetuate and deepen existing divisions within society, thereby ensuring, in the words of the sub-title of Willis' book, that 'working class kids get working class jobs'. The exact proportion of children whose work and/or behaviour is thought by different authors to fall short of their teachers' expectations or requirements is unimportant, at least for the present discussion. What matters is that most of the pupils they are talking about would be regarded on the Warnock Committee's criteria as having special educational needs.

Yet although politicians and educationalists on the right and the left agree about the education system's inadequacy with respect to a large minority of pupils, they reach their conclusions by totally different routes. The ground for the right-wing analysis was laid in the Black Papers of the 1970s (e.g.

Cox and Boyson, 1977) and developed in a longer critique by Boyson (1975). This is effectively summarized in Grace's (1987) review of the changing relationship between teachers and the state:

> Radical teachers, especially in inner-city schools, were portrayed as militant trade unionists intent on industrial action and work-place democracy on the one hand and as cultural and ideological subversives intent on a politicization of classroom practice on the other. These teachers, 'the trendies and the lefties', were, it was claimed, exploiting school and classroom autonomy to the full and for the wrong reasons (p. 214).

This view of themselves as radical subversives is generally greeted with slightly baffled amusement on INSET courses and by teachers taking post-qualification degree or diploma courses. It is certainly true that the view of teachers as cultural and ideological subversives was grossly overstated. Nevertheless, Grace is also correct in continuing to argue that 'the granting of classroom autonomy to teachers in Britain had always been premised on the implicit understanding that teachers would use this autonomy conservatively and not radically' (p. 214).

It was perhaps because the right-wing critique of the 1970s was so manifestly over-stated, though never denied by its exponents, that an additional argument was produced. This was that state education was preoccupied, simultaneously, with an educational élite of pupils and with the self interests of educational professionals (e.g. O'Keefe, 1987). The charge of preoccupation with an educational élite is reflected in Joseph's (1983) concern for the lowest attaining 40 per cent, and in Boyson's (1988) claim that we do as well as competitor countries with the education of the top 20 per cent, but fail with pupils of average and below average ability. The charge of self-interest retained the original picture of teachers as radical subversives when referring to the alleged excesses of hard-left LEAs, but adapted it when referring to the general body of teachers to depict them as preoccupied with their most intelligent pupils because they were easiest to teach. Self-interest was further evident in their concern with salaries, conditions of service and resources. At a time of continuing restrictions on public expenditure this image had undeniable attractions for the party in power.

Thus, the right attributed the failure of public education for less able and even average pupils to teachers' misuse of classroom autonomy for political purposes, to exclusive preoccupation with children who were easiest and most rewarding to teach and to a greater concern for their own salaries than for their pupils' needs. The left-wing analysis of the failure of state education for less able pupils was relatively straightforward. In summary, the problem lay in the conformity of teachers, not their radicalism. The education system was deeply involved in maintaining existing divisions within society, based on social class, race and gender. It was not simply that members of a middle-class profession could not realistically hope to meet the educational needs of working-class children. More important, by reflecting the interests of powerful groups within society, the education system would inevitably maintain existing stratification irrespective of the view of individual teachers.

Implications: Further Consensus?

The right-wing analysis of the ills of the education system led logically to three conclusions of relevance to the present discussion. First, the autonomy which teachers in Britain had enjoyed should be reduced. In no other Western country, perhaps no other country in the world, had teachers been given so much control over what was taught and over the way it was taught. Clearly, according to educationalists of the right, this power had been abused. The 'partnership' between the DES, LEAs and schools had become unequal, and the balance of power must be shifted. Since so many LEAs were either supine or subversive, the argument continued, the government must take the initiative. A national curriculum, if not a nationalized one, was the logical result.

Second, since the needs of pupils and the wishes of parents had so flagrantly been ignored, greater choice should be given to parents as 'consumers' of the education system. Giving parents greater representation on governing bodies and increased freedom to choose their children's school was a start. Mismanagement in some LEAs was so severe, though, that a more drastic measure was needed. Here the logical result was provision for parents to require governors to apply for grant-maintained status, thus opting out of LEA control.

Third, greater emphasis should be placed on the instrumental function of education in social and economic policy. Because the curriculum had been hijacked by teachers under the influence of left-wing sociologists, pupils were leaving school without the skills needed by the labour market in a rapidly changing economy. Even more important, they were leaving school with attitudes towards work and towards authority which equipped them neither to seek nor to hold down a job. The importance attached to the instrumental function of education is reflected in the explicitly vocational orientation of initiatives such as the Youth Training Scheme (YTS), the Technical and Vocational Education Initiative (TVEI) and the Certificate of

Pre-Vocational Education (CPVE). Significantly, personal and social education plays a major part in all these schemes.

At this stage I should perhaps repeat that I am not interested either in justifying or in criticizing the conclusions which followed from the right's analysis of the reasons for the perceived under-achievement of so many pupils. Nor am I interested in justifying or criticizing conclusions which follow from the radical left-wing analysis. They are, nevertheless, extraordinarily similar. Again, there are three obvious conclusions.

First, power should be removed from professionals. Since teachers are the agents, consciously or otherwise, of socially and economically entrenched interest groups, it is clear that their control over the curriculum must be drastically reduced. Since many LEAs are committed to the status quo, and in any case wouldn't know how to set about redefining the curriculum, the balance of power must shift towards the centre. A national curriculum would be an excellent starting point.

Second, since schools have so clearly failed to respond effectively to the needs of pupils and the wishes of parents, greater choice should be given to the people at grass roots level. The left's concept of the people differs, of course, from that of the right. Nevertheless, it would be as logical for the left as for the right to regard greater parental representation on governing bodies as useful starting points. What better means exist for challenging the vested interests of educational professionals?

Finally, the left could also join with the right in demanding greater emphasis on the instrumental functions of education. Only if all young people acquire the skills to become economically successful, will the existing social class, race and gender divisions in British society be reduced. Initiatives such as TVEI, CPVE and YTS could all be seen as logical products of this conclusion.

Both the right-wing and the left-wing analysis presented here lead logically to greater centralization of the curriculum and to reduced teacher autonomy. There are, of course, other right-wing and other left-wing analyses that would lead in different directions. My aim is merely to show that they *can* lead in the same direction, albeit for different reasons. Similarly, both the right and the left could, logically, welcome a policy that gave greater influence to parents within a framework that emphasized the vocational and instrumental functions of education. Whether one thinks of 'parents' as members of the Moral Majority, or as 'cells' or 'cadres' of Party Activists is irrelevant. My argument is that the main sections of the Act can be seen as apolitical. The question is whose interests it is most likely to serve. Will it, as the government professes to hope, raise the quality of education for pupils of below average ability, and enhance their employment prospects? Or will it, as its detractors argue, disadvantage them still further?

The National Curriculum

The need for a national curriculum is only contested by professional educationalists. It was accepted with little argument by politicians of all the main parties following James Callaghan's (1976) speech at Ruskin College. Nor has there been any public outcry to match that of professional interest groups. The confidence with which the government introduced the Act must have owed as much to recognition that teachers and academics were out of step and/or out of touch with public opinion as to its parliamentary majority. In so far as public debate took place, independent of professional input, it centred on the scope and details of a national curriculum, not on the need for one as a matter of general principle (Haviland, 1988).

Since a national curriculum is now widely accepted as necessary, what objections have special educators raised against the particular version to be found in the Act? I wish to focus particularly on the absence of any mention of personal and social relationships, the number and scope of compulsory subjects, and the provision that statements issued under the 1981 Act may exempt a child from all or part of the national curriculum's requirements.

No Place for Personal and Social Relations

Like the abolition of war, poverty and injustice, fostering positive personal and social relations has to be seen as *A Good Thing*. One could go further. For children whose family and social background have been impoverished and/or damaging, it must surely be *An Essential Thing*. My contention is that too many special educators both in mainstream and in special schools have for too long used this argument as a smokescreen for their failure to offer children with special needs *a special means of access* to the curriculum. Instead they have offered a *separate or modified* curriculum, often on the dubious grounds that this will provide greater scope for meeting children's emotional needs as well as their educational ones.

Two arguments can be put forward against including personal and social relations as a distinct topic in a national curriculum.'

(1) The concept itself is hopelessly imprecise. Personal and social development was considered at least as important in Hitler's Germany as in any late twentieth-century Western democracy. It seems doubtful, to say the least, whether the emphasis on developing values and attitudes in some tutorial schemes fits easily with a primary emphasis on preparation for working life. Yet both are aspects of personal and social development. There must be a powerful argument against including in a national curriculum a concept

that so obviously lends itself to political exploitation, either by politicians or by teachers.

(2) The legal right of teachers to concern themselves with pupils' personal and social development presumably rests in their role *in loco parentis*. Their moral right, however, is much more questionable. In one sense, of course, it is clear that schools *are* concerned with pupils' personal and social development. Any organization requires cooperation and/or constructive competition between members if it is to work effectively. To put it another way, schools cannot operate without rules, stated or implicit, and these rules reflect the values which the school wishes pupils to internalize. Thus, the rules, or expected way of behaving, together with the way they are enforced, will influence the values held by pupils which in turn will reflect, and be reflected in, their personal and social development.

This, however, is little more than a statement of the obvious. It certainly does not need to be formalized into a national curriculum. When they talk about the importance of personal and social development teachers generally mean more than this. It is here that the problem occurs, not least because it is disproportionately pupils of below average ability who are said to 'need' this kind of development. There is evidence that pupils with special needs resent and are distressed by removal from ordinary classes (Simmons, 1986). The limited available evidence suggests that children with special needs want experience of success *within* the mainstream curriculum. Provision of extra or alternative sessions in personal and social relations may be seen as offensively patronizing on the part of the teachers who claim, implicitly, to know the children's needs better than their parents or than the pupils themselves. As important, it can also be seen as a way of 'marginalizing' them from the core of the school's curriculum activities — a process described by Hargreaves (1983) in relation to pupil perceptions of community service programmes.

Size and Scope of the National Curriculum

The core subjects are English, Maths and Science. In addition, 'foundation subjects' will also form part of the national curriculum for all pupils, namely: history, geography, technology, music, art, physical education and (for secondary pupils) a modern foreign language. It has been argued that these compulsory subjects will take up too much time, leaving insufficient time for other topics needed by pupils with special needs. To justify this claim it is necessary to specify: (a) which curriculum areas are needed by the majority of pupils, but not by an arbitrarily selected minority regarded as having special needs; (b) what curriculum areas these pupils need, but the majority do not. One could, of course, say that the compulsory areas are too extensive for all pupils, but one would then still have to say what should go and what should replace it.

The claim that children with special needs have different and/or additional curriculum needs to other children is a familiar one. It has been used to justify providing them with an alternative, low-status curriculum that restricts rather than enhances their opportunities. This happens in special schools and units through the restrictions inevitably imposed by size. It also happens in some comprehensive schools where proliferation of options is used to shunt pupils of below average ability into a non-examination siding. The requirement that all pupils should have access to the full range of the national curriculum may make it more difficult for schools to marginalize their pupils with special needs.

The Exemption Clause

A statement of special needs may exempt a pupil from part or all of the requirements of the national curriculum. In addition, head teachers will have powers under Section 19 of the Act to modify or disapply all or part of the national curriculum in circumstances that are yet to be specified in regulations. However, the DES (1989) implies that head teachers will be encouraged not to make extensive use of this provision. It has been argued that these exemption clauses drive a hole through the integration spirit of the 1981 Act. Apart from the obvious point that some commentators have found this 'spirit' to have been heavily diluted by the 'escape clauses' regarding children who would continue to need special schooling (e.g. Tomlinson, 1982; Galloway and Goodwin, 1987), it is still difficult to make sense of this argument. Clearly, the national curriculum as proposed in the Act will be inappropriate for some pupils with special needs. For example, few pupils with hearing impairment and/or moderate or severe learning difficulties will benefit from learning a modern foreign language. For a larger number of pupils the attainment targets associated with each subject in the national curriculum will be unrealistic, at least at their own age-level. Yet it does not follow that these pupils should be offered a narrower, more restrictive curriculum, but rather that the attainment targets should be modified in the light of their abilities. The choice facing the government was really very simple. The requirements of the national curriculum could be stated so broadly that *all* pupils could be included, irrespective of the nature or severity of their learning difficulties. This would have satisfied professionals with vested interests in maintaining the status quo, but everyone else would have recognized that the issue had been fudged. Alternatively, the requirements could be formulated to include *most* pupils, with provision to exempt those for whom parents and professionals agreed that they were clearly impractical.

Attainment Targets and National Testing

A frequent criticism of the Act's proposals for national testing and publication of the results is that it will damage the self-esteem of the children who do badly. It isn't necessary to spend too long on this. From their first year in infant school children are aware of formal and informal practices which group them according to ability. These are evident in formal assessment procedures, for example reading tests, and, in many classrooms, in the seating arrangements. Teachers have always differentiated between children according to ability and progress; indeed, they must do so in order to cater effectively for the range of abilities that is found in any classroom. Children have always been aware of the process.

The objection, then, presumably lies in the public nature of the proposed testing at 7, 11, 14 and 16 and in the fact that parents will be told the results, both in absolute terms and in relation to the results of other children in the same school, other schools and nationally. The fear that parents will then place intolerable pressures on their children reflects the deep mistrust of parents that is endemic at all levels of the British school system (Marland, 1985). It is, however, probably a realistic anxiety in schools which have not established an effective, cooperative partnership with parents.

There is a peculiar arrogance in supporters of a system which more or less compels parents to hand their children over to strangers for a major part of their lives from the age of five, yet refuses to give them any precise information on what educational standards their children should have attained after a given time, let alone any objective guidance on their progress relative to other children. In the past, well-informed and articulate parents have generally been able to obtain the information they wanted. Parents of children with learning and adjustment difficulties all too often have felt themselves left, or kept, in the dark. While writing this chapter I heard from a mature student that her son has been placed in a remedial reading class without her knowledge or consent. It is worth mentioning only because it happens so frequently. At least the Act gives parents of children with special needs *some* information.

Two further points are worth mentioning. First, the Task Group of Assessment and Testing (DES, 1988) regarded the major purpose of national testing as diagnostic and formative. Providing a standard against which to measure progress was secondary to this. On the whole this report was favourably received by professionals. It accords broadly with the conventional wisdom of teachers and academics. However, a leaked letter from Downing Street revealed the Prime Minister's dissatisfaction with the report which 'places a heavy responsibility on teachers' judgements and general impressions' (Surkes, 1988). An outdated conventional wisdom holds that special needs must be identified and alternative programmes provided for the children concerned — a view reflected in Sir Keith Joseph's Lower Attaining Pupils Project. The radical critique, either from the right or from the left, holds that children underachieve partly because too little is expected of them, and partly because they receive insufficient and inappropriate help within the classroom. It follows that *all* children must have full access to the curriculum.

The second point arises from the Secretary of State's response to the interim report of the Mathematics Working Group (DES, 1987). The group, consisting mainly of professional educationalists, put forward the conventional view that programmes of study must be devised before setting attainment targets: in other words, decide on the curriculum, *then* decide what to test. In his reply Baker (1987) demanded a radical alternative to this: 'the programmes of study for mathematics will follow from the attainment targets which the group establishes'; in other words, decide what standard children should reach at each age level, *then* decide on the curriculum.

In each case the conventional wisdom leaves power and control in the hands of teachers. The radical alternative makes teachers more visibly accountable for the progress of pupils with special needs. It thereby has the potential: (a) to encourage teachers to give greater attention to their less able pupils; (b) to encourage parents to use the information they will be given to negotiate a more active role for themselves in their children's schooling. If the professional interests win the day, these possibilities may be lost.

Grant Maintained Status

A persistent argument against provision for schools to opt out of LEA control by seeking grant-maintained status is that grant-maintained schools will be reluctant to accept pupils with special needs. In particular, the argument goes, they will be reluctant to accept pupils with learning difficulties and with emotional and behavioural difficulties for fear that these pupils will lower the school's tone and drag down its results in national testing and public examinations. This is a legitimate point, but before accepting it we need to bear in mind two alternative arguments.

First, grant-maintained schools will have to make their admission policies clear. Since they are required to retain their existing character and status, the Secretary of State should presumably require them to state the catchment area from which they will in all normal circumstances accept pupils. Grant maintained schools will depend for their survival on active parental support. Certainly, examination results will be one way in which such support is obtained. A school's reputation in its catchment area does not, however, depend solely on its success with an academic élite of pupils. It also depends on the perceptions of parents of pupils of average and below average ability. Any board of governors which allowed a head teacher to establish a reputation for not caring about less able pupils would be foolish indeed.

The second argument concerns the motivation for seeking grant-maintained status. It seems to be assumed that only grammar schools and would-be grammar schools will seek to opt out. There is no reason why this should be the case. In some inner-city areas, parents of minority ethnic groups have established alternative evening and week-end schools for their children. Sometimes the motivation has been religious, but not always. Minority ethnic groups often have high academic aspirations for their children (Stone, 1981). In other inner-city areas politically active groups have been vocal in expressing their dissatisfaction with aspects of state schooling. Grant-maintained status could provide a welcome opportunity for parent activists to play a much larger part in running their children's schools than has previously been possible.

Conclusions

So could the GERBIL have been a Marxist mole? Curriculum control, active encouragement to local groups to pursue policies dictated by the centre, regular and rigorous monitoring of standards set from centre: none of these would be inconsistent with a Marxist philosophy. Members of the present government might be a little surprised, even worried, to receive congratulations from colleagues on the hard-left. They would profess to be less surprised if they were told that the Act could hold substantial benefits for a large majority of pupils traditionally regarded as having special educational needs – perhaps 18 or 19 of Warnock's 20 per cent. After all, they might say, the Act's aim was to raise the attainments of all pupils, especially those of lower ability.

I have argued that this is not *necessarily* a false claim. In retrospect, the education initiatives of the Labour governments of the 1960s and 1970s seem to have been based on a naive and atheoretical view of education as an intrinsic good. With the dubious wisdom of hindsight these initiatives seem to have been subverted by socially and economically dominant groups which had traditionally voted for the Conservative party. It would be ironic if the parent beneficiaries of a Conservative education bill turned out to be some of the government's most hostile critics. Outright opposition to the Act is misguided. It just might encourage parents and teachers of Sir Keith Joseph's 40 per cent and Warnock's 20 per cent to cooperate more actively in programmes that are intellectually more stimulating and vocationally more useful than what is currently on offer. If so, it will be interesting to see whether the pupils vote Conservative or Labour on reaching the age of 18. They might even decide to opt out by voting for one of the centre parties.

Note: This chapter was written in June 1988. Sixteen months later I retain my underlying optimism. Nevertheless, I recognize that my sections on the National Curriculum, Attainment Targets and Grant Maintained Status require more detailed analysis in the light of recent statutory orders, DES Circulars, curriculum working party reports and reports from the National Curriculum Council.

David Galloway
October 1989

References

BAKER. K. (1988) Letter to Professor Blin-Stoyle, re. Mathematics Working Group: Interim Report, London, DES.

BOYSON, R. (1975) *The Crisis in Education*, London, Woburn Press.

BOYSON, R. (1988) 'Follow the Lewes Priory Four', *Times Educational Supplement*, 18 March, p. 4.

BRENNAN, W. (1987) 'Once More into the Core', *Special Children* XIV (October), pp. 14–15.

CALLAGHAN, J. (1976) Speech by the Prime Minister at Ruskin College, Oxford on 18 October (Press Release).

CORRIGAN, P. (1979) *Schooling the Smash Street Kids*, London, Macmillan.

COX, C.B. and BOYSON, R. (1977) *Black Paper 1977*, London, Temple Smith.

DAVIE, R. (1987) *Review of Children's Services in the UK, 1987* (Report to the AGM by the Director of the National Children's Bureau), London, NCB.

DEPARTMENT OF EDUCATION AND SCIENCE (1978) *Special Educational Needs* (The Warnock Report), London, HMSO.

DEPARTMENT OF EDUCATION AND SCIENCE (1987) National Curriculum: Mathematics Working Group: Interim Report, London, DES.

DEPARTMENT OF EDUCATION AND SCIENCE (1988) National Curriculum: Task Group on Assessment and Testing, London, DES.

DEPARTMENT OF EDUCATION AND SCIENCE (1989) Draft Circular –/89: Revision of Circular 1/83: Assessments and Statements of Special Educational Needs: Procedures within the Education, Health and Social Services, London, DES.

FISHER, A. (1987) 'Fear for the Future of the "Forgotten Children"', *Times Educational Supplement*, 6 November.

GALLOWAY, D. and GOODWIN, C. (1987) *The Education of Disturbing Children: Pupils with Learning and Adjustment Difficulties*, London, Longman.

GRACE, G. (1987) 'Teachers and the State in Britain: A Changing Relation', in LAWN, M. and GRACE, G. (Eds), *Teachers: The Culture and Politics of Work*, Lewes, Falmer Press.

HARGREAVES, D.H. (1983) *The Challenge of the Comprehensive School: Culture, Curriculum, Community*, London, Routledge & Kegan Paul.

HAVILAND, D. (1988) *Take Care, Mr. Baker!*, London, Fourth Estate.

INNER LONDON EDUCATION AUTHORITY (1984) *Improving Secondary Schools* (The Hargreaves Report), London, ILEA.

JOSEPH, K. (1983) Address to C.L.E.A., 16 July.

LAWTON, D. and CHITTY, C. (1988) *The National Curriculum* (Bedford Way Paper 33), London, University of London Institute of Education.

MARLAND, M. (1985) 'Parents, Schooling and the Welfare of Pupils', in RIBBINS, P., (Ed.) *Schooling and Welfare*, Lewes, Falmer Press.

O'KEEFE, D. (1987) 'Schools as Self-Seeking Syndicates', *Economic Affairs*, April/May.

PETER, M. (1988) 'Picking up the Bill for Disruption', *Times Educational Supplement*, 22 April, p. 4.

STONE, M. (1981) *The Education of the Black Child in Britain*, London, Fontana.

SURKES, S. (1988) 'In Dispute over Whether to Help Parent or Pupil. What the letter from No. 10 said', *Times Educational Supplement*, 18 March, p. 6.

TOMLINSON, S. (1987) *The Sociology of Special Education*, London, Routledge & Kegan Paul.

WILLIS, P. (1977) *Learning to Labour: How Working Class Kids Get Working Class Jobs*, Farnborough, Saxon House.

Chapter 6

The Pre-school Years: Early Intervention and Prevention

Sarah Sandow

Today, the term 'prevention' sits oddly with early intervention, but during the 1960s and 1970s, early educators saw their work as essentially preventive. Compensatory education was envisaged as a system by which children who were growing up in what was seen as a disadvantaged environment might be helped to succeed in the 'advantaged' society. Such help was seen as preventing the operation of disadvantaging factors. It was a surprisingly short step from the prevention of disadvantage to the prevention of disability, and in each case, the professional workers concerned sought the same mediators: the parents of the children concerned. This was quite a novelty. Parents of children in ordinary schools, without handicaps or disabilities, were still viewed with some suspicion, kept at the school gates, discouraged from helping their children to read or write, and effectively 'de-skilled'. Accordingly there was no model to be taken from the involvement of 'ordinary' parents in education for the introduction of parents with children who had learning difficulties as tutors or therapists with those children. Perhaps because of these traditional barriers between parents and teachers, the first reports came from psychologists, and only later did teachers become involved. In view of the prevailing influence of behavioural psychology, it was natural that most reports of research dealt with the introduction of parents to behavioural techniques and their training in behaviour modification. This method of training children was also spreading in the schools for children with severe learning difficulties, transferred from the Ministry of Health to the Ministry of Education in 1971 and then called Schools for the Severely Educationally Subnormal (ESN(S)). The curriculum in these schools came under close scrutiny for the first time and methods of teaching along behavioural lines evolved in them which remained largely unknown in ordinary schools, which functioned on a mainly developmental 'child-centred' basis. Until the 1970 Education Act, there was little expectation that children, once placed in a Training Centre, could ever graduate to a 'real' school, and theoretically at least the inclusion of ESN(S) schools within the education system made this possible. Thus the hopes and aspirations of parents were recognized, and their skills as educators and therapists began to be utilized.

The Warnock Report (1978) (heavily influenced by psychologists) placed particular emphasis on the relations between parents and professionals in the field of special education in general and pre-school 'prevention' in particular. It may be useful to summarize the Report's view on early intervention and the involvement of parents.

In Chapter 5, the Report approved the several 'Portage Projects' then operating, but believed that the work should be the responsibility of qualified teachers. It advocated

> a comprehensive peripatetic teaching service which would cater, wherever possible, exclusively for children with disabilities or significant difficulties below school age (5.37).

These peripatetic teachers should:

> (i) assess children's educational needs on the basis of trained observation;
> (ii) work with parents towards an educational programme for their child in the light of his assessed needs;
> (iii) work directly with and teach children on a regular basis; and
> (iv) maintain contact with other professionals in the various services concerned with meeting the needs of young children with disabilities or significant difficulties and their parents;
> (v) encourage and participate in meetings of groups of parents of young children with special needs;
> (vi) put parents in touch with toy libraries, local forms of pre-school provision – playgroups, opportunity groups, day nurseries or nursery schools or classes in ordinary or special schools – and voluntary organizations (5.39).

The Report also advocated increased nursery provision for all children 'since this would have the consequence that opportunities for nursery education for young children with special needs could be correspondingly extended' (5.51).

The fifth chapter of the Report concluded by reiterating

> the crucial importance of early educational opportunities for children with disabilities or who are showing signs of having special needs, the role of parents as educators of their children and the need to provide them with skilled help, and the need for close cooperation between the different professions concerned.

The rôle of the 'named person' was delineated, and regarded as 'one of the cornerstones of the service . . . for parents of children with special needs' (5.72).

This concept was elaborated in Chapter 9, which was significantly entitled 'Parents as partners', an idea which has gained much currency (Mittler and Mittler, 1982).

Practice in the 1970s was characterized by a proliferation of intervention programmes, based on a deficit model. Where congenital disabilities were discovered, the deficit was assumed to be the child's, where disadvantage was a contributing factor, the deficit was assumed to be that of the parents. There was a gradual change as researchers rejected the deficit model largely under the influence of the newly emerging sociology of special education (e.g. Tomlinson, 1981 and 1982), but most still felt that some form of intervention was appropriate. Currently, we may observe a conflict between three approaches: (a) a simple behavioural model, epitomized by the Portage system (Smith, Kushlick and Glossop, 1977); (b) a parent support model, especially related to the time immediately after the condition is diagnosed, such as that offered by the Down's Syndrome association, or in the programmes designed by the Hester Adrian Research Centre (Cunningham and Sloper, 1978); and (c) an approach which regards most forms of intervention as suspect effectively devaluing and deskilling parents. This latter model has been promoted by the writers of the controversial Open University course 'Special Needs in Education' (E241) (Booth, 1983).

These three approaches relate partly but not completely to Raven's (1981) analysis. He also proposed three models:

(1) Children have not developed attitudes and abilities.
Solution: give them skills.
(2) Parents do not know how to foster these abilities and aptitudes.
Solution: give parents skills.
(3) 'School' has defined some children as failures and others as successes.
Solution: educate society to accept deviance.

However, Raven's second model does not necessarily offer any autonomy to parents, nor take account of the transactional and cumulative nature of family life. In fact, it reflects the beliefs cited by Nevin and Thousand (1986) that (1) parents are not willing or able to work with their handicapped child; (2) parents have unrealistic expectations; (3) parents do not know how to teach their child; (4) parents need professionals to help them; (5) parents contribute to the child's problem. As these authors point out, such attitudes foster an adversarial relationship between parents and professionals which is hardly conducive to positive action. It is particularly ironic that these attitudes were reported at a time when the superiority of educational experience provided in 'normal' homes over those provided at Nursery Schools was being reported, e.g. by Tizard and Hughes (1984). Unfortunately, there is evidence that professionals still maintain these views and couple with them the idea that not only are parents incompetent, but they are also fearfully dependent upon the professionals who serve them. The words 'anxiety', 'fear', 'resentful', 'desperate', 'confused', 'guilty', 'apprehensive', 'defended', occurred frequently in a series of interviews with professionals concerned with making statements of special need, where those professionals were asked to characterize parents' responses to the 'Statementing' process (Sandow, Stafford and Stafford, 1987).

As well as a model or rationale for the nature of the parent–professional relationship, there is also a rationale for the kind of intervention programme which is undertaken. While many programmes may be regarded as eclectic, drawing from a wide range of activities customary with young children in nursery schools or playgroups, other programmes are rooted in a specific developmental or neurological model. The programmes developed at the Honeylands Centre, Exeter (Rayner, 1977) exemplify the first, the second include the Portage programmes, and the Parent Involvement Project at the Hester Adrian Centre (Jeffree and McConkey, 1974) and the third, the neurological model, may be observed in, on the one hand, the Philadelphia Institute for Human Potential (Doman, 1974) and, on the other, Conductive Education, originating at the Peto Institute in Hungary (Cottam and Sutton, 1986).

Meisels (1985) asked four questions:

(1) What is the underlying developmental model or theoretical rationale for the early intervention programme?
(2) What is the intervention, and how does it relate to a theory of development?
(3) How is change in early intervention programmes measured?
(4) What are the neurological, biological, and socio-environmental characteristics of the infants enrolled in early intervention programmes? Early intervention for whom?

Meisels' first two questions seem at first to be complementary. However, this may not be the case. While programme designers may hold and express a view about development, and believe themselves to be designing interventions which reflect that view, the actual programmes may be essentially atheoretical. Thus, the developmental checklists of the Portage Project, which were derived from items in various infant intelligence tests, provide only a rough guide for the therapist, who will select targets in consultation with parents which may only approximate to the observed level of development. This may be because parents specifically seek progress in certain areas, or because the behaviour and development of the child may be idiosyncratic, and only imperfectly represented by the points attained on the checklists. Portage workers, among others, feel insecure when leaving the familiar path offered by 'normal' development. However, slavish adherence to this concept may prevent the therapist from observing the child himself with any objectivity. Hogg (1975) noted the atypical motor development of handicapped children, and proposed a less rigid approach to skills teaching which took account of individual learning patterns.

With respect to the measurement of achievement, Meisels, referring back to Bronfenbrenner's now classic (1974) paper, proposes that the criteria for success in early intervention now needed to be more clearly defined. Mere IQ increments would no longer do, especially as follow-up studies suggest that such gains are short-lived. Studies in the 1970s (including this writer's own: Sandow and Clarke, 1978; Sandow, Clarke, Cox and Stewart, 1981) concentrated on such gains, and their fugitive nature was apparent. The great variability of response within subject groups should have alerted us all to the inadequacy of a single factor model, or even of an interactive one. 'Childrens' development does not occur in a linear manner, but results from mutual transactions between children and their social and caregiving environments' (Meisels, 1985).

Nevertheless, it is currently the case that the most favoured models for early intervention (supported, for example, by Government through the Education Support Grants) remain those skills-based programmes such as the Portage model, which assume that competencies are simply transmitted from professionals to parents, easily measurable, and retained once learned. Similar assumptions are made about the viability of systems such as SNAP (Ainscow and Tweddle, 1989) in primary schools. It is perhaps not surprising, given a current situation in which the curriculum as a whole is seen increasingly as a set of skills to be taught and tested.

Meisels' fourth question relates to the characteristics of the children who are the intervention targets. In different programmes, these include 'at risk' and disadvantaged children as well as those identified as disabled or handicapped. The Warnock report, in seeking, laudably, to promote the continuum of special education, leads us, rather less appropriately, to regard these populations as similar or even unitary. However, the experience of parents and children in these groups may not be well matched, and their needs may not be equivalent (Sandow, Stafford and Stafford, 1987). In either case, measures of intelligence, which invite assumptions about the qualitative similarity of IQ changes regardless of their position on any scale, must be inappropriate as indices of individual progress. Badly used, early intervention, screening and a simple behavioural approach, which often go together, may promote the idea of something 'normal' of which special children fall short.

Booth (1983) goes so far as to suggest that early intervention is a 'prevention fantasy', because it is proposed as a simplistic 'cure' for a multifactorial interactive process, and because its practitioners ignore the mismatch between their easy prescriptions and the complexities of the lives and the societies for which they seek to compensate.

White and Casto (1985) analyzed 316 research articles (162 studies) describing programmes mainly for 'at risk' and disadvantaged children in the USA. They looked at subject characteristics, type of intervention, research design, outcomes and conclusions. They found that most presented results in terms of IQ data, and that 'good quality studies' had outcomes of approx. 0.5 S.D. of IQ. Examining concomitant variables, their main observations related to structure, parental involvement, training of agents, age of intervention, and maintenance of benefit over time. These may be summarized as follows:

(1) Degree of structure — supported: the greater the structure, the better.
(2) Involvement of parents — not supported: there was no evidence that programmes in which parents were involved were more successful than those in which they were not. White and Casto admit that this finding is counter to the received view and to popular intuition. However, the IQ measure may not be the best outcome measure for this group anyway. 'IQ has probably been measured as often as it has because it is easily available, relatively inexpensive to collect and psychometrically defensible . . . Other measures such as communications skills, mental health, social competencies, and daily living skills have been measured very infrequently.' They were less confident, however, that the involvement of parents was equally irrelevant in programmes for children with severe learning difficulties (SLD).
(3) Training of primary intervener — results were contradictory, in that there was no evidence in what the authors called 'high quality' studies, that professional trainers were any more successful as instructors than paraprofessional or volunteer trainers.
(4) Age at which intervention begins — there was a slight advantage only for early start but results were inconclusive.
(5) Maintenance of benefits from early intervention — after 36 months the gain for disadvantaged children was wiped out. There were not enough studies among children with SLD to draw a valid conclusion.

However, White and Casto take the view that extrapolation from disadvantaged and at risk children to those with SLD is not necessarily justified, though they found evidence that if early intervention programmes are not available, many disadvantaged or at risk children may become classified as having SLD. They conclude that, despite the instinctive view that early intervention of any kind must be a good thing, agents should not proceed on the basis of preference and intuition without properly controlled research. In fact, in a study concerned entirely with children with SLD, Sandow and Clarke (1978) found, contrary to expectation, that infrequent home visits were, in the medium term, more successful than frequent visits, and in the long term were no less successful.

Similar findings in respect of children with Down's Syndrome have been made by Cunningham and his associates (Cunningham, 1983, 1986, 1987). In his studies, intensity of programme and frequency of visits were shown to have a significant effect on outcome only at the very early stages, and this effect disappeared after the first eighteen months. However, those factors which correlated positively with later development were found to be social class, birth order, family size, parental education and gender. As Cunningham points out, these are precisely those variables found to have significance for ordinary children. Detailed comparisons with comparable groups not receiving intervention programmes (Lorenz, 1985; Cunningham, 1986) showed that the intervention groups were not advantaged with respect to later development, nor to the occurrence of behaviour problems, or family stress or cohesion. However, the parents in the intervention groups did show some differences: for example, in their willingness and ability to seek help, and their greater likelihood of entering full or part time employment. This suggests that these parents did show greater self confidence in their relations with agencies and in themselves as individuals. Children in the intervention groups were less likely to experience major health problems than control subjects, and more likely to have attended some sort of pre-school facility. Cunningham is tentative about the meaning of these positive outcomes, but suggests that mothers' attitudes to their children had been positively affected. Although the children in these samples showed advances relative to some groups previously reported, Cunningham suggests that the observed differences may have been due to increased expectations of children with Down's Syndrome, and changes in child-rearing practices occurring in the 1970s. The 'hidden deprivation' of past decades had been removed.

In his (1986) report to the funding agency (DHSS), Cunningham concludes by questioning the efficacy of child-focused models which appear to demand the investment of substantial time and effort by parents and therapists, but which seem to have such short-lived effects. He suggests that more attention should be paid to the interpersonal relationships within families and to a better understanding of developmental processes, with emphasis on communicative and interactional skills. He stresses the 'constant change of needs, resources, reactions and feelings in all families which influence how they construe and interpret and respond to each other's behaviour'.

This recognition of the changing context of a child's experience is echoed by Clark (1987) in a study of the integration of children with special needs in nursery provision, before and after the Warnock Report. She notes the emphasis in the 1970s on language deficits and compensation, and the tendency at that time to attribute successes to teachers' efforts at school and deficits to inadequacies at home. Now, she suggests, we are more sensitive to the influence of context on how competent children will tend to appear and to the importance of interaction with adults on children's language development. The potency of peers as educational resources is also recognized. The former emphasis on compensation meant that little attention was paid to what was actually being offered in school, it being assumed that whatever it was, it had to be an improvement on what was happening at home. Nevertheless, in spite of increased awareness of the importance of intra-familial interactions to children's language development and later school attainment, she found little evidence of a partnership between parents and professionals.

It appears that parents are still being effectively deskilled by professionals, mainly perhaps because many programmes have retained a transmission model, concentrating on skills teaching without regard to the many competencies brought to the parent–professional encounter by the parents themselves; often competencies which could not be easily identified. In 1966, Caldwell, Heider and Kaplan produced an 'Inventory of Home Stimulation' with which it was proposed that a home could be evaluated as an effective educational environment. Some years later, while considering the use of such an instrument, this writer observed many complex elaborate and productive interactions between parents and children in homes which would have thoroughly failed Caldwell's test. Today, it remains appropriate to ask how parents can be partners if we denigrate their abilities and reject their advice (Sandow, Stafford and Stafford, 1987).

An approach which takes account of the great variability within the population of families of children with special needs, such as that advocated by Cunningham, requires more and different skills in the intervening agent. Byrne and Cunningham (1985) propose that a successful paradigm for intervention must take account of three issues not usually considered together in the design of programmes: first, those factors which mediate vulnerability to stress in families; second, a consideration of families' material and practical needs; third, a consideration of those coping and adaptive mechanisms which have enabled families to cope with what seem, to the outsider, to be insuperable problems. They suggest that a study of family perceptions, value systems, aspirations, resources, relationships, and ecology, should inform the design of any intervention. Hence the demands on the agent for adaptability and a creative approach to programme design are infinitely greater than where a simple transmission model is followed. Buchan, Clemerson and Davis (1988) describe the operation of a home support scheme set up on these principles, where 'parent advisers' are trained in counselling as well as in behavioural management and where the needs and perceptions of parents are recognized and respected as individual and personal.

Social cognition, identified as a transactional process, has become popular in the 1980s as an appropriate post-Piagetian developmental approach. Butterworth (1982) characterizes this as the end of traditional demarcations between the social and the cognitive domain, and the recognition that 'a variety of aspects of behaviour and experience . . . have not previously been juxtaposed'. Cognitive development does not take place in a vacuum, even though it occupies a different slot in the University timetable than social psychology. Nor is it enough to say simply that positive social interaction facilitates cognitive development, as a hot oven facilitates the rising of a cake. Every cognitive advance alters the nature of the social relationship with which it is engaged. Early intervention with parents and children ought to be an area in which the validity of such an approach is recognized. Bronfenbrenner's (1974) dictum, that the key element in successful pre-school education was 'the involvement of parent and child in verbal interaction round a cognitively challenging task' indicates as much. In such a system, as Byrne and Cunningham (1985) point out, the distinction between outcomes and predictors becomes blurred, for 'any of the variables used may function as either predictor or outcome measures, depending on the aim of the research'. Further, outcome measures should not be limited to measureable gains on checklists, but should also encompass 'indices of family members' satisfaction with their lives, their stress and anxiety levels, relationships within the family and their social integration'.

It appears that in the 1970s lip-service was paid to a transactional model but researchers were actually clinging to simple outcome measures. Perhaps this was due to a combination of factors. First, the habit of thinking in simplistic behavioural terms, for qualitative measurement was unfashionable; second, the need to justify a method to sponsors and collaborators by immediate positive results; third, the heady feeling induced by the conviction that psychology was about improving situations and helping people, not merely about examining behavioural phenomena. Finally, the fact that so many programmes were in their infancy, and were conducted against a background in which the importance of early experience was taken for granted (despite the evidence displayed in, for example, Clarke and Clarke, 1975) meant that insufficient time was allowed for long-term evaluation. 'Hawthorne effects' were taken as evidence of real progress, although such evidence was paltry, to say the least. Holmes (1982), for example, claimed that: 'intensive attention for one hour every day can compensate sufficiently to develop intelligence and school adjustment' on the basis of minimal IQ changes in a sample of six pre-school children.

Passionate conviction in the unique quality of a simple behavioural approach combined with a commendable altruism informs most of the publications based on the Portage project. It has the effect of making even the most complex problem appear simple. Westmacott and Cameron (1982) outline crisply a framework for 'selling behavioural psychology to parents and teachers' as follows:

1. List assets
2. List problems
3. State priority problem
4. State desired outcome
5. Examine the controlling conditions
6. Agree the intervention
7. Implement the intervention
8. Monitor the outcome
9. Evaluate the outcome: if success, go back to 2; if failure, go back to 4.

It is not merely this process which is questionable, but the implied simplicity of its various parts. Would that we could always 'examine the controlling conditions' efficiently! It is the stuff of human experience that, so often, we cannot. Here the Portage system makes assumptions about the relevant skills for 'behaviour managers' and 'behavioural engineers'. Sturmey and Crisp (1986) note that 'the staff training literature has focused excessively on manager and engineer skills at the expense of identifying and training consultant skills'.

Despite all this, Portage remains the most frequent choice for LEAs wishing to improve their pre-school services, aided by the application of Education Support Grant funds. In this as in other cases (for example in the treatment of young offenders) Governments adopt simplistic solutions for which there is no evidence. 'Street level bureaucrats' as Weatherley and Lipsky (1977) identified them, have to find ways to deal with the demands made upon them, and often do so in a way which is intuitively logical and appropriate, even if, as in the case of the Portage project, it has not been effectively evaluated. It seems that belief in the supreme importance of early experience, and in the compensatory effectiveness of early intervention, has so far proved resistant to any evidence to the contrary.

> . . . intuitive scientists gain the illusion that their theories are more logical and empirically buttressed than is really the case. They are

> even apt to believe that their theories enjoy 'independent support' and to rely on such support in maintaining those theories when their original evidential basis is challenged and discounted (Ross, 1981).

Within the Portage movement itself, as within the wider context of early intervention, there are signs that a more supportive, less didactic approach is developing. Counselling, as a central function rather than as an optional extra, is beginning to emerge (Le Poidevin and Cameron, 1985). A social-cognitive approach, which encourages us to see the environment and the individuals within it as a transactional, developing progression of encounters, rather than a framework within which individuals develop in an essentially isolated way, should enable therapists to respond more sensitively to the needs of parents, and even to recognize that there may be cases where intervention is unnecessary and inappropriate. The simple behavioural model of the 1970s must give way to a more complex but less imperious approach to the facilitation of human development.

The evaluation of early intervention programmes must develop into a system where factors other than measurable cognitive advances are considered important. Changes in the attitudes and confidence of parents, such as are evidenced by Cunningham (1986) and by Buchan *et al.* (1988) must be recognized as appropriate indicators of success. Perhaps if these had been understood in the 1970s, the early disappointments of the Headstart programmes, and the emergence of the later 'sleeper effects', might have been better understood. An understanding of the ecology of family life as a developing entity, rather than as a more or less effective cocoon for the child with SLD, must be recognized. Unfortunately, such nebulous concepts are hard for bureaucrats to cope with, pressured as they are for tangible results and measurable outcomes. We must beware of Stedman's (1977) 'press to do well' now, as much as we were then.

References

AINSCOW, M. and TWEDDLE, D. (1979) *Preventing Classroom Failure: an Objectives Approach*, London, Wiley.

BOOTH, T. (1983) *Special Needs in Education (E241): Eradicating Handicap, Unit 14*, Walton, Open University.

BRONFENBRENNER, U. (1974) *A Report on Longitudinal Evaluations of Pre-school Programs 2 Is Early Intervention Effective?* Washington DC, Department of Health Education and Welfare, Publ. No. (OHD) 74–25.

BUCHAN, L., CLEMERSON, J. and DAVIS, H. (1988) 'Working with families of special needs: the parent adviser scheme', *Child: care health and development*, *14*, pp. 81–91.

BUTTERWORTH, G. (1982) 'A brief account of the conflict between the individual and the social in models of cognitive growth', in BUTTERWORTH, G. and LIGHT, P. (Eds) *Social Cognition: Studies of the Development of Understanding*, Brighton, The Harvester Press.

BYRNE, E.A. and CUNNINGHAM, C.C. (1985) 'The effects of mentally handicapped children on families — a conceptual review', *Journal of Child Psychology and Psychiatry*, *26:6*, pp. 847–64.

CLARK, M.M. (1987) 'Early Education and Children with Special Needs', *Journal of Child Psychology and Psychiatry*, *28:3*, pp. 417–27.

CLARKE, A.M. and CLARKE, A.D.B. (1975) *Early Experience: Myth and Evidence*, Methuen.

CALDWELL, B., HEIDER, J. and KAPLAN, B. (1966) *Inventory of Home Stimulation*, Paper presented at meeting of the American Psychological Association New York, September 1966.

COTTAM, P. and SUTTON, A. (1986) *Conductive Education*, London, Croom Helm.

CUNNINGHAM, C.C. and SLOPER, P. (1978) *Helping your Handicapped Baby*, London, Souvenir Press.

CUNNINGHAM, C.C. (1983) *Early Development and its Facilitation in Infants with Down's Syndrome*, Report to DHSS, University of Manchester Hester Adrian Research Centre.

CUNNINGHAM, C.C. (1986) *The Effects of Early Intervention on the Occurrence and Nature of Behaviour Problems in Children with Down's Syndrome*, Summary of Report to DHSS, University of Manchester, Hester Adrian Research Centre.

CUNNNINGHAM, C.C. (1987) 'Early intervention in Down's Syndrome', in HOSKING, G. and MURPHY, G. (Eds) *Prevention of mental handicap: a world view*, Royal Society of Medicine Services International Congress and Symposius series No. 112, London, Royal Society of Medicine Services Ltd.

DEPARTMENT OF EDUCATION AND SCIENCE (1978) *Report of the Committee of Enquiry into the Education of Handicapped Children and Young People (Warnock Report)*, Cmnd 7212, HMSO.

DOMAN, G. (1974) *What to do about your Brain Injured Child*, London, Jonathan Cape.

HOGG, J. (1975) 'Normative development and educational programme planning for severely educationally subnormal children', in KIERNAN, C.C. and WOODFORD, F.P. (Eds) *Behaviour Modification for the Severely Retarded*, Amsterdam, Elsevier, Associated Scientific Publishers.

HOLMES, E. (1982) 'The effectiveness of intervention for preschool children in day and residential care assessment, follow-up and implications for policy', *New Growth 2:1*, pp. 17–30.

JEFFREE, D.M. (1976) *Parental involvement in facilitating the Development of Young Handicapped Children (P.I.P.)*, Manchester, University of Manchester, Hester Adrian Research Centre.

LE POIDEVIN, S. and CAMERON, J. (1985) 'Is there more to Portage than education?', in DALY, B., ADDINGTON, J., KERFOOT, S. and SIGSTON, A. (Eds), *Portage: The Importance of Parents*, Windsor, NFER Nelson.

LORENZ, S. (1985) *Long term effects of early intervention in infants with Down's Syndrome*, unpublished Ph.D. Thesis, University of Manchester.

MEISELS, S.J. (1985) 'The efficacy of early intervention: why are we still asking this question?', *Topics in Early Childhood Special Education 5:2*, pp. 1–11.

NEVIN, A. and THOUSAND, J. (1986) 'What administrators need to know about systems that limit or avoid special education referrals', *Planning and Changing 17:4*, pp. 195–208.

RAVEN, J. (1981) 'Early Intervention: a selective Review of the literature', *CORE 5:3*, p. 81.

RAYNER, H. (1977) *The Exeter Home Visiting Project: the psychologist as one of several Therapists*, paper read at Annual Conference of the British Psychological Society.

ROSS, L. (1981) 'The "intuitive scientist" formulation and its developmental implications', in FLAVELL, J.H. and ROSS, L. (Eds) *Social cognitive development: frontiers and possible futures*, Cambridge University Press.

SANDOW, S. and CLARKE, A.D.B. (1978) 'Home Intervention with parents of severely subnormal pre-school children: an interim report', *Child: care health and development 4*, pp. 29–39.

SANDOW, S., CLARKE, A.D.B., COX, M.V. and STEWART, L. (1981) 'Home Intervention with parents of severely subnormal preschool children: a final report', *Child: care health and development* **7**, pp. 135–44.

SANDOW, S., STAFFORD, D. and STAFFORD, P. (1987) *An agreed Understanding?: parent-professional communication and the 1981 Education Act*, Windsor, NFER-Nelson.

SMITH, J., KUSHLICK, A. and GLOSSOP, C. (1977) *The Wessex Portage Project: a Home Teaching Service for Families with a Pre-School mentally Handicapped Child*, Wessex Regional Health Authority Health Care Evaluation Research Team, Research Report 125.

STEDMAN, D.J. (1977) 'Important considerations in the review and evaluation of educational intervention programmes', in MITTLER, P. (Ed.) *Research to Practice in Mental Retardation: Care and Intervention, Vol. 1*, London, Butterworth.

STURMEY, P. and CRISP, A.G. (1986) 'Portage Guide to early Education: a Review of Research', *Educational Psychology 6:2*, pp. 139–57.

TIZARD, B. and HUGHES, M. (1984) *Young Children Learning*, London, Fontana.

TOMLINSON, S. (1981) *Educational Subnormality: a study in decision making*, London, Routledge & Kegan Paul.

TOMLINSON, S. (1982) *A Sociology of Special Education*, London, Routledge & Kegan Paul.

WESTMACOTT, E.W. and CAMERON, J. (1982) 'Selling Behavioural psychology to parents and teachers', *Association of Educational Psychologists Journal 5:9*, pp. 24–8.

WEATHERLEY, R. and LIPSKY, M. (1977) 'Street level bureaucrats and institutional innovation: implementing special educational reform', *Harvard Educational Review 47*, pp. 171–97.

WHITE and CASTO (1985) 'An integrative review of early intervention. Efficacy Studies with At-Risk Children: implications for the handicapped', *Analysis and Intervention in developmental disabilities 5:1–2*, pp. 7–31.

Chapter 7

The Modified Curriculum: Help with the Same or Something Completely Different

Harry Daniels

This chapter is concerned with the aspects of the education of children who are described as having moderate learning difficulties. It will examine selected aspects of the recent history of educational development in the light of current speculations on reform. A descriptive model of curriculum modification will then be proposed. The intention is to provide a frame of reference for considering the relationship between the education of children with special educational needs and their mainstream peers.

The Recent History

The 1944 Education Act, whatever else it did, extended the four categories of children for whom special provison was made under the 1921 Act. It also invoked the notion that associated with these new categories of disability of mind and body were appropriate forms of provision. Children were to be diagnosed, principally by medical authorities, as being members of particular disability groups with which particular curriculum forms and, in most cases, schools were associated. It also designated one group of children, those with a measured IQ below 50, as being outside the scope of education and it was not until 1970 that all children were considered as candidates for schooling.

During the years that followed there was a consistent trend in influential reports such as Plowden (DES, 1967) and Newsom (DES, 1963), away from an analysis of individual deficiency and towards an interactionist (Wedell, 1980) or transactional view of causation, an important corollary of this being the, albeit somewhat slower, general move away from the use of normative assessment devices. Whereas the 1944 Act relied, in part, upon IQ tests and the 11 plus for its implementation, by the time the Warnock Report was published in 1978 (DES, 1978) criterion-based assessment formed a far greater part of the evolving model of 'good practice'. Indeed it could be argued that the Warnock Report acted as a useful summary of mid-seventies educational thinking rather than as a sudden inspired innovation. By arguing that as far as possible all children should be educated with their community peers it was espousing the more general 'comprehensive education for all' demand. In the years that have followed Warnock, reports such as those of Hargreaves (ILEA, 1984), Fish (ILEA, 1985), Thomas (ILEA, 1985) and Swann (DES, 1985) have both reaffirmed and in their different ways extended this debate.

Rather than arranging provision in different schools to deliver different curricula to diagnosed disabilities, the community school was to provide the modifications required to enable all children to make progress and to have equal opportunity to access common experiences in the curriculum. (Table 7.1 provides a summary of this analysis.)

The forty-four years that have elapsed since the 1944 Act was implemented have then witnessed a remarkable transition. Whereas children with special educational needs (SEN) went to a special school with a special curriculum there is now much more official emphasis on SEN children going to a mainstream school where the curriculum is modified to meet their needs.

So much for rhetoric! In reality the situation is rather mixed. The extent to which LEAs adopted the comprehensive ideal was and is reflected in the rate of referral to a form of education that was special in both location and function. The purpose of the chapter so far has been to illustrate an underlying general trend towards what might loosely be called integration. That is, a move towards making the same educational experience accessible to all children.

The 1988 Education Act

The new categories of provision to be created by the 1988 Education Act are of a different nature to those created by the 1944 Act. They will be of locus of control of the school (LEA or opted out) and of statemented or unstatemented access to the curriculum. The requirements of the National Curriculum may be disapplied or modified on a long term or temporary basis in particular cases or circumstances or in the light of assessments of individual special needs. Whatever form provision takes during the implementation of this Act it is clear that the intention is to reverse many elements of the trend outlined above.

The exact blend of assessment devices to be used is not yet clear although there is some evidence from the Black (TGAT) report (DES, 1987) that

Table 7.1 Recent influences on the development of special education

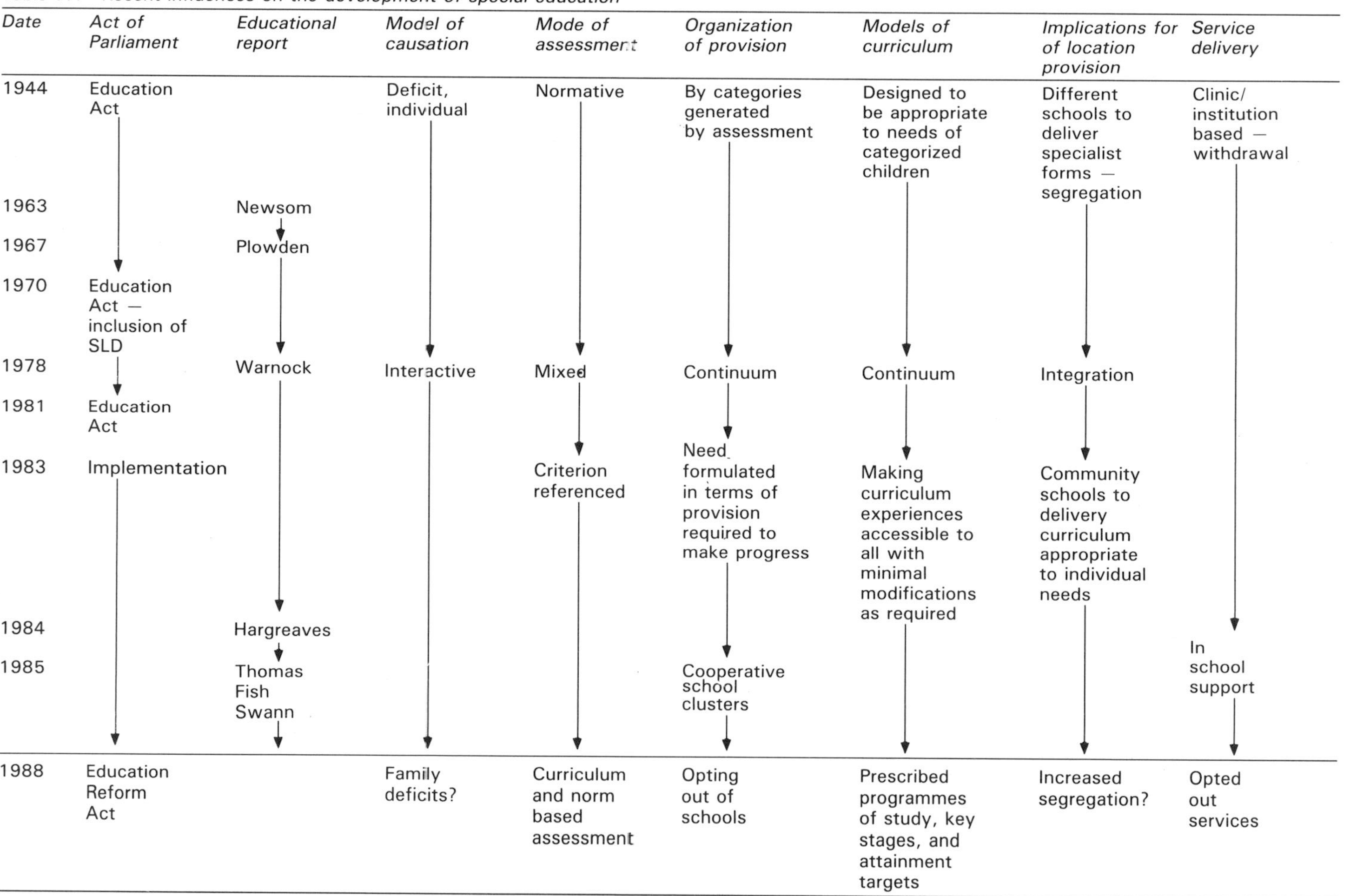

Date	Act of Parliament	Educational report	Model of causation	Mode of assessment	Organization of provision	Models of curriculum	Implications for of location provision	Service delivery
1944	Education Act		Deficit, individual	Normative	By categories generated by assessment	Designed to be appropriate to needs of categorized children	Different schools to deliver specialist forms — segregation	Clinic/ institution based — withdrawal
1963		Newsom						
1967		Plowden						
1970	Education Act — inclusion of SLD							
1978		Warnock	Interactive	Mixed	Continuum	Continuum	Integration	
1981	Education Act							
1983	Implementation			Criterion referenced	Need formulated in terms of provision required to make progress	Making curriculum experiences accessible to all with minimal modifications as required	Community schools to delivery curriculum appropriate to individual needs	
1984		Hargreaves						
1985		Thomas Fish Swann			Cooperative school clusters			In school support
1988	Education Reform Act		Family deficits?	Curriculum and norm based assessment	Opting out of schools	Prescribed programmes of study, key stages, and attainment targets	Increased segregation?	Opted out services

elements of criterion referencing will persist as it doubtless will within GCSE and many of the post-14 curriculum initiatives. Major questions arise as to the extent to which all children will be educated together in the future and also to whether curriculum modification will become curriculum separation.

The DES and Welsh Office Note of 1984 (DES, 1984) announced that the modified curriculum for children with moderate learning difficulties should contain a 'strong emphasis on personal and social development and therefore work in subjects such as home economics' (p. 4). This echoes the suggestions made in the Hargreaves Report (ILEA, 1984) that the curriculum for all secondary aged pupils should embody a strong commitment to fostering personal and social development. There was no conflict at this level between what was to be the 'modified' and what was to be the 'mainstream'. However, the Education Act does not stipulate that this influence should be represented in the core and foundation subjects of the National Curriculum.

Placement in special school always has been much more than a matter of level of intelligence (Gulliford, 1985), and it now seems that the instructional practice of the National Curriculum presumes levels of social compliance in schools. The Secretaries of State of Education and Home Affairs are both considering what to do with the parents of children whose personal and social development has not involved the acquisition of the competencies required for the instructional practice of the National Curriculum. Here, possibly, is the return of deficiency, this time of the family. The report of the Elton Committee drew attention to the possibility of making parents liable in civil law for their children's behaviour (DES, 1989). At present it seems, unlikely that the Secretary of State will implement this suggestion; however, the notion of parental culpability may well find some other form of expression. The result may well be that as schools are compelled to make a form of mainstream provison that denies much space for personal and social development, it will marginalize certain groups of children into separate provision, the stated intention being to compensate for the deficits in socialization.

Just as the Warnock Report could be seen as an expression of educational trends at the time, the 1988 Education Act may be seen as the expression of a very different set of ideological intentions.

The Curriculum

The Warnock Report, in asserting that the goals of education for children with SEN were essentially the same as those for all children, clearly expressed an orientation towards the questions as to whether the special curriculum should be 'special'. Warnock's two major goals referred to increased knowledge and understanding on the one hand and progress towards independence on the other, the extrinsic and intrinsic educational goals. This assertion was developed by the HMI document 'A view of the curriculum' (HMI, 1980) which added that 'a common policy for the curriculum in this sense cannot be a prescription for uniformity' (p. 2). They went on to outline the need for a broadly based definition of curriculum responsibility, and state that the means by which these goals may be realized was a matter for 'professional judgment'. This contrasts sharply with the 1988 Act which, whilst it defines a balanced and broadly based curriculum in terms similar to those of Warnock,

(a) promotes the spiritual, moral, cultural, mental and physical development of pupils at the school and of society; and
(b) prepares such pupils for the opportunities, responsibilities and experiences of adult life (DES, 1988).

It then proceeds to stipulate the means of assessment and curriculum configuration. The scope for professional judgment is therefore limited. Yet again the Act may be seen as a reversal of recent trends. Before proceeding to examine the influences that have been and are brought to bear on professional judgment concerning means, it seems appropriate to consider the current definition of the children being considered.

The DES and Welsh Office Note outlined three levels of curriculum: mainstream plus support, modified and developmental; the definition of the modified curriculum being:

> a curriculum similar to that provided in ordinary schools which, while not restricted in its expectations, has objectives more appropriate to children whose special educational needs would not properly be met by a mainstream curriculum. Children requiring such a curriculum may be described as having moderate learning difficulties (DES, 1984).

A somewhat tautologous and unhelpful definition. The note does proceed to suggest a few differences between the mainstream and modified curricula such as the removal of single subject sciences and foreign language instruction. (This raises some interesting questions concerning the predicament of children for whom English is not the first language!) The population to whom this definition applies form by far the largest group in Special Education (Fish, 1985). Yet the reader is offered little in the way of guidance as to what 'modified' means in practice and, as Wilson points out, there is a growing demand for clarity: 'Each Special School will need to specify and in writing what functions it can perform, what needs can be met and what special facilities and curricula are offered' (Wilson, 1981, p. 8).

With the demise of the placement of children into a category of school and the rise of accountability in all sections of education, there is a demand to explicate the relation of what counts as special and mainstream in a particular context.

Brennan's survey report for the Schools Council in 1979 made it quite clear that LEAs had not developed a consistent attitude or policy about the detail of curricula in special schools. He also revealed the lack of relation between the few written school curriculum documents he found available to inspection and what actually went on in classrooms (Brennan, 1979).

Certainly at the time of the publication of the Warnock Report there was a very confused response to Brennan's early definition of the curriculum problem:

> The real curricular problem is that of accepting the content limitations required to achieve quality of learning in the basic subjects whilst avoiding an educational programme which is sterile, unexciting and inadequate for both personal richness and social competence (Brennan, 1974, p. 59).

The nature of appropriate forms of curriculum modification remain elusive, perhaps all the more because of the imminent changes in the definition of the mainstream curriculum.

An attempt will now be made to produce a model of curriculum modification. The intention is to give practitioners a way of describing the way in which they make modifications which are additional to or otherwise different from the mainstream curriculum. This will hopefully enable those in the field to reflect on the extent to which they are delivering a special curriculum or modifying the mainstream curriculum in the light of individual learning requirements.

The Modified Curriculum: a Descriptive Model

It seems appropriate to use Warnock's two goals as factors in a general description. For the purposes of this model these elements of firstly knowledge and understanding and secondly preparation for adult life will be considered separately; this is not to imply that they remain separate in practice. It is clear that any particular school selects and combines curriculum elements in its practice. As Gagne notes: 'If the various kinds of learning outcomes and the ways of analyzing learning requirements are combined in a rational and systematic manner, it is possible to describe a total set of ideas that constitute a theory of instruction' (Gagne, 1985, p. 243). This distinction between the extrinsic and intrinsic goals will be portrayed as a continuum between a focus on mainstream school work and as a focus on the requirements of adult life.

The children for whom special modifications were constructed were considered by many to be slow in learning. The principal of modification from this perspective may be simply as Wilson states 'tempering the wind to the shorn lamb' (Wilson, 1981, p. 11). The result when applied to the mainstream situation is what Brennan (1979) terms the 'watered down' curriculum. Here traditional subject matter is simply reduced in amount and level of complexity. When applied to adult life, work situations are also reduced in complexity and the demands of production reduced. This is seen in training centres and many work experience schemes. The next aspect of modification to be considered relates to the control over the selection of work for children. In particular it relates to the criteria by which the children will be evaluated, the locus of control over the speed of progression and also the control over the sequence of instruction.

Objectives and Process Based Approaches

There has been a long running and often bitter debate in the field of curriculum theory as to the best way to control children's learning through the curriculum. This debate, that has popularly become known as the process versus objectives argument, has tended to focus on issues related to the nature and levels of learning and as to the way in which educational intention may be specified. Skilbeck attempts to resolve the major tension between those who wish to specify the processes in which children are to engage and those who wish to specify the outcomes of their learning by reformulating processes as outcomes with a high degree of generality (Skilbeck, 1984). For the purpose of this analysis, attention is drawn to the pole positions of those who focus on learning outcomes and those who focus on contexts that will enable children to learn. These two approaches will now be considered for both mainstream school and adult life foci. It will become clear in the course of the analysis that there is an unequal distribution of Brennan's elements of content across these systems of control (Brennan, 1985). The way in which skills, knowledge, attitudes and values distribute across the process/objectives divide is not uniform. It is easier to state a skill or an aspect of knowledge in precise terms as a desirable outcome than it is an attitude. Equally it is likely that a teacher aiming to facilitate the acquisition of certain attitudes will specify the context in which children will be required to engage in certain processes. This does not, however, imply that any one method of specification can never be used with a particular aspect of content in education (Skilbeck, 1984). Indeed, in special education many aspects of the curriculum considered to be beyond specification or 'hidden' in mainstream schooling become planned (Tomlinson, 1981; Brennan, 1985). The process/objectives dimension itself consists of many related continua. One continuum is between those who conceive of learning as an active process on the part of the learner and those who see the learner as passive. Another associated continuum relates to the degree of structure required for children with learning difficulties to learn successfully, that is between seeing the child as benefiting only from structured learning and from spontaneous or incidental learning. There are therefore at least four associated continua of belief about the nature of the learning experience for children with learning difficulties. This is summarized in Figure 7.1

Figure 7.1 Continua of belief about the nature of the learning experience

The Learner:	Active	______________	Passive
Specification of Curriculum:	Processes	______________	Objectives
Nature of Learning Situation:	Spontaneous Incidental	______________	Structured
Emphasis:	Contexts	______________	Outcomes

Again, as Skilbeck has shown, various aspects of these issues may be selected and combined in a variety of ways (Skilbeck, 1984). The extreme pole positions need not co-occur.

Whilst Thomas (1985) and Swann (1985) have shown that the objectives approach has enjoyed some considerable popularity of late, it is not without its critics and detractors. Swann is particularly critical of the way in which psychological research has been used to justify the objectives approach to the Special Needs curriculum. He echoes the sentiments of Goddard (1983) and Thomas (1985): '. . . attempts to justify educational practices with psychological research conducted in isolation from the precise nature of these practices and from their context are beset with problems' (Swann, 1985). The question as to whether the objectives approach will go out of 'fashion' as implied by Thomas (1985) remains to be seen. The fact remains that there is a continuum of degree of specificity of strictures by which learning situations may be controlled and these may be focused on processes in contexts and/or outcomes.

Stenhouse (1975) draws attention to the differential degree of application that the objectives and process models find in different aspects of education. Education, he claims, comprises at least four different processes: training,

Figure 7.2 Four processes of education

	Focus	Evaluation
TRAINING	Acquisition of skills	Capacity in performance
INSTRUCTION	Learning of information	Retention
INITIATION	Familiarization with social values and norms	Capacity to interpret the social environment and to anticipate reaction to one's own action
INDUCTION	Introduction into thought systems — the knowledge of the culture	Understanding as evidenced by capacity to grasp and to make for oneself relationships and judgments

After Stenhouse (1975), p. 80.

instruction, initiation and induction. Figure 7.2 summarizes his definitions of these processes.

Whilst he acknowledges that the objectives model gives a 'reasonably good fit' in the case of training and is 'appropriate' in instruction, Stenhouse (1975) emphasizes that the problem in the objectives model lies in the area of induction into knowledge. 'Education as induction into knowledge is successful to the extent that it makes the behavioural outcomes of the students unpredictable' (Stenhouse, 1975, p. 82). Thus if this argument is applied to the model under development here, training and instruction on the one hand and induction and initiation on the other would be correlates of the process/objectives dimension. Applying the principles of specification through objectives and a process based formulation to the Mainstream School/Adult Life distinctions yields the configuration illustrated in Figure 7.3.

Mainstream School Focused Objectives

There are important distinctions to be made in this category between objectives which are generated by an analysis of the tasks of instruction, objectives based upon the differential diagnosis of individual strengths and weaknesses of children, and objectives based on a model of thinking skills. The first, known as the Task Analysis model, specifies a task's behavioural components and its prerequisites. The second attempts to diagnose those abilities that are considered to underlie academic learning. The third involves an analysis of the cognitive functions or thinking skills which, it is hypothesized, enable academic performance.

Figure 7.3 Curriculum modification for SEN: a model

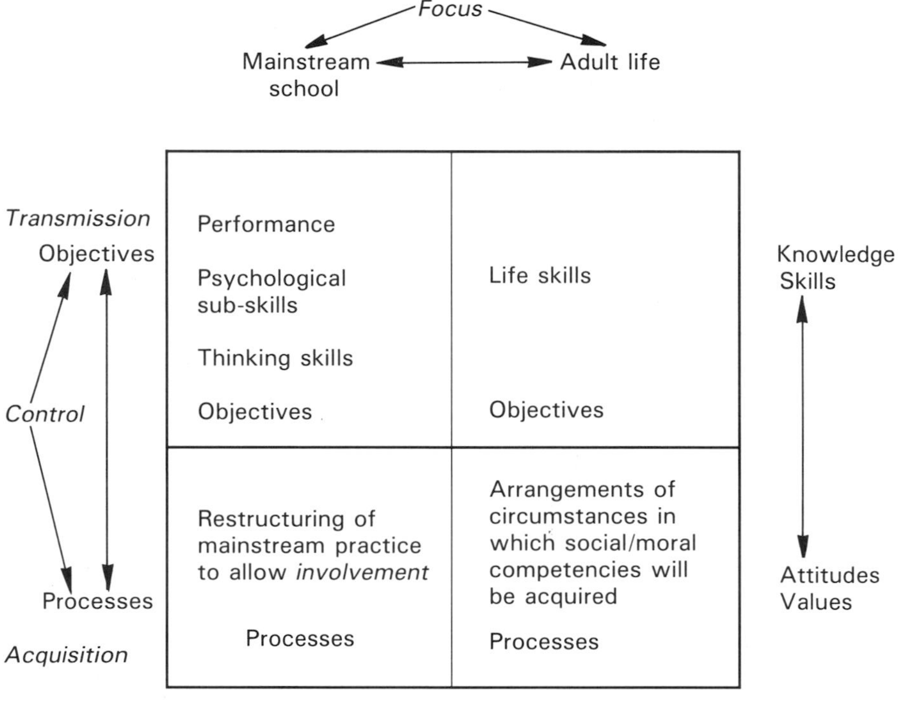

The Task Analysis Model

The intention here is not to describe in detail the various aspects of the task analysis model. Rather this section will discuss the principles of modification that are applied.

As mentioned above, this model is most often and easily applied to skills and knowledge. When consideration is given to the special curriculum the question becomes: What skills and what knowledge? Wilson (1981) admits that 'the list of important skills could be extended almost indefinitely', yet returns to a formulation of basic skills as the basis for planning the curriculum. 'Planning the curriculum with special relation to basic skills is particuarly relevant to special schools, because their pupils so often have to be taught in school skills which other children acquire naturally in the family situation' (Wilson, 1981, p. 15).

Again, here is the reference to a spontaneous learning deficit. The existence of this deficit is as much a matter of debate as are the suggestions for intervention. There is now available a considerable body of technical information relating to the sequencing (e.g. Posner and Strike, 1976), assessment and evaluation (e.g. Ainscow and Tweddle, 1979) of basic skills and yet there is a vociferous lobby which questions the nature of basic skills teaching. Here then is a principle of curriculum modification used in the creation of instructional tasks for children with learning difficulties. This principle justifies the translation of mainstream activities into their supposed component skill elements. These elements are then analyzed into the sequences of instructional tasks. The form that the sequence takes is usually a function of the content and/or the theoretical model of the skill adopted by the teacher.

Herein lies the potential for the misapplication of the approach. Objectives based teaching was designed to be embedded in an overall experimental teaching approach in which teacher-generated sequences of instruction were regarded as hypotheses as to a child's teaching/learning requirements. If a particular orthodoxy of sequence predominates then the difficulty that some children have in learning may well be compounded. By its very specification the approach rests a high degree of instructional control with the teacher. If this position is abused and children's own learning strategies are ignored, then difficulties ensue (Daniels, 1988). The objectives approach can be used as a tool to investigate and assist children's learning; it can also be used as a form of pedagogic blunderbuss.

Thus it is possible to consider at least two points at which this process is arbitrary, firstly in the translation of complex activities into component skills, and secondly the arrangement of skills into sequences. Advocates of the approach insist that treating the translation processes as an operation of hypothesis testing enables the most efficient instructional form to be produced and delivered.

Differential Diagnosis Ability Training

The differential diagnosis ability training approach assumes that psycholinguistic and perceptual motor abilities are necessary for learning basic academic skills. Children's learning abilities are explained in terms of their weakness in a profile of these abilities. The child's curriculum is then modified to provide training in the appropriate abilities. The assessment devices and materials devised by Frostig and Horne (1964), Kephart (1960) and Kirk, McCarthy and Kirk (1968) were and are commonly used. Criticisms of the approach come from both psychological sources (e.g. Ysseldyke and Saliva, 1974; Hammill and Larsen, 1974) and sociological sources (e.g. Carrier, 1988a and b; and Kronick, 1976). The essence of the criticisms appears to focus on the nature of the relationship between the abilities in question, training and academic performance. It is undoubtedly true that some disabilities cause academic failure; the question remains as to whether all failures are caused by disabilities and thus whether training in abilities will be effective. The general psychological factors under consideration are auditory abilities (e.g. auditory discrimination and memory), visual abilities (e.g. visual discrimination and spatial relationships), cross sensory perceptual abilities (e.g. auditory-visual integration) and psycholinguistic abilities (e.g. auditory sequential memory and verbal expression). Arter and Jenkins (1979) question whether these abilities exist as such and, if they do, whether they can be validly and reliably tested. They remain unconvinced of the efficacy of the testing procedures and question the value of teaching based on test results.

There are those who consider that ability training should be used in conjunction with task analysis (Smead, 1977) and those who reject both forms (Heshusius, 1986). However, in practice, materials designed for ability training purposes are still widely used in Special Schools albeit not always with an explicit understanding of the theoretical base of the practice.

To summarize, the differential diagnosis of within child abilities and the subsequent modification of the curriculum in line with the strictures of learning disability theory have been subject to considerable criticism. Despite the writings of both psychologists and sociologists, the theory continues to influence special educational practice. The principle that operates is one which calls for an analysis of the psychological subskills thought to underlie academic achievement. Deficiencies in these abilities are then the subject of training. The child's abilities are analyzed rather than the task.

Mainstream Focused Thinking Skills Approaches

A theme which emerges from much recent research relates to the ability of children with learning difficulties to use information flexibly once it has been acquired. Studies that are concerned with children knowing when, where and how to use information once it has been acquired now form an important and rapidly expanding aspect of psychological research into the nature of special educational needs (Sperber and McCauley, 1984; Campione, Brown and Ferrara, 1982; Evans, 1986; Borkowski, Reid and Kurtz, 1984; Brown, 1978). The term metacognition has been viewed as 'an epiphenomenon recently elevated and dignified with a new title but really the stuff that problem solving literature has been concerned with all along' (Brown, 1978). Although the term is now widely used, it appears to mean different things in different research programmes. Flavell (1976) offered the definition of a metacognition as referring to: 'One's knowledge concerning one's own cognitive processes and products of anything related to them' (Flavell, 1976). In the research literature this definition has been further refined and an important distinction drawn:

> This distinction between knowledge and the use of the knowledge also emerged in the metacognition section, where we reserved the term metacognition for knowledge about cognition (more specifically memory) and distinguished it from executive control, the process whereby we select, monitor and generally oversee our own cognitive activities (Campione, Brown and Ferrara, 1982).

Campione *et al.* argue on the basis of current research findings that instructing metacognition did not seem to result in improvement on tasks whereas training in self management routines did. The question of interest is as to how one investigates and makes use of such findings. Borkowski, Reid and Kurtz (1984) recommended research into the application of specific forms of what they term metacognitive training for modifying cognitive deficiencies in impulsive and retarded children. Certainly many schools are experimenting with forms of strategic training. Rectory Paddock School (1983) have outlined an approach to the training of control processes in children with severe learning difficulties.

The same issues are developed with Feuerstein's Instrumental Enrichment programme. He concentrates on the training of cognitive regulatory functions (e.g. self control and self regulation) achieved via the mediation of a supportive teacher. Feuerstein characterizes cognitive deficits in children with learning difficulties in a way that is consistent with the literature cited above. They are purported to lack systematic data gathering, checking, monitoring and self regulating mechanisms. They are also supposed to follow instructions blindly, lack adequate question asking skills and tolerate contradictions and inconsistences happily. 'They have a tendency to treat each problem as a new problem, regardless of relevant prior experiences, and generally develop learning sets slowly, transferring the effects of past learning reluctantly' (Feuerstein, 1979). It is important to add to this somewhat damning description the phrase 'in school'. To circumvent this set of behaviours the instrumental enrichment package is now being used in many secondary and special schools. Despite somewhat inconclusive evaluation reports (Weller and Craft, 1983; Shayer and Beasley, 1987), attempts are being made to offer the package as described by Feuerstein to children with learning difficulties.

> The salient characteristic in Instrumental Enrichment is its conscious, intentional, focused and volitional nature. The student is made aware that a certain concept is to be taught; he is made to focus on that concept and gradually to perfect his abilities with relationship to it. It is deemed of the utmost importance that his awareness and cooperation in this effort be enlisted and it will not be left to chance that perhaps he will come to understand the purposes and logic behind the disparate exercises (Feuerstein, 1979, p. 18).

When reviewing conditions for transfer of training of cognitive instruction Butterfield and Ferretti (1984) conclude that quicker learning and more ready transfer results if problems are grouped according to the similarity of underlying psychological processes. 'The practical importance of these findings on transfer is their implication that classroom curricula should be organized around the psychological problems underlying the material to be taught' (Butterfield and Ferretti, 1984, p. 331).

One clear feature that many authors have noted is that retarded children consistently need direct and explicit instruction before they will show signs of behaving strategically (Belmont and Butterfield, 1977; Brown, 1978; Campione and Brown, 1984). Also, it seems that some children abandon routines when instruction is withdrawn. That is, if transfer of trained routines is required then additional specific training is needed (Brown and Campione, 1979, 1981). This problem is also addressed by aspects of the Direct Instruction method (Englemann and Carnine, 1982). There is, then, a growing body of literature which focuses the attention of educators on the need to design programmes which explicitly train children to transfer information once it has been acquired, the central argument being that this ability underlies performances that are taken as indicators of intelligent behaviour in school.

Mainstream Focused Process Based Approaches

Whilst it is only in the early stages of implementation it is evident that one of the effects of GCSE will be to require those children who study for it to engage in much more problem solving, investigational work than was previously the case. Mathematics and science show these changes in orientation most clearly. Process based work has been evident in 'good primary practice' since the days of the Plowden Report. However, relatively little has been written on the topic of process based approaches in Special Education. Goddard (1983), Power (1981), Sinha (1981), Wood (1981) and Swann (1985) are representative of the field. Much of the emphasis on process based work has been focused on language work and pays particular attention to the contexts in which children are most likely to acquire competence. This emphasis on the tacit acquisition of competence is the hallmark of studies which seek to suggest modifications to teaching contexts rather than pupil outcomes.

Goddard (1983) offered his staff principles of procedure which he considered would ensure an adequate context to enable children's learning to take place. The recently published Open University Course with its associated readers Booth, Potts, Swann (1987), and Coulby and Booth (1987), follow in this tradition. The change from an objectives approach to a process orientation in two books by the same authors (Ainscow and Tweddle, 1979 and 1988) is perhaps made more startling when the fundamental theoretical antecedents are considered.

The suggestions for the modification of the context of learning involve changing the modality of instruction and response as well as the formulation of appropriate support for the child when it engages with the problems set. The organization and management of learning contexts and the analysis of the support required to allow children to gain access to the experiences open to others in the classroom has also been the focus of a number of recent texts, e.g. Thomas and Feiler (1988). Elements of this approach and of the behavioural task analytic approach are being combined in what are termed ecological approaches (Apter, 1982). These approaches suggest the need (to differing degrees) for systematic attention to environmental/contextual system change. Thomas (1985) has ventured to suggest why these approaches are meeting with resistance in the field.

> The fact that ecological perspectives have not been used more often as an escape route from the closed loop of individually based approaches has, of course, not a little to do with the constraints imposed upon employers (made more powerful by the influence of the 1981 Act) who are perturbed less (in the main) about the idea of individual change than about the idea of institutional change (Thomas, 1985).

The principle which operates here is of modification of the context in which the child is seen actively to go about acquiring understanding.

Adult Life Focused Approaches

As Fish (1985) has stated, there is a sense in which the whole school curriculum prepared the individual for adult life from the earliest years. Special Schools have often been praised for their efforts in preparing different forms of leavers' programmes for their pupils (Brennan, 1979; Wilson, 1981). These arose out of the schools' concerns about the extra problems for children with learning difficulties in making the transition from school to adult life.

> The traditional academic curriculum, however, often leaves out social and life skills and relies on families to cultivate them. Aspects of preparation for leaving school have entered into the programme of less academic pupils, but it has been in Special Schools where most thought has been given to developing leaving courses (Fish, 1985, p. 96).

This is not to imply that adult life focused work consists exclusively of social and life skills work; as Gulliford (1985) has stated, there are many preparatory courses which take place in workshops and industrial units designed to provide realistic work settings. These can, of course, be combined with a variety of link courses with local colleges and work experience schemes.

However, partly as a response to what are seen by some as the demands of post-industrial society (Hopson and Scally, 1981) and as the particular difficulties of children with learning and behaviour difficulties (Gulliford, 1985), social and life skills teaching has assumed a position of some importance in the secondary curriculum of many schools for a selection of the pupil population. It is important to see the social and life skills approach as only a form of social education. Moore (1984) and Lee (1980) discuss seven approaches to social education, one of which is skills training.

> The seven approaches can be briefly summarized in terms of what is involved for the learner: Information-based: reception of knowledge and information with either theoretical or practical relevance in the social education area. Enquiry-based: practice in a variety of modes of enquiry through a search for knowledge. Creative: self-expression through the practice and/or appreciation of the creative arts. Experiential: participation in activities considered to be inherently socially educative. Awareness-raising: participation in and reflection on group activities and experience. Skills training: structured practice in tasks, behaviours and strategies. Modelling: spending time with adult 'non-teachers' (Lee, 1980).

Viewed from the perspective of this section which is concerned about the principles that control the modification of teaching, it may be argued that information based and skills training are more open to objectives based work, whereas experiential, creative and enquiry based work are more open to a process approach.

Adult Life Focused Objectives Based Approaches

Implicit in objectives based approach is the assumption that the content matter can be transformed into a set of objectives. Attempts at this process have been criticized by a variety of commentators.

> They run the risk of encouraging the facile view that successful living can be reduced to the identification and acquisition of a number of unambiguous social skills (Wilcox *et al.*, 1984, p. 31).

The reality is that we know precious little about the nature of social

> and life skills – about, that is, the awesomely detailed and subtle ways in which we organize our everyday social interaction . . . In the absence of any systematic body of knowledge, there can be no adequate curriculum or pedagogy (Atkinson *et al.*, 1980, pp. 13–14).

Despite these and many other criticisms the social and life skills objectives based modifications to particularly the secondary school curriculum are becoming increasingly widespread (Gulliford, 1985). This is partly due to the influence of initiatives in Further Education and training through the Manpower Services Commission and the Further Education Curriculum Review and Development Unit. A considerable proportion of this work is heavily influenced by the work of Argyle (1967) who drew an analogy between motor skills and social behaviour. The descriptions devised for the motor skill process were applied to social skills and the model used a reference point in identifying specific causes of poor interaction. Objectives generated by this and/or other similar models (e.g. the self empowerment model of Hopson and Scally, 1981) are delivered in work preparation or transition courses in many special schools. Here the boundary between school work and everyday work is deliberately blurred and school subjects tend to disappear into a generalized course. However, as is the case with almost all forms of objectives based teaching, there is a high degree of control over what the children actually do, the order they do things in and how quickly they do them. This is what Dickinson and Erben (1983) declare to be the 'pedagogy of technicisation'.

Here, then, is a principle of modification which attempts to translate complicated forms of social and vocational behaviour into specific programmes. Whilst these attempts have been dismissed as 'gestures of naive educational utopianism' (Wilcox *et al.*, 1984, p. 105), they nonetheless represent a considerable proportion of the programmes being planned for secondary aged pupils in special and mainstream schools.

Adult Life Focused Process Based Approaches

Concern here is with modifying the contexts in which children acquire those competences which will facilitate their transition to adult life. In terms of Lee's (1980) approaches to social education, attention would be directed towards creative or experiential work. Power's critique of formal objectives based social skills teaching is indicative of some of the areas explored in process based approaches.

> Two other problems in the social skills learning area also need considerable attention from special educators. First of all, there is

> the frequent and redundant (and hence boring and off-putting) painstaking teaching in school of skills already naturally and easily learned from parents and siblings at home. The need for very close liaison between school and home in this area cannot be overemphasized. Secondly, it must be asked whether schools are desirable environments for teaching social and life skills anyway (Power, 1981, p. 439).

This clearly denies Wilson's (1981) assertion that Special Needs children have to be taught that which other children 'acquire naturally' in the family situation.

Emphasis within a process based approach to social education would tend to be on the contexts in which children were placed and on the ways in which they would be encouraged to work. Rather than being formally taught to, say, cooperate or show good work habits the teacher would attempt to create situations in which they could and would acquire such competences. Just as an objectives based approach to teaching is more amenable to the transmission of skills and knowledge, a process approach is perhaps more suited to the creation of situations in which children will acquire attitudes and value sets. Thus the moral component of the schooling may assume a high profile in process based approaches.

In summary, process based approaches to adult life focused schooling find expression through the principle of creating situations considered appropriate for the acquisition of attitudes and values.

Curriculum Shape

The discussion so far has focused on the principles of control regulating what may be taught and what may not be taught in school and also the specification of educational practice in Special Schools. Attention now turns to the nature of the differentiation of what counts as content within the curriculum.

Clearly the whole curriculum may not be compartmentalized in the same way. Indeed, the differing orientations within systems of control towards aspects of knowledge have different demands in terms of organization. As Tansley and Gulliford (1960) have stated:

> If the curriculum content is compartmentalized into subjects it is less easy to provide those broad experiences and real life situations which are so necessary. If correlation is emphasized, the basic subjects are likely to suffer because of difficulty of control and continuity; teaching may become subservient to the project and not related to the individual (Tansley and Gulliford, 1960).

This same tension is described by Wilson (1981) in terms of the psychological needs of children on the one hand and that 'school subjects represent the accumulated knowledge of our society' (p. 14) on the other. A curriculum may then be partially described in terms of the position it occupies on a subjects/projects continuum. The way in which knowledge is selected for combination into what are often arbitrary subjects in schools (e.g. Integrated Studies) has been the focus of much public debate. The debate is set to continue as there is no stipulation within the 1988 Act as to the shape, in terms of timetabled subjects, that the National Curriculum should assume. Special Schools, if they believe that their pupils only have capacity to learn a limited amount, often prioritize content. These priorities or even the system used to prioritize content may change with age. For instance, whilst the secondary curriculum may be organized around subjects, the primary curriculum may attend more to experience.

> For those working with very young or handicapped children, however, it is very clear that a timetable based on subjects lays too much stress on transmitted knowledge and skills and too little on the child's experience. Since young children exploring their environment may be acquiring linguistic, mathematical and social concepts through the same activity, the division of learning into subject compartments seems inappropriate (Wilson, 1981, p. 14).

Brennan advocates a broad based version of curriculum construction which involves a three level prioritization process across knowledge, skills, attitudes and values (Brennan, 1985). This represents a development from Tansley and Gulliford's (1960) notion of an essential core of basic skills and peripheral curriculum of activities into the designation of content that must, should or could be included in the child's schooling. Here a curriculum shape or structure would possibly involve different control systems at different levels. Brennan further distinguishes between function learning and context learning. Where function learning is 'essential learning which must be established in the behaviour of the pupils if they are to face the problems of later life with a reasonable level of success', context learning 'is the assimilated learning which is the background or context of pupils' behaviours and allows them to relate to and maintain contact with the natural, social, emotional and aesthetic aspects of their environment' (Brennan, 1985, p. 75). Clearly, here, function learning is more likely to be controlled through objectives and context learning through a process based approach.

Account may be taken of issues of curriculum balance, continuity and progression from the perspectives of local mainstream school subjects, areas of experience, skills, attitudes and values embedded in the particular shape chosen (Wilson, 1981; Brennan, 1985).

In terms of curriculum modifications for special needs, control seems to assume a higher practical priority than organization or curriculum shape. It is true that popular accounts of curriculum modification claim a psychological justification for integrated day primary schooling (e.g. Wilson, 1981; Blenkin and Kelly, 1983). However, there appears to be no psychological justification for any particular curriculum shape at secondary level. Here it seems issues of power govern the shape of the curriculum. As Goodson (1983) argues, the maintenance of the existing differential status of school subjects in the secondary curriculum can defeat new contenders for curriculum space despite the newcomers' possible greater potential for the education of children.

The principle of modification at issue here, then, is one which regulates the relationship between the contents of lessons. On the one extreme all lessons may be the same. Justifications for this approach, usually project or theme based, relate to theories of learning and development and thus to the psychological needs of the child (Wilson, 1981). On the other hand a great number of subjects may be presented and justified in terms of relations with those of other institutions.

The Intentions of Whole School Approaches

The burgeoning literature on whole school approaches to working with children with special needs in mainstream schools is in part an outcome of the systems analysis of schools as advocated by psychologists such as Gillham (1981). A necessary part of this systems analysis must be attention to selection and combination of curriculum modifications. The approach adopted by a particular school in part represents an expression of its own priorities and overall intentions. Different selections reveal different orientations to children and intention of schooling.

In the past much of the practice of special schools has been orientated towards concerns over the regulation of children's behaviour. Therapeutic approaches were employed in many special schools. Many of the children sent to these schools had in some way offended the social and moral codes of their previous schools. In general the schools themselves were not held accountable for the academic achievements of their pupils. Their intentions were formulated in terms of adjustment, the development of caring attitudes and emotional stability. However, with the lack of attention to instructional practice itself as anything other than a context for the acquisition of social and moral competence, they were profoundly segregationalist in both theory and practice.

The Warnock Report and the 1981 Act shifted the balance to the predomination of modification of instructional practice. Under this formulation it is argued that children will behave in an acceptable way because of the limitations imposed on them by the demands of work. Allied to this is the argument that successful learning enables children to adjust emotionally. A gross simplification of these two approaches yields the tension between a segregationist caring form of provision and an integrationist positive teaching approach. Under the guidance of GCSE the mainstream system is moving towards a more process based stance. It is clear that some children will continue to need direct tuition in order that they may make progress. This tuition may derive its objectives from a variety of sources. However, if the sources are not within the mainstream framework, then the curriculum for children with special needs will inevitably become completely different from their peers. If they are to remain in curriculum contact with their peers the modifications selected by teachers must seek their rationale from the same source as the mainstream curriculum. In other words they need the same experiences but in some cases require support to benefit from them. In a sense they require a form of positive discrimination: more help in achieving the same ends.

The worry is that when these children are seen to fail as judged against academic or social criteria they will be given something completely different: an entirely objectives based approach when their peers are engaged in GCSE, or a process based adult life focused approach while their peers are acquiring specific skills and knowledge.

Conclusion

The practice of special education abounds with a range of curricular exotica. Some are historical remnants, echoes of previously fashionable psychological theories. Some represent poles of ongoing philosophical and psychological debates concerning the nature of causation and views of learning.

Their origins are not of as much importance for the children as their position relative to those practices which hold sway in the mainstream. If we want to achieve functional integration, only those modifications which enable children both to participate in mainstream practice and make progress should be selected from those available. One of the many changes made by the 1988 Act is to alter the implication of the term 'modification'. The Warnock report drew attention to three elements of modification: access, curriculum and climate. The 1988 Act can also be interpreted as implying that modification should be used to enable children with special needs to make progress towards the same goals as their mainstream peers. Sadly, it could be used to introduce profoundly segregationist practice into our system of schooling. Enabling all children to have access to the National Curriculum will be a great challenge, one that can only be met by a collective response to individual difficulty. It calls for the sensitive application of those modifications which support children's progress rather than divert them into educational backwaters.

References

AINSCOW, M. and TWEDDLE, D.A. (1979) *Preventing Classroom Failure*, London, Methuen.

AINSCOW, M. and TWEDDLE, D.A. (1988) *Encouraging Classroom Success*, London, David Fulton.

APTER, S.J. (1982) *Troubled Children, Troubled Systems*, New York, Pergamon.

ARGYLE, M. (1967) *The Psychology of Interpersonal Behaviour*, Harmondsworth, Penguin.

ARTER, J.A., JENKINS, J.R. (1979) 'Differential diagnosis prescriptive teaching: A critical appraisal', *Review of Educational Research*, 49, pp. 517–55.

ATKINSON, P., SHONE, D. and REES, T. (1980) 'Labouring to learn? Industrial Training for Slow Learners', in BARTON, L. and TOMLINSON, S. (Eds) *Special Education: Policy, Practices and Social Issues*, London, Harper & Row.

BELMONT, U.M. and BUTTERFIELD, E.C. (1977) 'The instructional approach to developmental cognitive research', in KAIL, R.V. and HAGEN, J.W. (Eds) *Perspectives on the Development of Memory and Cognition*, Hillsdale, Erlbaum.

BLENKIN, G. and KELLY, A.V. (Eds) (1983) *The Primary Curriculum in action: a process approach to educational practice*, London, Harper & Row.

BOOTH, T. and COULBY, D. (1987) *Producing and Reducing Disaffection*, Milton Keynes, Open University Press.

BOOTH, T., POTTS, P. and SWANN, W. (1987) *Preventing Difficulties in Learning*, Milton Keynes, Open University Press.

BORKOWSKI, J.G., REID, M.K. and KURTZ, B.E. (1984) 'Metacognition and Retardation: Paradigmatic, Theoretical and Applied Perspectives', in BROOKS, P.H., SPERBER, R. and MCCAULEY, O. (Eds) *Learning and Cognition in the Mentally Retarded*, London, Lawrence Erlbaum.

BRENNAN, W. (1974) *Shaping the Education of Slow Learners*, London, R.K.P.

BRENNAN, W. (1979) *Curricular Needs of Slow Learners*, Schools Council Working Paper 63, London, Evans/Methuen Educational.

BRENNAN, W. (1985) *Curriculum for Special Needs*, Milton Keynes, Open University Press.

BROWN, A.L. (1978) 'Knowing when, where and how to remember: A problem of metacognition', in GLASER, R. (Ed.) *Advances in Instructional Psychology*, Vol. 1., Hillsdale, Lawrence Erlbaum.

BROWN, A.L. and CAMPIONE, J.C. (1979) 'Memory Strategies in Learning: Training children to study strategically', in PICK, H.L., LESKOWITZ, H.W., SINGER, J.E., STEINSCHNEIDER, A. and STEVENSON, H.W. (Eds) *Psychology from Research to Practice*, New York, Plenum Press.

BROWN, A.L. and CAMPIONE J.C. (1981) 'Inducing flexible thinking: a problem of access', in FRIEDMAN, M., DAS, J.P. and O'CONNOR, N. (Eds) *Intelligence and Learning*, New York, Plenum Press.

BUTTERFIELD, E.C. and FERRETTI, R.P. (1984) 'Some extensions of the instructional approach to the study of cognitive development and a sufficient condition for the transfer of training', in BROOKS, P.H., SPERBER, R. and MCCAULEY, C. (Eds) *Learning and Cognition in the Mentally Retarded*, London, Lawrence Erlbaum.

CAMPIONE, J.C. and BROWN, A.L. (1984) 'Learning ability and transfer propensity as sources of individual differences in intelligence', in BROOKS, P.H., SPERBER, R. and MCCAULEY, C. (Eds) *Learning and Cognition in the Mentally Retarded*, London, Lawrence Erlbaum.

CAMPIONE, J.C., BROWN, A.L. and FERRARA, R. A. (1982) 'The zone of proximal development: implications for individual differences in learning', in ROGOFF, B. and WERTECH, J.V. (Eds) *Children's Learning in the Zone of Proximal Development, New Directions for Child Development No. 23*, San Francisco, Jossey Bass.

CARRIER, J.G. (1982a) 'Masking the social in Educational Knowledge', *American Journal of Sociology* Vol. 88 No. 5, pp. 948–74.

CARRIER, J.G. (1983b) 'Explaining educability: an investigation of political support for children with learning disabilities', *British Journal of Sociology of Education* Vol. 4 No. 2.

DANIELS, H. (1988) 'Misunderstanding, Miscues and Maths', *British Journal of Special Education* Vol. 15 No. 1, pp. 11–13.

DEPARTMENT OF EDUCATION AND SCIENCE (1963) *Half our Future* (The Newsom Report), London, HMSO.

DEPARTMENT OF EDUCATION AND SCIENCE (1967) *Children and their Primary Schools* (Plowden Report), London, HMSO.

DEPARTMENT OF EDUCATION AND SCIENCE (1978) *Special Educational Needs* (The Warnock Report, London, HMSO.

DEPARTMENT OF EDUCATION AND SCIENCE (1981) *Education Act 1981*, London, HMSO.

DEPARTMENT OF EDUCATION AND SCIENCE (1984) *The Organization and Content of the Curriculum: Special Schools*, London, HMSO.

DEPARTMENT OF EDUCATION AND SCIENCE (1985) *Education for All: The Report of the Committee of Inquiry into the Education of Children from Ethnic Minority Groups* (The Swann Report), London, HMSO.

DEPARTMENT OF EDUCATION AND SCIENCE (1987) *National Curriculum: Task Group on Assessment and Testing: A report*, London, HMSO.

DEPARTMENT OF EDUCATION AND SCIENCE (1988) *The Education Reform Act*, London, HMSO.

DICKINSON, H. and ERBEN, M. (1983) 'The technicisation of morality and culture: a consideration of the work of Claude Grignon and its relevance to Further Education in Britain', in GLEESON, D. (Ed.) *Youth Training and the Search for Work*, London, Routledge & Kegan Paul.

ENGLEMANN, S. and CARNINE, D. (1982) *Theory of Instruction: Principles and Application*, New York, Irrington.

EVANS, P.L.C. (1986) 'The Learning Process', in COUPE, J. and PORTER, J. (Eds) *The Education of Children with Severe Learning Difficulties: Bridging the gap between theory and practice*, London, Croom Helm.

FEUERSTEIN, R. (1979) *The Dynamic Assessment of Retarded Performers: The Learning*

Potential Assessment Device, Theory, Instruments and Techniques, Baltimore, University Park Press.

FISH, J. (1985) *The Way Ahead*, Milton Keynes, Open University Press.

FLAVELL, J.H. (1976) 'Metacognitive Aspects of Problem Solving', in RESNICK, L.B. (Ed.) *The nature of intelligence*, Hillsdale, Lawrence Erlbaum.

FORD, J., MONGON, D. and WHELAN, M. (1982) *Special Education and Social Control: Invisible Disasters*, London, Routledge & Kegan Paul.

FROSTIG, M. and HORNE, D. (1964) *The Frostig program for the development of visual perception: Teachers' Guide*, Chicago, Follett.

GAGNE, R. (1985) *The Conditions of Learning*, 4th ed., New York, Holt, Rinehart & Wilson.

GODDARD, A. (1983) 'Processes in Special Education', in BLENKIN, G.M. and KELLY, A.V. (Eds) *The primary curriculum in action: a process approach to educational practice*, London, Harper & Row.

GOODSON, I.F. (1983) *School Subjects and Curriculum Change*, London, Croom Helm.

GULLIFORD, R. (1985) *Teaching Children with Learning Difficulties*, Oxford, NFER/Nelson.

HAMMILL, D.D. and LARSEN, S.C. (1974) 'The effectiveness of psycholinguistic training', *Exceptional Children*, 41, pp. 5–14.

HESHUSIUS, L. (1986) 'Paradigm shifts and Special Education: A response to Ulman and Rosenberg', *Exceptional Children*, February, pp. 461–5.

HOPSON, B. and SCALLY, M. (1981) *Life Skills Teaching*, London, McGraw-Hill.

INNER LONDON EDUCATION AUTHORITY (1984) *Improving Secondary Schools* (The Hargreaves Report), London, ILEA.

INNER LONDON EDUCATION AUTHORITY (1985) *Equal Opportunities for ALL?* (The Fish Report), London, ILEA.

INNER LONDON EDUCATION AUTHORITY (1985b) *Improving Primary Schools* (The Thomas Report), London, ILEA.

KEPHART, N.O. (1960) *The slow learner in the classroom*, Columbus, Chic., Merrill.

KIRK, S., MCCARTHY, L. and KIRK, N. (1968) *Illinois Tests of Psycho-linguistic Abilities*, Urbana, University of Illinois Press.

KRONICK, D. (1976) 'The importance of a sociological perspective towards learning disabilities', *Journal of Learning Disabilities* Vol. 9 No. 2.

LEE, R. (1980) *Beyond Coping: Some Approaches to Social Education*, London, FEU.

MOORE, R. (1984) *Education and Production: A generative model*, unpublished Ph.D. thesis, University of London.

POSNER, G.J. and STRIKE, K.A. (1976) 'A categorization scheme for principles of sequencing content', *Review of Educational Research* Vol. 46 No. 4, pp. 665–90.

POWER, D.J. (1981) 'Principles of curriculum and methods development in special education', in SWANN, W. (Ed.) *The Practice of Special Education*, London, Basil Blackwell and Open University Press.

RECTORY PADDOCK STAFF (1983) *In Search of a Curriculum*, 2nd ed., London, Robin Wren Publications.

SHAYER, M. and BEASLEY, F. (1987) 'Does instrumental enrichment work?', *British Journal of Educational Research* Vol. 1 no. 2.

SINHA, C. (1981) 'The role of psychological research in special education', in SWANN, W. (Ed.) *The Practice of Special Education*, London, Basil Blackwell and Open University Press.

SKILBECK, M. (1984) *School Based Curriculum Development*, London, Harper & Row.

SMEAD, V.S. (1977) 'Ability training and task analysis in diagnostic prescriptive teaching', *Journal of Special Education* Vol. 11, pp. 113–25.

SPERBER, R. and MCCAULEY, C. (1984) 'Semantic Processing Efficiency in the Mentally Retarded', in BROOKS, P.H., SPERBER, R., MCCAULEY, S. (Eds) *Learning and Cognition in the Mentally Retarded*, London, Lawrence Erlbaum.

STENHOUSE, L. (1975) *An Introduction to Curriculum Research and Development*, London, Heinemann.

SWANN, W. (1985) 'Psychological Science and the Practice of Special Education', in CLAXTON, S. *et al.* (Eds) *Psychology and Schooling: What's the Matter?*, Bedford Way Paper No. 25, Institute of Education, University of London.

TANSLEY, A.E. and GULLIFORD, R. (1960) *The Education of Slow Learning Children*, London, Routledge & Kegan Paul.

THOMAS, J. (1985) 'What Psychology had to offer Education – then', *Bulletin of The British Psychological Society* 38, pp. 322–6.

THOMAS, S. and FAILER, A. (Eds) (1988) *Planning for Special Needs*, London, Basil Blackwell.

TOMLINSON, S. (1981) *Educational Subnormality: a study in decision making*, London, Routledge & Kegan Paul.

TOMLINSON, S. (1981) *A Sociology of Special Education*, London, Routledge & Kegan Paul.

WEDELL, K. (1980) 'Early identification and compensatory interaction', in KNIGHT R.M. and BAKER, D.J. (Eds) *Treatment of Hyperactive and Learning Disordered Children*, Baltimore, University Park Press.

WELLER, K. and CRAFT, A. (1983) *Making up our minds: An exploratory study of instrumental enrichment*, London, Schools Council.

WILCOX, B., DUNN, J., LAVERCOMBE, S. and BURN, L. (1984) *The Preparation for Life Curriculum*, Beckenham, Croom Helm.

WILSON, M. (1981) *The Curriculum in Special Schools*, London, Schools Council.

WOOD, D. (1981) 'Theory and Research in Classrooms: lessons from deaf education', in SWANN, W. (Ed.) *The Practice of Special Education*, London, Basil Blackwell and Open University Press.

YSSELDYKE, J.E. and SALVIA, J. (1974) 'Diagnostic prescriptive teaching: two models', *Exceptional Children* Vol. 41, pp. 181–5.

Chapter 8

The Needs of Hearing-impaired Children and Integration

Brian Fraser

The integration of hearing-impaired children into ordinary classes was a major development in the education of the deaf in the 1960s. Small-scale experiments had been attempted in different LEAs in the UK and at various times since the latter years of the nineteenth century. The development was accelerated in the late 50s by the improved detection facilities; by research results which highlighted the fact that there were in ordinary schools, significant numbers of children with previously undetected hearing losses, and by the technological development of electronic aids to hearing. Local education authorities responded to these developments by establishing units for partially hearing-impaired children attached to ordinary primary and secondary schools and by creating services designed to support partially hearing children found in mainstream classes. In some instances these two developments were combined into an integrated service for hearing-impaired children which was developed into a school-like structure with a head teacher, senior teaching staff and assistant teachers. Most LEAs had until this time relied upon out of authority placement of children with more severe impairments and more obvious special educational needs. Large urban authorities had day schools for the deaf which catered for children from within that authority and from neighbouring boroughs and counties. There was a well established network of residential schools for the deaf and for the partially deaf. Any advice sought by LEA came from these existing provisions, from a small team of specialist HMI, or from the Department of Education of the Deaf at the University of Manchester. The establishment of embryo services for hearing-impaired children changed much of this. This change occurred in three ways. Firstly, the appointment of a specialist teacher of the deaf generally initiated a programme of ascertainment to determine the numbers of children in ordinary schools with hearing loss. Such a programme would be a simple questionnaire asking schools and health authorities to identify those children known to have hearing losses. In several instances this was extended by initiating a screening programme in cooperation with health authorities more properly to detect all children whether known to have a hearing loss or not.

The second type of change related to what most teachers of the deaf appointed to LEAs saw as their priority work: that is, the guidance and counselling of parents of pre-school aged children from the age of initial diagnosis. By the late 1950s there was a developing awareness in the child health services of the need for early identification of hearing loss in babies and young children in order that habilitative programmes could be initiated. Such early identification led to the timely fitting of hearing aids thus maximizing the use of any residual hearing. This was coupled with regular ongoing sessions of parent counselling and guidance usually conducted in the home. This work had been pioneered in the University of Manchester and had been seen to produce dramatic effects upon the development and verbal communication skills in deaf children (Watson and Pickles, 1957). By developing intensive pre-school services which often meant working with babies from as young as 7 or 8 months of age the nature of needs of hearing-impaired children of 5 years was seen to change. Many who without such early support would have previously required the specialist help of schools for the deaf or partially hearing, were now able to take up places in the normal school system albeit with some degree of supportive specialist help.

The third type of change initiated by the appointment of specialist teachers of the deaf in LEAs relates to the source of professional advice. Most authorities, and certainly all of those without special schools for children with hearing impairment, depended for educational advice upon out-authority sources — either day or residential schools or university or clinical centres which had developed expertise in matters related to the education of the deaf. With appointment of a LEA based specialist teacher, authorities tended to turn more to this person for advice and guidance on matters related to the placement of children with hearing loss and the development of educational facilities. Such advice and guidance was placed in the context of local needs and expectations and tended more closely to reflect the wishes of parents and of the educational services.

An examination of the official statistics related to the classification and placement of hearing-impaired children from the late 1940s to the present day demonstrates the effects of these developments. In 1947 there was a rate of 6.83/10,000 of children being educated in special schools or classes for hearing-impaired children; of these 5.1/10,000 were classified as deaf and 1.73/10,000 as partially hearing. By 1967, twenty years later, the ratio had increased to 8.61/10,000 but now 3.93 were classified as deaf and 4.68 as partially hearing. Figures for other school children wearing hearing aids were first collected in 1957 (perhaps because the first widely available NHS transistorized hearing aid was not issued until 1956!). In that year these were only 1.03/10,000 of the school population (there were, in special schools and classes, 7.23/10,000). By 1967 8.07/10,000 of the school population were in the mainstream sector wearing hearing aids. This represented nearly half of the known school aged population of hearing-impaired children (DES, 1968). More recent figures (BATOD, 1983) show that of the known population of school aged children with hearing impairment, only 13.6 per cent are in special schools for the hearing-impaired; 15 per cent are in units for hearing-impaired children attached to mainstream schools and 71.3 per cent are in local mainstream schools receiving support from visiting teachers of the deaf.

Needs of the Hearing-impaired Child

The special educational needs of the hearing-impaired child are complex and arise from several different sources. These can be divided into those which are associated with the impairment and those which are concerned with the environment (Fraser, 1984). There is a temptation, as with all impairments, to impute the condition with the blame for the resultant handicap. The deficit is seen to be the focus both of the problems and of the habilitation efforts. Increasingly it is being recognized (Webster, 1986) that such a view is too narrow in its conceptualization and is likely to result in a restricted and restricting developmental programme.

The needs of the hearing impaired children are the same as for any children. Circumstances compounded of factors inherent in the condition and externally in society and its organization conspire to prevent the adequate meeting of these needs. The needs can be divided into three main categories. Whilst these may seem to be discrete they are mutually influencing and really have to be seen as a global handicapping package. These three categories are:

(1) interpersonal communication;
(2) sensory deprivation;
(3) societal attitudes.

1. Interpersonal Communication

Because of limited auditory experience the child with hearing loss is offered limited opportunities for the reception of spoken language. This will have an inevitable affect upon language production. Limited expressive language

Figure 8.1: The effect of auditory deficit upon language competence

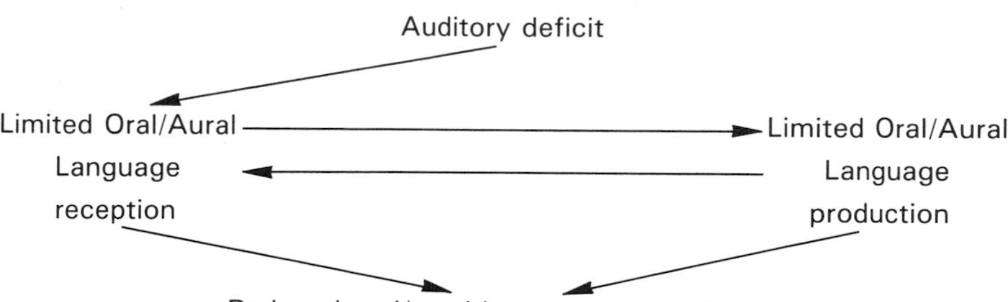

skills will also affect language reception. The overall effect will be limited language ability. (See Figure 8.1.)

For the most part children with hearing losses integrated into mainstream schools will have developed skills in verbal language. These skills may not be of the same order as other children in the same class. The children with hearing loss may have language competence which is restricted by between several months and several years. It is not uncommon to meet children placed in units for hearing-impaired children who spend at least some of their time in the mainstream class, who may, at 8 or 9 years of age, have the linguistic skills more normally associated with hearing children of 2–2½ years. The source of this language deficit lies not wholly in the hearing loss. Wood *et al.* (1986) have identified a strong influence in the patterns of language offered to the child and we will return to this later in this chapter. In the meantime it is worth considering the effects of limited language ability and to do this we must first consider the functions of language. These can be seen to be threefold — cognitive, social and abstract.

Language is the medium used for categorization of experience, for organizing the material and social word in order that relationships between and among things and society can be ordered. This is the cognitive function of language. It permits of a fine and flexible system of categorization and is exemplified by the specifically created Linnaean system for classifying plants and animals.

The second function of language relates to the exchange of common elements of experience. This is the interpersonal communication component which permits of easy exchange of experiences occurring at present, in the past and those which are anticipated in the future. It is this aspect of language which is instrumental in developing the shared understandings which are essential for functioning in any society (Newson, 1978). These shared understandings can be the private and excluding feelings and concepts enjoyed and practised within a family, church, political party or workplace or they can be the wider understandings of the macrocosm contributed to by tradition and literature. In this latter respect the experiences, ideas and observations of Chaucer, Shakespeare, Johnson or of Jane Austin contribute to the common language code.

The final function of language is that which is concerned with abstract experiences, that is with feelings, emotions and with moral and spiritual ideas. The most flexible and precise way of expressing abstract ideas is through a linguistic code. Music, art, dance and other media can be used but none has the precision and infinite flexibility of language.

A child who has restricted language ability will have limitations imposed within each of these three functions of language. As each of these is concerned with experience there will be an essential reduction in the level of experiences available to the child. We will return later to the effects of limitation on the range of available experiences.

2. Sensory Deprivation

The child with hearing loss does not just have privations related to language. There will also be problems related to other aspects of environmental communication. The child will be unaware of some sounds in his environment which for the hearing person signify a need to alter behaviour to accommodate the signalled change. The ringing telephone bell or a warning shout will cause most of us to cease our immediate activity to attend to the new, and auditorally signalled event. Hearing is being used here at one of its most basic levels, as a warning sense. Hearing as such is a mandatory sense and functions in all places and at all times. It only ceases to operate for physiological or for psychological reasons. Hearing is unlike vision, the other sense concerned with information from sources distant to the organism. Hearing is a sense over which humans can exercise no control, there is no auditory equivalent of the eyelid or of the averted gaze. The child with a hearing loss will be denied many experiences to which he has not been alerted by this background sense of hearing. He will also be exposed to many experiences of which he has had no auditory warning. The combined effect of these will be a reduction of level of experiences compared to those available for a person with normal hearing and a very much less secure and more potentially frightening environment than that experienced by most of us.

A further aspect of the effect of deprivation or limitation of hearing as a sense is that which relates to temporal sequencing. Auditory information is organized in time, it is temporal information. Visual information is spatial and as such is available for more detailed scrutiny than is an auditory signal which has gone as soon as it has been produced. There is no way in which sound can be frozen for re-examination in the same way that sights can be photographed. To be able to relate one sound to another and to intepret an auditory experience, such as spoken language (and even its visual representation, the written word), temporal sequencing skills are necessary. It can be argued that as the sense of hearing is concerned solely with temporal information then the exercise of this sense is important in the development of temporal sequencing skills. In people with normal hearing this exercise has been operating since before birth! Deprivation or limitation of hearing will effect the development of temporal sequencing skills and this in turn will affect the ability to process and to develop conventional language skills. It is interesting to note here that the Sign language developed in many deaf communities is a language system which does not have the same temporal conventions as verbal language. The early detection of hearing loss and the early fitting of hearing-aids to utilize residual hearing is an important factor in promoting the development of temporal sequencing skills in deaf children. There are many who argue (Morris, 1978) that little use can be made of residual hearing by profoundly deaf children. Such arguments are based upon analyses of segmental components of language and of the amount of auditory information potentially available for the deaf child. This is a narrow view of the problem and is one which is akin to the apocryphal aeronautical engineer's view of the bumble bee. The bumble bee, it will be remembered, has a mass and a weight which combine with a weak musculature and limited wing capacity to prevent the possibility of flight. Fortunately the bumble bee is too preoccupied to heed these warnings and goes about her business giving us much pleasure in the process. Similarly very many hearing impaired children with seemingly impossible hearing losses develop efficient oral language skills by utilizing very limited auditory information. Something has been left out of the limiting analysis. It may be that there is very restricted segmental information which is available, even with very powerful hearing aids, to some deaf children but there are available the supra-segmental components of language, that is the prosodic features of rhythm, intonation, stress and pause. In addition there are also available redundancies within the speech signal which are associated with these segmental features. These redundancies give cues to the manner and production of specific phonemes and experience in their use can greatly enhance speech reception. Importantly, however, amplification makes available the opportunity for exercising residual hearing and thereby acquiring these critically important language processing skills.

3. Societal Attitudes

This category produces handicapping effects which are not a direct consequence of the hearing loss. The effects are a consequence of the reactions to the deaf child by the society in which the child is operating and they impinge upon all areas of development both related and unrelated to the presenting deafness. Keogh (1975) has argued that the initial problems for children with impairment may be related more to how they are viewed by other people than to the degree or the type of disability.

Fraser (1984) has examined major and interrelated factors which fall into this category. These are:

(a) the social role of sickness:
(b) preconceived notions of abilities and expectations.

(a) The social role of sickness

There is a clearly defined role for a person who is ill. Sick people are exempted from the obligations of work, school and other social responsibilities. There is an implicit need for the sick person to receive help and the associated release from obligations is given to assist that person to recover. It could be argued that the responsibility of the sick person is to become well and that societal concessions are made in order to facilitate recovery. Now it also could be argued that this has little to do with deaf children. Such children are not sick in the usually accepted sense, they merely deviate from some vague social norm. It must be remembered however, that deafness, like other impairments, has strong medical connotations. Diagnosis and assessment of the condition necessarily involves an important medical component. The deaf child may be initially detected in a routine screening test of hearing conducted by a health visitor. Subsequent examination will be made either by the family doctor or by a clinical medical officer and referral will be made to hospital consultants in paediatrics and otology. Lengthy clinical investigations are inevitable and necessary and in the eyes of parents and teachers the child will come to be seen naively as being in some vague way sick. We have seen how society views sick people and there is no reason to suppose that the child with deafness will be treated differently. Such a child is likely to be released from expectations and obligations with a consequent affect upon the range of potential experiences available. One can only wonder about the effect upon parents when the child fails to 'get better': how will this influence their future behaviour with the child? Society has limited patience with sick people and whilst adequate provision is made in the early stages of an illness, anyone who has the effrontery not to get better is viewed seemingly with some opprobrium and will receive the sanctions of limited material assistance.

(b) Preconceived notions of abilities and expectations

Closely related to the social role of sickness, indeed a consequence of it, are the conceptions that society has of the disabled person's capabilities and limitations. Such conceptions are based upon simply conceived half-truths and myths which often result in lowered expectations of performance. Such prophecies of performance have an unfortunate way of becoming self-fulfilling and the behaviour expected becomes the behaviour given. Keogh (1975) has demonstrated that the expected future of handicapped children is often seen as limited and as a result the children are exposed to limited educational programmes. She argues that it is often the outcomes or goals of special education which are modified and not necessarily the organization or teaching techniques. This in effect means that it is possible for some special education programmes to add to handicap by limiting opportunities and experience. It is not just special school *per se* which can produce such limitations. Cope and Anderson (1977) have demonstrated that programmes in special units in mainstream schools can be just as limiting. Lynas (1986) has shown that the attitudes of teachers in mainstream classes towards hearing-impaired pupils placed in those classes can be similarly limiting.

One effect of expectations related to the way in which parents view the deafness in their child. Parents are likely to adopt child rearing practices which are different from those adopted with non-disabled siblings. One source of this could be the response of the child to the hearing loss. Another is that the parents become so involved with the child's functional impairment that they fail to respond to other needs that the child may have.

Early Detection and Parent Counselling and Guidance

It is clear that the responsibility for the habilitation of a deaf child is not something which can be picked up at the start of schooling even when this may be nursery based at 3 years. There are many influences upon the development of a career in handicap and for that handicap to be as limited as possible it is important that all of these are taken into account in educational planning. It is important that the audiological aspects are well catered for, that the child be fitted with the best possible amplification systems for his hearing loss. It is important that the child is exposed to a language environment which is likely to facilitate rather than hinder language acquisition. It is important that the child be given opportunities for exposure to the range of experiences necessary for maximizing cognitive and social and emotional development and for developing the adaptational ability and learning skills necessary for accommodating to living in a wide community and adjusting to change with flexibility. An important key to meeting such needs is early detection associated with guidance and counselling of parents.

All Community Health Districts operate some form of screening programme designed to detect hearing loss in infants and young children. The success of such programmes varies considerably. Both Gregory (1975) and Clarke (1978) have demonstrated that there is often a breakdown in such programmes. Many children are not detected either because they are not brought to the clinic or because faulty techniques or misinterpretation of responses results in the child being passed as having normal hearing. This is not necessarily because of inadequate training of the Health Visitors who normally conduct such tests but is rather the result of inadequate monitoring of their work. The Health Visitors Association has stressed the need for continuing supervision and refresher training but financial constraints upon the NHS preclude the universal adoption of such practices. The result is that there is a very patchy picture of practice with some authorities successfully identifying over 90 per cent of children with congenital hearing loss within the first year of life and others not detecting such children until well into the second or third year.

After diagnosis, programmes of counselling and guidance are made available in all local education authorities. These interventions should be exercises in adult education: counselling to help parents to adjust to the reality of the hearing loss and guidance to promote the development of parenting skills which will maximize development. This is the theory. The reality often falls short of this and the source of this deficiency can be traced to the training of personnel. Traditionally the professional involved in parent counselling and guidance work is a teacher of the deaf. Most of those engaged in this work are employed on a visiting basis within a service for hearing-impaired children. Whilst some specialize in work with pre-school aged children very many are what could be termed generic teachers of the deaf. As such they will carry a mixed case load which will include hearing-impaired children placed in primary and secondary schools as well as pre-school aged children. They may also have responsibility for young people in future education and for liaison with Careers Advisory Services. Their training will be related for the most part to the needs of school-aged children and as people who are primarily teachers, the emphasis of their training will be upon schooling. Their understanding of child development and psychology will be related to children from 5 up to adolescence with some people who have specialized in nursery and infant work extending this understanding down to 3. Guidance and counselling work with parents of pre-school aged deaf children requires skills of a different professional order. It is axiomatic that the personnel concerned need knowledge of early child development and particularly of the early development of communication skills. Also needed are skills in counselling and in adult education. Work with pre-school aged hearing-impaired children is not an exercise in child teaching. It is unlikely that the visiting teacher will be able to see the child for more than an hour a week. Little will be achieved in this time simply by working with the child yet the writer's observations and those of his students would suggest that this is the most common form of practice with such children. The teacher will see her role as one of direct intervention with a child and there is no doubt that such work is very satisfying and any small change in child behaviour resulting from such practice will do much to heighten self-esteem. The exercise is not concerned with short term behavioural changes; rather, it is concerned with the promotion of an environment in which learning and development will be facilitated and enhanced. Teacher satisfaction is unlikely to be immediate and results of interventions may not be apparent until long after the child has moved on from the care of his teacher.

It is important not to lay the blame for inappropriate practices at the feet of the teachers. These people are simply classroom practitioners who have been transmuted into a situation for which they have had inadequate preparation. Most initial training courses for teachers of the deaf pay only theoretical attention to parent guidance and counselling work. There are some few routes to deeper understandings but because of their very specialist nature appealing to a minority group of professionals these have to be provided either infrequently or on a national level. It is unlikely that many teachers of the deaf will have opportunities for attendance under the new INSET arrangements. The guidance skills can be seen to lie within the range of professional expertise of teachers even though these may be adapted to a situation very different from the classroom. The same cannot be said about counselling. Lutterman (1979) and Darling and Darling (1982) have demonstrated the complexity of response of parents to deaf children and have highlighted the difficulties of intervening in a positive and a constructive way. The enormities of the problem are such that the best advice to anybody without a professional understanding of counselling skills would be to keep off and seek advice. This does not generally seem to be advice which would be well received. Whilst in most cases careful professional conselling may not be required there will always be situations where this is not the case and where lasting damage to relationships and to mental health could result from inappropriate responses. Perhaps in the absence of adequate training for teachers others and more appropriately trained professionals should be used. A mark of a professional is that person's flexibility of response to a situation; another mark is to know the limitations of his or her expertise and a preparedness to back away and asks for timely advice and help. These are strong arguments for a multi-disciplinary approach to this work with different professional groups recognizing the limitations of their own practices and cooperating closely to deliver a programme which will more adequately meet parent needs. Perhaps this could avoid the practice which is beginning to develop where different groups, educationalists and social workers, are competing to offer similar programmes, programmes which may seem to parents to offer conflicting advice.

Modes of Communication

Before addressing the concept of integration or mainstreaming as it relates to hearing-impaired children it is necessary to consider that aspect of the education of the deaf which dominates all discussion of principles and practice — that is the question of what is generally described as methodology of education. This phase is interesting in itself; it implies an educational approach which relates to clearly defined principles of child development and learning. To a teacher of the deaf this broad educational reading is often too sophisticated and the response given to a question directed to ascertain such information would be related almost exclusively to the mode of communication used and in only one or two instances would the mode of communication carry implications of underlying developmental principles.

The modes of communication used in the education of the deaf are many, and like many educational crazes, they come and go (who in normal schools still uses ITA: how many teachers under 35 know what ITA is?). The main systems in use will be described briefly here but for a more detailed and carefully reasoned account the reader is referred to Lynas *et al.* (1988) who provided a critical and comprehensive account of the main systems currently in use.

On the surface there seems to be a bewildering and complex range of modes of communication used in the education of deaf children. These can be divided into three main groups although some advocates of the modes described could well take me to task for assigning their particular system to a particular category. The three main categories are:

1. Oral
2. Total Communication
3. Sign Language

As has been suggested, the difficulty is where a particular approach should be assigned. Some people using a Total Communication approach might argue that they are following what is essentially an oral approach whilst others may see their system more closely related to Sign Language. Advocates of the use of Sign may argue that some systems of signing cannot be properly described as Sign Language. There is not, and never has been, a unanimity of agreement in the education of the deaf!

1. *Oral Approaches*

These approaches can be divided into two, the traditional oral and the oral/auditory. There is a third system which could be closely allied to the traditional oral mode called Cued Speech. This had a vogue some ten years ago but is now seldom seen in this country.

(a) Traditional oral

The emphasis in this system was upon the development of language through the use of lip reading skills and a systemized approach to language teaching Visual cues other than lip patterns are de-emphasized, even to the extent, in some instances, of teachers having to keep their hands in pockets whilst talking to deaf children. Because it was assumed that deaf children were unable to 'catch' language by overhearing and otherwise incidentally then highly structured forms of language had to be taught and learned by using contrived exercises not unlike the traditional approach used for teaching second languages (Andrews, 1988).

(b) Auditory/oral

This approach may seem to the casual observer to be a *laissez-faire* system with nothing constructive happening apart from an insistence that the deaf child wear hearing aids. There is no apparent attempt to teach language skills and, indeed, there seems to be little or no level of special skills required from the teacher of the deaf. The superficial appearance belies the underlying principles and these are twofold. The first relates to the use of residual hearing and the presumption is made that in all but very rare cases, deaf children have elements of residual hearing which can be utilized in the acquisition of spoken language skills. This has been discussed earlier in this chapter. By fitting appropriate hearing aids as early as possible the child will be enabled to develop listening experience which will facilitate the acquisition of the 'top down' skills necessary for the interpretation of spoken language. Hearing aids need to be worn consistently and it is essential that they be maintained at optimal levels of efficiency. This requires rigorous attention from teachers and parents early in the child's life but as he matures so can he assume greater responsibility. The hearing aid will, with correct use, eventually become integrated into the child's personality and will become as indispensable as spectacles are to a person with myopia. What the hearing aid will not do is to compensate for the hearing loss in the way in which spectacles may compensate for a myopic condition. The hearing aid will, as its name implies, aid hearing and will provide another element of information in the complexity of signals which go to make up conventional human language.

The second underlying principle relates to the nature of input provided for the child and it is this which is of critical importance. If the input is wrong then the system will not work. (This of course applies to any mode of communication — if all that is put in is garbage then garbage as the end product is all that can be expected.)

The auditory/oral approaches are dependent upon the principles of normal language acquisition. It is argued that the usual interactions between infants and young children and their parents are uniquely structured and that they facilitate the acquisition of language. The child brings to this interactional process a language acquisition ability, the adult brings a language enabling device. If either is missing or is exercised inappropriately then the child is unlikely to develop adequate and efficient language skills. Earlier we discussed the possibility of the development of inappropriate interactional behaviours by parents, and Wood *et al.* (1986) have demonstrated that similarly inappropriate behaviours can be adopted by teachers. It is these which could contribute more to language deficiency and deviance in hearing-impaired children than the hearing loss itself. There is now a considerable corpus of knowledge on early language acquisition and an increasing literature on the place of interactions (see Wells, 1981, 1985) in this process. It is the application of practices derived from such researches which is positively influencing this particular approach to the acquisition of language skills by deaf children.

2. Sign Language

Within many communities of deaf people there has been developed a language code based upon a manual system of arbitrary signs. This system varies from community to community and in the UK is known as British Sign Language (BSL). In the USA it is known as American Sign Language (ASL). Within BSL there are many 'dialects' into which Sign users have to tune themselves. The language system is a language in its own right with its own system of rules and conventions (Kyle and Woll, 1985). It is also a language which bears no relationship to the spoken language of the wider community. The syntax and organization are completely different. Indeed so different is the organization that spoken language users find it difficult to comprehend the difference. One example of this difference is sufficient as an illustration. In spoken language a sequential convention is followed with one idea following on from another thus influencing the organization and the importance of syntax. In Sign this convention is far less important. Sign is a spatially as well as a sequentially organized communication system and as such it is possible to express several ideas simultaneously thus removing the need for the strict conventions of grammatical structures that apply in spoken languages.

It has been postulated that Sign is the natural language of deaf people and that deaf children should therefore be educated in Sign as a first language and that the language of the wider community should be introduced as a second language once proficiency in the first language had been achieved. There are some attractions in this argument but a closer examination reveals the difficulties. Language acquisition depends, as has been discussed, upon the unique interactions between the child and care giver in a conversational mode with the adult adopting a language register which is contingent upon the child's developing linguistic need. This implies a linguistic fluency upon the part of the adult. Very few adults are fluent enough in Sign to make this appropriate register adjustment and it is unlikely to be achieved where the adult is learning the language as a second language from its basics. Some very few deaf children are born of deaf parents who may themselves use Sign as the first language in the home and in such situations acquisition of Sign by the child will follow the normal patterns of first language acquisition. However only 3 per cent of severely or profoundly deaf children have both parents who are deaf and only a further 7 per cent have one deaf parent (Lynas *et al.*, 1988) and not all of these parents will be Sign users. For deaf children to develop Sign as a first language there needs to be an intensive programme of Sign language teaching to parents and to teachers so that they may gain the linguistic fluency that is required for the necessary register adjustment. This is patently not realistic. An alternative would be to use Sign users from the deaf community to provide appropriate input and in a few instances this is happening in classes of deaf children. It obviously presents enormous difficulties for very young children in their own homes and valuable early language acquisition opportunities will be lost.

Wood, Wood, Griffiths and Howarth (1986) have pointed out that schooling is a recent development in social engineering and that schools are not organized to provide the 'intimate, two-way, reciprocal and contingent interactions that seem best suited to the development of communication skills between adults and children'. Indeed, they point out that schools are more likely to achieve an opposite state of affairs. Even with a fluent signer in the classroom the child is unlikely to get the quantity of interactions necessary for language acquisition and if this input is not reinforced adequately by appropriate interactions in the home then it is unlikely that optimum language development will occur. It is worth reflecting upon the degree of exposure to contingent linguistic interactions that a normal hearing child receives and which would appear to be necessary for the development of the linguistic competence of a normal 5-year-old. If we assume that such a child has a modest five hour of interaction with an adult every day (and research by Wells (1981) would suggest a much higher order) then in each year from birth that child will be exposed to 1,825 hours of conversation. By the time he enters school his total conversational experience will be 9,125 hours. The deaf child in school with a deaf adult will have five hours schooling a day, the adult will have to divide her attention between other children but in theory may be able to offer one hour of conversation to each child. With a five day week and a forty week school year the child will receive 200 hours of conversational interaction each year. This is a long way short of the 1,825 hours which seem to be necessary for the linguistic development of the normal hearing child. Without increased opportunities for conversational interactions high orders of linguistic skills are unlikely to develop regardless of the mode of communication used.

Programmes of first language teaching in Sign are being tried. Their outcomes are uncertain and there is no available evidence to show that a child exposed to such a programme will necessarily be in a better position to acquire English as a second language after developing Sign skills.

3. Total Communication

This mode of communication is currently very fashionable in the United Kingdom whence it was imported from the United States ten or twelve years ago. The basis for the approach is the use of as many systems of access to language information as possible. The child is exposed to language through auditory, lip read patterns and through the use of some form of signed system. The child is thus presented with a wide variety of linguistic information in which the message is protected by a sort of communication overload. Practitioners of Total Communication use English as the language of instruction and this is presented verbally and with either Signed English or Signs Supporting English. In the former signs based upon British Sign language are presented in the conventional word order of English simultaneous with the verbal message. In Signs Supporting English verbal patterns are still used normally but with signs used to support the message. There is no attempt to replicate the spoken message although the supporting signs should coincide with spoken elements.

The practices have been in use for a very long time. Thirty years ago it was common to find schools for the deaf who, whilst espousing an oral policy of education, nevertheless practised what was described as the 'combined method'. Perhaps one of the reasons why Total Communication has become so popular is that it lent credence to existing practices. Formalized Total Communication is relatively new in this country and there are very few children who have been exposed to the practice for the whole of their school careers so there is not yet any clear evidence to support the claims of its practitioners. This is not the case in the United States where the research evidence is beginning to suggest that language is not being acquired in the accelerated way that was anticipated (for a critical review see Lynas *et al.*, 1988). One of the problems with this approach is that it divides the child's attention and they are then likely to concentrate upon one signal and to ignore others. Research has shown that even the best practitioners fail to provide complete oral or complete manual messages so the child receives a debased lingusitic input. Total Communication has been described as a mule (*Special Children*, 1987). Like the mule it is a product of two different beasts and like the mule it is infertile, producing proficiency neither in spoken or written English nor in Sign.

A final criticism of Total Communication is that it is not total. Normal spoken language has several elements. There are the segmental components of the sounds of speech and phonemes, which combine to form words. There are also the very important non-segmental or prosodic features of rhythm, intonation, stress and pause which are reinforced by synchronous movements of the hands, arms and body. Finally there is the body language of position and facial expression. A slowing down of verbal rate, necessary when presenting a simultaneous signed element, will reduce the important information carrying prosodic component and will lead to distortions of body language. The child will, as a consequence, be provided with reduced information.

Integration of Hearing-impaired Children: Current Practice and the Future

The developments which have consolidated in services for hearing-impaired children which can be seen all over Britain were initiated by a desire to meet the needs of children who were already in mainstream schools. These children had special needs which were seen to be rooted in mild to moderate hearing losses, and visiting teacher of the deaf services and units for hearing-impaired children were established to meet these. Gradually, and very properly, the type of child served by such facilities changed. More children with greater degrees of hearing loss and with special needs of a greater magnitude were included and services expanded better to accommodate the change. As more children were placed in mainstream schools so the size and actual numbers of special schools for hearing-impaired children declined. Places in such schools were costly, particularly for shire authorities with widely scattered populations who were dependent upon residential facilities for those children requiring special school placement. Strong economical as well as psychological and sociological grounds were put forward for making provision within the ordinary school system and this accelerated the reduction in the use of special schools for the deaf and partially hearing. There were also strong educational grounds. Studies such as that conducted by Conrad (1977) demonstrated limited educational outcomes in children leaving such establishments and this encouraged local education authorities to think that they could do better by hearing-impaired children, or at least, no worse. Another important factor in the move to integrated provision was parental wishes. Parents were no longer prepared to see their children taken off to a boarding school, even on a weekly basis. There are seeds in these developments for what could be regarded as radical change, particularly so in the light of changes already occurring in the educational system as a result of the Education Reform Act. Not all radical change could be seen as positive or forward in its inclination. This change could have an effect upon the goodwill necessary to implement any integration programme. We will go on to explore this now.

Goodwill

Any integration programme for any group of children with disability is strongly dependent upon goodwill: the goodwill of the parents of other children; the goodwill of teachers; the goodwill of the school as a system, and the goodwill of the local education authority. These four sources of goodwill are closely linked. Let us take each in turn.

Parental interest in schools and education tends to have a limited horizon and one which is limited to and by what they see as the interests of their child. The collective good of the school may be encompassed within this horizon but only in so much as it contributes to this narrow focus. Anything which is seen to hamper specific parental interest is likely to be responded to with suspicion at the best and hostility at the worst and clear reassurances are needed to convince parents that the education of their child is not likely to be affected by the presence in his class of a child with a hearing aid and a need for greater class teacher input (greater teacher attention for one child means less for mine therefore the schooling of mine is likely to suffer!). With clear national attainment targets being set, parental desire is for overt achievement and anything which may be deemed to interfere with this is not likely to be tolerated. At the best of times our community is not very tolerant of difference but in the current climate of individualism the more liberal view of a broader acceptance is decidely unfashionable. The limits of acceptable normality are shrinking and are likely to shrink further. As schools begin to opt out of local authority control (by parental wish) one wonders how many parents will feel encouraged to have accepted into their own child's class a child who may be seen as requiring attention which could be detrimental to the rest.

By the same token, mainstream class teachers are likely to be less willing to accept hearing-impaired children for similar reasons, reasons which may be seen to emanate from self-interest. There is likely to be pressure for norm based results and the child with a need could be the child who is not acceptable because such a child may be seen as one who is likely to fail to achieve adequate grades or to create pressures which prevent other children achieving adequate grades. Studies of teachers in mainstream schools have shown them to be inadequately prepared and naive about the needs of hearing-impaired children and to exhibit behaviours which are not always appropriate (Tobin, 1972; Lynas, 1984). Ironically, it may be that hearing-impaired children with the greatest needs may be acceptable in many classrooms. There are increasing numbers of such children who are placed in the mainstream class with an amanuensis/interpreter. The class teacher has little to do with this arrangement, leaving this person to provide all of the support and translation which she or he may think is necessary. Whether such placement and support could be deemed to be integration is another matter. The deaf child may be integrated into aspects of the curriculum but may have little opportunity to share in the more general life of the school or the class. This writer recalls visiting a secondary school and watching with mounting embarrassment and incredulity whilst a chemistry teacher, clearly regarded as a soft touch by a mainstream class, valiantly tried to teach three groups of about ten normally hearing children each of whom had a small project in hand. Whilst he attended one group the others exhibited a rowdiness which was well beyond the levels of acceptability. Missiles were projected, furniture toppled, hilarity was enjoyed and education and learning were in abeyance. In the midst of this riot were four deaf children working with their specialist teacher and seemingly oblivious to the fun of the greater group. If true integration were happening then these children too would have been making their contribution to the general mayhem.

Another source of goodwill is the school as a system and understandably this is likely to be constrained by the demands of regular norm referenced assessments. The school will be encouraged to see itself in a market place and will see its position to a very great extent determined by results. Children seen to deviate from its predetermined conception of normality are likely either to be refused admission or referred for statementing and for special education placement. The school as a system will also be responsible for its own financial management and may, as a result, be less than enthusiastic about replacing faulty specialist auditory equipment or providing adaptations to suit the needs of one or two children. Schools which have opted out of local authority control will also have opted out of the services generally provided and without the back-up of specialist visiting teachers of the deaf may find the cost of purchasing such specialists advice and input too heavy a drain on a finite budget.

The final area of goodwill is one which related to the local education authority itself. With local financial management the LEA will be left with a considerably reduced sum of money. Out of this various mandatory and quasi-mandatory services must be maintained. The National Curriculum will require inspectors, and the statementing procedure, psychologists. Educational services for hearing-impaired children with costly visiting teachers of the deaf may be deemed to be very low priority and are indeed seen as an item of discretionary expenditure. As revenue falls as a consequence of schools opting out, such a service could be regarded as a very expensive luxury. As schools take and retain fewer hearing-impaired children the need for such a service will be seen to disappear. The children so displaced are very likely to find themselves in some form of generic special needs placement with perhaps a token advisory teacher of the deaf on the staff. This is not very far fetched; such provisions already exist for children with severe mental handicaps who, whilst showing a common learning problem, may have diverse individual impairments. The introduction of such a policy may be accelerated by the existing practices of many local authority services for hearing-impaired children. Many of these have policies of not preparing statements of special educational need unless a child is to be referred for special schooling. Many of these authorities operate policies of integration for all but a very few of their children with hearing loss. To service this policy a large team of specialist and advisory teachers is maintained with children being supported in their ordinary classes several times a week. That such children have special educational needs is without doubt but without statements it may be difficult to convince the accountants in county hall of the need for services. The rhetoric of Warnock and the 1981 Education Act saw the statement as an instrument which would be a protection for the child and would apply whether the child was placed in the mainstream sector or in a special school By denying the child a statement of need for a costly and intensive service, that service could be withdrawn and diminished.

Units for Hearing-impaired Children

There is no clearly outlined description of what a unit for hearing-impaired children is and how it should operate. Such provisions range from a single specialist teacher of the deaf placed in a mainstream school and responsible for the support of a small group of children with hearing losses who are fully integrated into ordinary classes, to a multi-specialist teacher provision with groups being taught perhaps for some of their time in specialist non-integrated classrooms. It is not unusual to find very specialized units where one teacher and a welfare assistant may be responsible for a group of about six children aged between 5 and 11 years with a wide range of needs and who are being contained in a non-integrating setting in a mainstream school and taught by manually based modes of communication. The educational justification and viability of such provision must be seriously in question.

Little is known about the practice of specialist teachers in units, particularly where such classes are not part of a wider service for hearing-impaired children. Some authorities organize their provision within a global service which includes visiting teachers of the deaf and units. Such a service would have central finances and unit provision would not draw upon the finances of the host schools. There is an obvious disadvantage in such a system in that the specialist unit teachers would feel that they had divided responsibilities and loyalties both to the mainstream school and to the service for hearing-impaired children. This disadvantage is outweighed by the opportunities for wider monitoring, supervision and planning allowing for the provision of a more flexible service and more flexible response to need.

Practices in units vary considerably. In some the purpose of the provision is seen as being to develop skills in the child which will permit the child to integrate into the mainstream. In others a blanket locational integration programme operates, with children being given support in the mainstream class by either the teacher of the deaf or by someone who is described as an integration assistant. These people will act as an interpreter or amanuensis particularly where the child has very limited language skills and where the policy is for manual support. This practice poses several concerns. One is related to the functioning of the integration assistant. Generally such people are not teachers and have little understanding of the principles of language acquisition. Observation of their work raises serious questions about the ability of such a system to facilitate language development. With adequate training this may be possible but the levels of knowledge and expertise observed by this writer would suggest that much needs to be done. Another source of anxiety relates to the limited range of opportunities available for hearing-impaired children to interact directly with the curriculum. With a regular system of one-to-one support the child has fewer opportunities for exercising personal responsibility in the learning process. The child will be exposed to high levels of external control in the classroom and such an external locus of control is a major factor in the development of learned helplessness. The child could, as a result of such practices, have handicap enhanced. Obviously there is a great need for care to be taken in developing such intensive support practices. In some situations the mainstream teacher and the specialist teacher have reduced the heavy control profile by developing a team teaching approach and making the support less overt.

Visiting Teachers of the Deaf

This group of teachers are one of the least understood of all educational professionals. Little is known of their functioning because no evaluative exercise into services has been conducted. This writer has observed many and varied practices. At one extreme it is possible to see careful educational support for the hearing-impaired child in the mainstream class based upon comprehensive assessment of auditory, lingusitic and educational needs and provided by frequent visits which involve close cooperation with the class and subject teacher and the home. At the other extreme the visiting teacher of the deaf will be little more than a checker of hearing aids and a person who advises on the most suitable seating position in the classroom. In the first instance the teacher will have a small and stable case load not dissimilar in size to the number of children that she would have if she were class based. In the second instance the teacher is likely to have a case load of perhaps 90 to 100 or even more with little opportunity to respond to anything but superficial needs unless a crisis develops. When this happens it is likely that the focusing of all energies on this situation will deny other children support and make it more likely that other crises will develop. Accountability of visiting teachers of the deaf seems high in some authorities and low in others.

A major problem seems to relate to an identification of good practice. Roles have been identified for visiting teachers of the deaf and most local authorities will have clearly defined job descriptions. The problem associated with implementation seems to be two-fold; one aspect is realistically sized case loads, and the other is a system of monitoring. It is unlikely that without the former anything but a fire brigade service will be provided. Without the latter there are too many opportunities for limited and inefficient educational programmes to be practised. In authorities where there is a clear hierarchical structure with experienced and authoritative head teachers who can provide leadership and represent the interests of hearing-impaired children and their services then both of these factors of case load size and of monitoring will be met. Where there is not adequate leadership (and this is generally because the education authority has not structured the service adequately or because the leadership is divided over too diverse a range of specialist areas such as integrated visually handicapped children and language disordered children) then the service for hearing-impaired children is likely to be potentially less than adequate.

There is one area of work which is central to most, if not all, visiting teacher of the deaf services and that is educational audiology. This is a service which provides an assessment of the child's auditory functioning related to the child's educational and developmental needs. It involves the testing of hearing and the provision of appropriate sources of amplification and of the monitoring of auditory functioning. This is a costly process both in personnel and in equipment. Educational audiologists generally have a specialist university qualification in the science of audiology and have skills and expertise which cross educational and medical boundaries. The close association with these two disciplines has meant that in some instances such services have been jointly funded by the local education authority and the associated district health authorities. This is not a widespread financial practice but the in depth audiological assessment of children is. This results in very close cooperation between services for hearing-impaired children, school health services and the ear, nose and throat departments of local hospitals. This facility could be seen by financially pressed education authorities as more properly the province of medicine and therefore not as something which should be met out of an educational budget. Whilst such an argument could be seen to have attractions there is no doubt that this is an educational service as its provision means that all auditory needs can be met in an educational setting. The educational success of the majority of hearing-impaired children would be of a considerably lower order if educational audiological facilities were not available.

The Future

That changes will occur in the organization of services for hearing-impaired children is certain. The nature of these changes is less than certain. A gloomy prospect has been presented in these pages with the needs of hearing-impaired children becoming less well catered for in some authorities than may be desirable for developments and education. However, there are certainly some current practices which it could be argued are not necessarily providing an educational or developmental response which is contingent upon the hearing-impaired child's needs.

One change which will almost certainly occur is a reduction in the numbers of hearing-impaired children deemed to be acceptable in mainstream schools. This will result in more children being placed in existing special schools for the deaf, the development of larger and probably less integrated units attached to mainstream schools but separately funded, and a number of children placed in schools similar to the old educational priority area schools where additional resources will be made available for a wide range of special needs. At the same time there is likely to be an increase in the number of local education authorities which are moving to a generic provision for all children with special educational needs. This is likely to mean that the teachers supporting hearing-impaired children are unlikely to have deep understanding of the auditory, linguistic and sensory needs unique to such children.

Those services for hearing-impaired children which survive will be those which are coordinated and centrally funded and are seen to provide for a continuum of need across mainstream placement and special class and unit provision. Such services will provide audiological and educational assessment and will have a clear policy of educational planning and intervention. These services will depend for the bulk of their financing upon the local education authority but should be prepared to enter the market-place and to sell their services to schools which are outside local authority control. Whilst these schools — and they will be opted-out schools, City Technology Colleges (CTCs), and schools in existing independent sector — may be more reluctant to take hearing-impaired children there will be pressure from parents for acceptance of their child. There may be opportunities for centrally funded schools to seek an increase in their grant under section 89 of the Education Reform Act in order to respond to the special educational needs of individual children. As these schools will be outside local authority control they would not necessarily have to use the services provided by the immediate local authority. Parents may wish for their child's needs to be responded to in a particular way and may request that facilities of a service be purchased which best matches their wishes. There is a possibility here for a greater element of parental choice in the type of provision available for a child.

The course of future developments for hearing-impaired children within mainstream settings can only be speculated upon. The 1988 Education Act is not yet fully implemented and the regulations, orders and circulars associated with it have still to appear. A major result of the debate surrounding the passage of the Great Educational Reform Bill and its emergence as an Act has been the navel contemplation that it has promoted. Mainstream schools and special services have all been behoven to examine their practice. Parents of all children have looked more critically at what education services are providing. Such reflection can result in better educational practice, a practice which is contingent upon comprehensively assessed need. Unfortunately, a broad consideration of educational principles and practice is often not central in the minds of officials and administrators. The accountant dominates much official thinking and generally has a narrower view of needs and provision than does the professional. Educational provision which will result in a reduction of handicap in a child is likely to be costly but if this cost is balanced against the long term costs of handicap to a community then it can be seen to be an investment which will be to the future financial good of that community. This is a crude financial argument which takes no account of humanitarian social responses but in a crude financial climate it may be the only argument which would be listened to.

References

ANDREWS, E.M. (1988) 'The relationship between natural auralism and the maternal reflective way of working', *J. Brit. Assoc. Teachers of the Deaf*, 12, 3, pp. 49–56.

CLARKE, M.H. (1978) 'Preparation of deaf children for hearing society', *J. Brit. Assoc. Teachers of the Deaf*, 2, 5 pp. 146–54.

CONRAD, R. (1979) *The Deaf School Child*, Harper & Row.

COPE, C. and ANDERSON, E. (1977) *Special Units in Ordinary Schools*, University of London, Institute of Education.

DARLING, J. and DARLING, R. (1982) *Children Who Are Different*, The C.V. Mosby Company.

DES (1968) *The Education of Deaf Children* (The Lewis Report), HMSO.

FRASER, B.C. (1984) *Society, Schools and Handicap*, National Council for Special Education.

GREGORY, S. (1976) *The Deaf Child and His Family*, George, Allen & Unwin.

KEOGH, B. (1975) 'Social and ethical assumptions about special education', in Wedell, K. (Ed.) *Orientations in Special Education*, John Wiley and Sons.

KYLE, J.G. and WOLL, B. (1985) *Sign Language: The study of deaf people and their language*, Cambridge University Press.

LUTERMAN, D. (1979) *Counseling Parents of Hearing Impaired Children*, Little, Brown & Co.

LYNAS, W. (1986) *Integrating the Handicapped Into Ordinary Schools: A study of hearing-impaired pupils*, Croom Helm.

LYNAS. W. HUNTINGTON, A. and TUCKER, I. (1988) *A Critical Examination of Different Approaches to Communication in the Education of Deaf Children*, The Ewing Foundation.

MORRIS, T. (1978) 'Some observations on the part played by oral teaching methods in perpetuating low standards of language attainment in severely and profoundly deaf pupils', *Brit. J. of Teachers of the Deaf*, 2, 4, pp. 130–35.

NEWSON, J. (1978) 'Dialogue and development', in LOCK, A. (Ed.) *Action, Gesture and Symbol: The Emergence of Language*, Academic Press.

SPECIAL CHILDREN (1978) Editorial, *Special Children*, 8, p. 2.

TOBIN, M.J. (1972) 'The attitudes of non-specialist teachers towards visually handicapped pupils', *Teacher of the Blind*, 60, 2, pp. 60–64.

WATSON, D.M. and PICKLES, A.M. (1957) 'Home training', in EWING, A.W.G. (Ed.) *Educational Guidance and the Deaf Child*, Manchester University Press.

WEBSTER, A. (1986) *Deafness, Development and Literacy*, Methuen.

WELLS, C.G. (1981) *Learning Through Interaction*, Cambridge University Press.
WELLS, C.G. (1985) 'Language and learning: an interactional perspective', in WELLS, C.G. and NICHOLLS, J. (Eds) *Language and Learning: An Interactional Perspective*, Lewes, Falmer Press.
WOOD, D., WOOD, H., GRIFFITHS, A. and HOWARTH, I. (1986) *Teaching and Talking With Deaf Children*, John Wiley and Sons.

Chapter 9

Integrating Visually Impaired Pupils: Issues and Needs

Michael Tobin

Introduction

The most cursory examination of the history of the education of visually impaired children in the United Kingdom reveals that the state has relied heavily upon charitable institutions. The setting up of the first school for blind children in Liverpool in 1791 was soon followed by other foundations, and as the Vernon Committee (DES, 1972) put it, 'All the pioneer work for the blind was carried out by voluntary bodies' (*ibid.*, p. 1). The educationally handicapping consequences of blindness were recognized publicly in the 1889 report of the Royal Commission on the Blind, Deaf, and Dumb (culminating in Education Act of 1893) where it was recommended that there should be compulsory schooling for blind children between the ages of 5 and 16. It was not until the 1944 Education Act, however, that partially sighted pupils were given a separate status, although the actual use of the term 'partially sighted' had been one of the recommendations of a Board of Education Committee set up in 1931. It is interesting to observe that the Vernon committee had noted (*ibid.*, p. 2) its predecessor's conclusion that such children should be educated in the ordinary elementary schools of the time. The further boost given to the integration movement by the Warnock Committee (DES, 1978) has inevitably given rise to new problems since the hard-won experience and expertise of the teachers in the special day and boarding schools cannot be quickly and easily transferred to their non-specialist colleagues. The members of the Warnock Committee had foreseen the nature of many of these problems, and in so far as there have been any failures in implementing their general recommendations, the blame must lie in our unwillingness as a nation to provide the necessary resources; the requirements of the 1988 Education Reform Act have major resource implications, and it is imperative that they be recognized.

Part of the blame must also be laid at the door of the research community: the spate of survey investigations has not been paralleled by projects specifically targetted upon crucial aspects of assessment, curriculum needs, and methods of teaching. There is now some urgency for research that will be of direct practical value to 'mainstream' teachers who are presented with pupils dependent either upon nonvisual modes of learning or upon low-vision and other optical aids. The low incidence and prevalence of severe visual impairment are themselves factors that militate against the development of understanding among non-specialist teachers, especially where cost-effectiveness is the prime determinant of funding for in-service training and for the kind of research that such training presupposes.

Definition of Visual Disability

The great Education Act of 1944 used as its definition of blind pupils those who had 'no sight or whose sight is or is likely to become so defective that they require education by methods not involving the use of sight'. The same Act, as slightly modified in 1959, define partially sighted pupils as those 'who by reason of defective vision cannot follow the normal regime of ordinary schools without detriment to their sight or to their educational development, but can be educated by special methods involving the use of sight'.

For the ophthalmologist providing the diagnosis which allows the local Social Service Departments to place a child on one of the registers (although actually registration is voluntary and may be refused by the family), the working criteria for blindness are a distance visual acuity of 3/60 Snellen or less in the better eye after optimal correction by lenses. This effectively means that inability to read at more than three metres the standard symbols legible by most people at 60 metres can lead to classification as blind. If there is a marked contraction in the width of the visual field, even if acuity is as good as 6/60, this can also constitute blindness. Vision between 6/60 and 6/18 can lead to registration as partially sighted. The criteria are such that most blind people have some potentially useful residual vision and, by definition, all partially sighted people have sight useful for some purposes.

With very young children, and those with other disabilities, it may be difficult or impossible to measure acuity with any great accuracy. In addition, the standard conditions under which testing is done do not mirror those in which learning and other everyday activities are carried out. Measurement of acuity, therefore, is not always totally reliable and it takes little account of the subject's ability to use his intelligence and past experience to make sense out of the stimuli falling upon the retina of the eye. Knowing a child's distance acuity tells us little about how willing and able he is to use his sight in the classroom situation.

Numbers of Visually Impaired Pupils in Schools

Specialist peripatetic teachers frequently report that their appointment to post has led to massive upward revisions of estimates of the numbers of visually impaired children within their Local Education Authorities. The inadequacy of the data base was noted some twenty years ago by the Vernon committee (DES, 1972) when its members were trying to predict the number of special school placements that would be needed over the next decade. The difficulty arises from:

(i) the criteria used for determining whether a child is registrable as blind or partially sighted; they are not, as discussed above, absolutely rigidly applicable, and the results of testing are not easy to interpret;
(ii) delays in registering very young children as visually impaired, due in part to parental reluctance and in part to the desire of the ophthalmologists to await further and more reliable objective evidence;
(iii) failure to diagnose visual impairment in some children who are severely additionally impaired (sensorily, physically, or mentally);
(iv) failure to register children whose visual impairment is diagnosed but whose other impairments are thought to be so severe as to outweigh the significance of poor or non-existent sight;
(v) the fact that the DES and DHSS do not use the same age groupings; the DHSS statistics, for example, record numbers in the age-ranges 0–4, 5–15, and 16–49 years, and it is therefore not possible to deduce from them the numbers of subjects in the age-range 16–19, i.e. those still eligible for education at secondary school level.

The most up-to-date figures of the numbers of registered blind and partially sighted people in England are for the year ending 31 March 1986 (DHSS, 1987). These reveal that there were 378 registered blind and 177 registered partially sighted children in the age-range 0–4 years and 1,519 and 1,768 respectively in the age-range 5–15 years. An independent survey commissioned by the Royal National Institute for the Blind (RNIB, 1986) seems to suggest that the numbers on the official registers in 1981 represented less than:

16 per cent of the 'registrable' blind in the age-range 0–4 years;
47 per cent of the 'registrable' blind in the age-range 5–15 years;
8 per cent of the 'registrable' partially sighted in the age-range 0–4 years;
50 per cent of the 'registrable' partially sighted in the age-range 5–15 years.

Other, indirect evidence supporting the contention that the official figures are underestimates of the true situation comes from an investigation by Colborne Brown and Tobin (1982a) whose aim was to locate 'educationally blind' children who were not attending specialist schools for the visually impaired. A response rate of some 85 per cent of LEAs revealed nearly 1100 pupils in various other kinds of educational settings. It was estimated that at the time there were another 1100 in the specialist schools. Given, therefore, the 15 per cent of Authorities that did not respond, it is clear that there were and still are many more children than those recorded on the registers, even if the RNIB's consultants' calculations are at the top end of the range of estimates.

Perhaps the most important matter of concern arising from these discrepancies is the possibility that many children, especially those with multiple disabilities, are not having sufficient cognizance taken of the educationally handicapping consequences of their visual difficulties. This will probably result in failure to assess their needs, and associated failure to provide appropriate visual and tactual aids, and to ensure regular input from fully qualified, specialist teachers. The loss to the individual child will always be hidden.

Financial Costs

It is frequently claimed that integration is not a cheap option, and in their detailed examination of the matter Hegarty *et al.* (1981) have agreed that 'any direct comparison of costs would be meaningless' (p. 278). It is undoubtedly true that caution should be exercised in making such comparisons, if only because it is rarely the case that like is being compared with like; for example, numbers of pupils are likely to differ, with all the consequences this has for economies of scale. Where attempts have been made to estimate the costs of integration, a distinction has been made between recurring and non-recurring costs, as in the examples cited by the RNIB (1987a and b). The non-recurring charges for 1984/5 in providing for a newly-blinded 13-year-old pupil amounted to £4642, with the bulk of this being attributed to additional teaching, and only £1000 being spent on equipment. The recurring costs amounted to £7141, a third of which was spent on transport, the other major element (approximately 26 per cent) being accounted for by braille tuition. The second example is for integrating a 17-year-old blind student in a college of further education. Non-recurring costs in 1984/5 were £5459, of which 70 per cent was for the purchase of an electronic braille writer and a braille embosser. The recurring costs were £2645, giving a total of £8104. To these, of course, must be added the unspecified sums that are the appropriate proportions of the total cost of running any school; as Knight (1980) has said, few headteachers of non-specialist schools are able to provide data of this kind. A not untypical special school for visually impaired children in the north of England has annual fees of just over £7800 for day and £11,500 for residential pupils. Given the difficulties of knowing whether comparison of like with like is being made, the safest inference is that cost differences are probably not great, and the key question then turns on the quality of the education.

Implementing the Curriculum: Needs and Opportunities

Among the thirteen research topics which the Warnock Committee singled out as in need of attention (DES, 1978, p. 322) the only specific reference made to the curriculum was in relation to the 'slow learner in the ordinary school'. One inference to be drawn from this is that the Committee did not see the curriculum as being a major problem area for the other groups of pupils. Reinforcement for this interpretation may be found in the kinds of research grants made available. Directories of non-medical research, such as that produced by Newcastle Polytechnic's Handicapped Persons Research Unit (Sandhu *et al.*, 1988), show a preponderance of survey, evaluation, and database projects, with a corresponding dearth of references to curriculum and teaching investigations. It would seem easier to raise funding for relatively quick survey work, which require less 'content' and 'experiential' knowledge, than for projects requiring a longer time-span and staff with experience and expertise in the subject matter and in the methodology of teaching.

While for the able partially sighted pupil the main problem is a technical one concerned with how to facilitate access to the normal curriculum, the situation is more complex for the learner who is blind. In addition to finding solutions to problems in the reading and writing of braille and the production of tactile diagrams, there are other curricular needs. Time is required for the teaching of orientation and mobility, for enhancing the use of the other senses, and for developing social, self-help and independence skills. A question that is not being adequately addressed at present is whether and how these additional elements in the curriculum can be accommodated without losses elsewhere. Perhaps the difficulties will only become crucial when more pupils of average and slightly below average ability are integrated. Current successes with very able children cannot be taken as proof that these fears are illusory; in fact, even with regard to the most intellectually gifted pupils, the survey-type investigations have not probed deeply enough to ascertain whether there are any hidden curricular restrictions. What is now indicated is an action research programme that might show how time and specialist input could be manipulated to permit the implementation of a full curriculum as well as the additional components essential for the blind child. Among the hypotheses to be tested might be: whether extra time can be made by slightly extending the length of the school day; whether journey times to and from school can be used for formal mobility training; and whether greater efficiency can be achieved by the setting up of small teams of volunteers (parents, teachers and fellow pupils) to tape record introductions to and summaries of key chapters of texts. Even with the most efficient use of time and resources to mitigate the handicapping consequences of blindness, there will still remain, however, the fact that full-scale integration may debar the blind child from the pleasure of representing his school in, for example, football, cricket and other team-game sports. This is a sphere where the special schools, through their regional and national networks, do provide unique opportunities for important personal and social achievements.

The information technology revolution is being heralded as one means of guaranteeing equality of opportunity and access to the broadest possible curriculum. However, in evaluating the benefits of micro-computers for the visually impaired pupil in an integrated setting, it is possible to argue that the very flexibility of the technology poses new problems by its encouragement of unconventional approaches to the lay-out of text, graphs, and other illustrative matter. For the partially sighted, the painstaking development of accurate left-to-right and other systematic scanning techniques may be subverted by facilities that allow elements of the display to be switched around the screen so that the 'page' is no longer a familiar, highly predictable array. Nevertheless, the advantages massively outweigh the costs. The need of the short-sighted reader to get very close to the textbook he is reading results in the blocking out of the external light source; since the micro-computer's visual display unit is itself light-emitting, there is no such loss of light. Moreover, with synthetic speech output, the ability to enlarge the print size, and other options allowing individual choice of colour and contrast between figure and background, the new technology does offer greater accessibility to information. At present, the emphasis has been upon creating methods of controlling the computer (see, for example, Spencer *et al.*, 1987 and Hawley *et al.*, 1987). This is arguably the way to proceed, since it is asserting that the curricular needs of these pupils are the same as those of their non-handicapped peers.

This will, undoubtedly be the case in the secondary school, but at the pre-school and junior-age levels there are basic prerequisites in visual perception and psycho-motor skills that can be more easily developed and monitored by means of the new technology. Here again, the 'back-lit', light-emitting nature of the visual display unit, the availability of touch-screens and joysticks, and other modes of controlling what can appear upon the screen, are encouraging the production of software specifically designed to exercise and refine these skills (Spencer *et al.*, 1987; Spencer and Ross, 1988; and Spencer and Ross, 1989). The immediate need is for pump-priming funding to generate the production of such software. Databases containing information on what has been produced are necessary, but funding bodies should be giving priority to design and production; in the absence of a grand theory of educational technology and evaluation, a pragmatic approach will certainly be adopted by teachers who will be the arbiters over which software deserves to survive.

Surveys of Provision

The most useful surveys of provision would be those in which extensive use is made of examples. Hegarty *et al.* (1981) make this very point; unfortunately, their own survey, ranging widely over many educationally-handicapping disabilities, does not include an extended and finely detailed case-study of how the curriculum was organized and delivered for a blind or partially sighted pupil in an integrated setting. An earlier study (Jamieson *et al.*, 1977) did make such an attempt with four case-studies of pupils, none of whom was so severely disabled as to make braille essential for reading. Although a non-specialist teacher would learn little about techniques of teaching or about ways of modifying the content of lessons to make them more readily understandable by a student, Jamieson and her colleagues have brought out the importance for successful integration of attitudes and motivation, on the part of the child, her teachers, and her family.

One of the drawbacks of studies such as those of Hegarty *et al.* (1981) and Jamieson *et al.* (1977) is that even the most careful of research teams do not always differentiate between braille and print readers but are often wont to state quite categorically that special needs can be met in the ordinary school if adequate provision is made, despite the fact that the data at hand are derived from observational investigations comprising very few children. Even where the database is much larger, as in the Croll and Moses (1985) survey of teachers' attitudes towards integration, there remain problematical issues since the label 'visual handicap' would seem to imply blind and partially sighted subjects, when in fact 'none of the 428 classrooms in the sample contained a blind child' (Croll, personal communication).

Another large scale survey of integration, that by Colborne Brown and Tobin (1982a, 1982b, and 1983), has revealed among other things the degree of satisfaction experienced by families, but it has not shown directly how teachers can go about improving the quality of education provided to educationally-blind pupils in integrated settings. Some fine detail is provided by Stockley (1987) in her survey which contains a short section of case-histories on ten children, some of whom were totally blind; even here, nevertheless, the overall effect is to cause the reader to raise questions rather than to find answers. Fortunately, the Royal National Institute for the Blind is endeavouring to build on this, filling the gap by means of its *Integration Bulletin*, inaugurated in 1987 and containing practical information and advice based upon the experience of its contributors who are practitioners in the classroom and the peripetatic services.

Assessment

The Warnock Committee members placed considerable emphasis upon assessment, prescribing its main requirements, analyzing its various stages, demanding a 'multi-professional' input, and calling for regular monitoring of the child's progress and changing needs. Hegarty *et al.* (1981) have gone on to argue that monitoring is 'particularly important in integration' (*ibid.*, p. 379) since the special-needs pupils will be receiving help from a variety of sources, with each having perhaps only a partial understanding of the individual child's development. The comprehensive approach advocated, and the organizational system required to record the knowledge obtained, will be acknowledged as the ideal to which we should aspire. Among its many presuppositions are the existence of valid and reliable assessment instruments and a cadre of specialist teachers and psychologists trained in their use and interpretation. While there has been a growth in the number of teachers having additional specialist qualifications in the teaching of visually handicapped children — due largely to the expansion of the 'distance teaching' course at Birmingham University — there are still vast areas of the curriculum (and of the underlying prerequisite cognitive, perceptual and social skills) for which there are no procedures standardized on representative samples of the populations of blind and partially sighted pupils. Integration, almost by definition, implies that all learners must be assumed to have much in common with one another, certainly in terms of their major educational goals. This in turn entails common standards of appraisal, with each child's attainments gaining their significance in part from comparison with those of his age peers. For the teacher, this will require the administration of the same tests(s) to all pupils in the class. In so far as blindness and partial sight have educationally handicapping consequences, these will have to be taken into account. For the purposes of setting appropriate targets and diagnosing individual needs, there will also often be the requirement for tests that allow comparison with the group, or appropriate sub-group, of visually disabled learners. Such multiple comparisons — with the fully sighted, with the blind or partially sighted, and with the pupil's own particular sub-group of the visually disabled – are essential if a comprehensive assessment is to be undertaken and associated teaching programme implemented.

At present we are far from being able to equip teachers in integrated settings to do this. At the stage of entry to school, there are three instruments available to the teacher. The Reynell-Zinkin Scales (Reynell, 1979) are readily useable by an experienced teacher of infants, since their administration relies mainly upon observation by the teacher, coupled with presentation of tasks to elicit verbal responses. They give an indication of areas of difficulty being experienced by the child in such things as social adaptation, sensori-motor understanding, exploration of the environment, and receptive and expressive language skills; they also permit comparisons to be made with partially sighted, blind, and fully sighted children of the same chronological age. The Schools Council's 'Look and Think Checklist' (Tobin *et al.*, 1978) is for use with children aged 5 to 11 years, and claims to measure visual perceptual skills relevant to classroom activities. This, too, is easily used by non-specialist teachers, and will quickly yield the kind of information that an experienced teacher would gather informally over an extended period of classroom observation. Although primarily concerned with assessing the child's visual perception, and thus making clear to the teacher how well he can use any residual vision, the Checklist also elicits information about basic cognitive skills concerned with the correct use of words related to size and space and to a variety of relational concepts. The third instrument, the Williams Intelligence Test for Children with Defective Vision (Williams, 1956) covers the age range 3 years 6 months to 16 years and is designed for use with subjects who are or would be registrable as blind or partially sighted. It is now rather dated, both in content and in the way in which it provides information, the major outcome being a global intelligence quotient. For children in integrated settings, the other information that can be drawn out from it will depend upon the user's experience with such tests and upon familiarity with visually impaired children. Its importance lies in the fact that it was developed for use with, and standardized upon, such children; it therefore concentrates chiefly upon verbal abilities, saying little if anything about non-verbal reasoning, spatial imagery, and speed of information processing.

The only other important complex of skills for which there are standardized tests available is in the area of braille reading. The Tooze Braille Speed Test (Tooze, 1962) and the Lorimer Braille Recognition Test (Lorimer, 1962) are straightforward word-recognition tests, the first requiring no knowledge of fully-contracted braille, the second making use of the contractions that are an important space-saving characteristic of Standard English Braille. There is also a standardized braille version of the Neale

Analysis of Reading Ability (Lorimer, 1977) which allows teachers to assess a braillist's reading speed, reading accuracy, and reading comprehension simultaneously. For the partially sighted pupil, there is no such instrument available, but experience has shown that the standard print version of the Neale test can be coped with by most partially sighted readers. The age of all three tests now makes them suspect on the grounds of content and standardization: changes have occurred in the theory and practice of assessment of reading; and the population of visually impaired children is thought to contain a much larger proportion of multiple impaired pupils. New procedures that reflect these changes are needed. It is unlikely that a single test can adequately measure the range of abilities of the learners now to be found in specialist and integrated settings, especially if it is to be both diagnostic and normative in function.

The rate at which information can be processed has recently become more widely recognized as a factor of significance in learning and problem-solving (*vide*, for example, Elliott, 1983). Reading is, of course, the skill in which speed of visual information processing most obviously manifests itself at school. For the learner with severe visual problems, the special schools made it possible to alleviate the handicapping effects on learning to some degree by means of small classes and by extending the duration of schooling. Integration, with all that it implies in size of class, progression through the school with the age-groups, and studying the same texts more or less in unison, could be seen as likely to aggravate these difficulties. It has been argued above that it would be unacceptable to restrict the number of subjects studied at secondary school level. That this may be happening may be inferred from Jamieson *et al.* (1977, p. 185): 'If the teacher is unsure, there is perhaps a natural tendency to "play safe" and lower expectations . . . excusing the child from certain academic tasks . . . [and] excluding him or her from project work.' The decision by parents and advisers to opt for placement in the neighbourhood school ought to be based upon adequate information about a matter of this kind so that aids and compensatory and alternative teaching methods can be adopted (for example, by the use of tape-recordings, additional lessons on how to improve reading efficiency, and appropriate magnification of text). For the professionals responsible for providing the information, there must be a means of initially assessing this skill and an awareness of the importance of regular monitoring, both by reading speed tests and by an instrument such as the Speed of Information sub-scale of the British Ability Scale (Elliott, 1983). As has been shown (Mason and Tobin, 1986), there is considerable variation in performance among partially sighted pupils. While some achieve scores placing them in the top quartile of normally sighted children, the majority score at much lower levels, with no evidence that increase in age enables them to attain parity with their fully sighted peers.

There is as yet no similar assessment procedure for use with blind pupils, although braille reading, as demonstrated by Lorimer (1977), is much slower, the 'perceptual window' being no greater than the width of the finger pad by means of which the tactile symbols are identified. Work is, however, being prosecuted by Mason (personal communication) at Birmingham University to provide teachers with a means of measuring speed of processing by touch.

Specific learning difficulties should not debar children from integrated placements, but failure to assess in key areas of functioning can lead to setbacks in achievement that may be mistakenly attributed to other causes — lack of intelligence, poor motivation, laziness. In these circumstances, inexpert assessment can impose additional handicapping burdens. In willing integration as an end, society must will adequate means to ensure that needs are precisely identified; unless that is done, society's satisfaction in the attainment of its goal will be entirely spurious.

Conclusion

The implementation of the 1988 Education Reform Act will pose new challenges. Fortunately, there has been a wide-scale acceptance of the Act's insistence that its 'general principles . . . apply to all pupils and must be reflected in all special arrangements' (DES, 1989). However, the requirements of the National Curriculum, especially those sections concerned with attainment targets and assessment arrangements, will place severe pressure upon the LEAs, especially those that are still in the process of setting up support systems in mainstream schools. The mastery of braille is a prerequisite for competence in the foundation subjects, but the presence of teachers, qualified and experienced in the teaching of this skill, will be a crucial factor in determining whether the specified levels of attainment can be reached in a time-span that does not put blind pupils too far out of step with their fully-sighted peers. For partially sighted children, the generally slower speed at which visually presented information is decoded will also have its effects upon the likelihood of the attainment targets being achieved at the expected ages. In integrated settings, the National Curriculum may serve to bring the educational consequences of visual disability into sharper focus since there will not be the same easy availability of experienced colleagues for teachers to seek advice from. In that case, the design and production of well-validated assessment instruments may be given a higher priority than in the past.

In so far as the Act also requires that the whole curriculum must encompass aspects of personal and social education, then time must be found for regular and systematic mobility training and for the development of daily-living skills. Neither of these substantive areas of need can be ignored if integration is to be meaningful. The question of how they are to be accommodated within the framework of a National Curriculum in which chronological age is to be given so much more emphasis has already been touched upon. What research can do is to evaluate the relative effectiveness of various solutions that can be mooted, e.g. summer schools, additional teaching (involving a longer working day or week), formal education at an earlier age, and the raising of the minimum leaving age. What must not be given serious consideration is a reduction in the number of curricular options open to the visually disabled learner. One test of the nation's commitment to the National Curriculum will be its willingness to provide the finance for teachers and researchers to carry out the necessary work.

References

COLBORNE BROWN, M.S. and TOBIN, M.J. (1982a) 'Integration of the educationally blind: numbers and placement, *The New Beacon*, May, LXVI, 781, pp. 113–17.

COLBORNE BROWN, M.S. and TOBIN, M.J. (1982b) 'Integration of the educationally blind: information from questionnaire to parents', *The New Beacon*, November, LXVI, 787, pp. 281–6.

COLBORNE BROWN, M.S. and TOBIN, M.J. (1983) 'Integration of the educationally blind: parents' opinions and general conclusions', *The New Beacon*, July, LXVII, 795, pp. 169–74.

CROLL, P. and MOSES, D. (1985) *One in five. The assessment and incidence of special educational needs*, London, Routledge & Kegan Paul.

DEPARTMENT OF EDUCATION AND SCIENCE (1972) *The education of the visually handicapped* (Report of the Committee of Enquiry appointed by the Secretary of State for Education and Science in 1968), London, HMSO.

DEPARTMENT OF EDUCATION AND SCIENCE (1978) *Special Education Needs* (Report of the Committee of Enquiry into the Education of Handicapped Children and Young People), London, HMSO.

DEPARTMENT OF EDUCATION AND SCIENCE (1989) *National Curriculum. From policy to practice*, Stanmore, Department of Education and Science.

DEPARTMENT OF HEALTH AND SOCIAL SECURITY (1987) *Registered blind and partially sighted persons at 31 March, 1986, England*, A/F86/7, London, DHSS.

ELLIOTT, C.D. (1983) *British Ability Scales*, Windsor, NFER-Nelson.

HAWLEY, A., JEFFERYS, S., ROSS, M., SPENCER, S. and TOBIN, M.J. (1987) 'Electronic publishing and visually handicapped learners', *The New Beacon*, LXXI, 844, pp. 253–5.

HEGARTY, S., POCKLINGTON, K. and LUCAS, D. (1981) *Educating pupils with special needs in the ordinary school*, Windsor, NFER-Nelson.

JAMIESON, M., PARLETT, M. and POCKLINGTON, K. (1977) *Towards integration. A study of blind and partially sighted children in ordinary schools*, Windsor, NFER.

KNIGHT, B. (1980) 'What does a school cost to run?', *Education*, 22, pp. 199–200.

LORIMER, J. (1962) *The Lorimer Braille Recognition Test*, Bristol, College of Teachers of the Blind (now available from the Association for the Education and Welfare of the Visually Handicapped).

LORIMER, J. (1977) *Neale Analysis of Reading Ability adapted for use with blind children. Manual of Directions and Norms.* Windsor, National Foundation for Educational Research.

MASON, H. and TOBIN, M.J. (1986) 'Speed of information processing and the visually handicapped child', *British Journal of Special Education*, 13, 2, pp. 69–70.

REYNELL, J. (1979) *Manual for the Reynell-Zinkin Scales. Development scales for young visually handicapped children — Part 1, Mental Development*, Windsor, National Foundation for Educational Research.

ROYAL NATIONAL INSTITUTE FOR THE BLIND (1987a) *Integration Bulletin, No. 3*, London, Royal National Institute for the Blind.

ROYAL NATIONAL INSTITUTE FOR THE BLIND (1987b) *Integration Bulletin, No. 4*, London, Royal National Institute for the Blind.

SANDHU, J., MURRAY, P. and RICHARDSON, S. (1988) *Directory of non-medical research relating to handicapped people, 1988*, Newcastle, Newcastle-upon-Tyne Polytechnic, Handicapped Persons Research Unit.

SPENCER, S. and ROSS, M. (1988) 'Visual stimulation using microcomputers', *European Journal of Special Needs Education*, 3, 3, pp. 173–6.

SPENCER, S., and ROSS, M. (1989) 'Closing the gap', *Special Children*, 28, pp. 20–21.

SPENCER, S., ROSS, M., TOBIN, M.J. and BLENKHORN, P. (1987) 'Centre Computer Base for visually handicapped children, students, and adults', *British Journal of Visual Impairment*, V, 2, pp. 67–9.

STOCKLEY, J. (1987) *Vision in the classroom. A study of the integration of visually handicapped children*, London. Royal National Institute for the Blind.

TOBIN, M.J., CHAPMAN, E.K., TOOZE, F.H.G. and MOSS, S.C. (1979) *Look and Think. A handbook for teachers*, London. Royal National Institute for the Blind/Schools Council.

TOOZE, F.H.G. (1962) *The Tooze Braille Speed Test*, Bristol, College of Teachers of the Blind (now available from the Association for the Education and Welfare of the Visually Handicapped).

WILLIAMS, M. (1956) *Williams Intelligence Test for Children with Defective Vision*, Windsor, NFER.

Chapter 10

The Education of Children with Physical Impairments: Curriculum Developments, Integration and Prospects

Barbara Riddick

Before and After the Warnock Report

In order to examine the education of physically impaired children in the ten years since the publication of the Warnock Report in 1978, it is necessary to know something about the identification and education of this group prior to the Report. Related to this is the question that is often raised as to whether the Warnock Report significantly shaped the course of thinking about special needs or largely reflected changes that were already taking place. This is of particular relevance to physical disability where research into the educational needs of this group of children especially in relation to integration had been carried out since the early 1970s, notably the studies by Elizabeth Anderson (1973) on integration into the ordinary primary school and Anderson and Cope (1977) on the function of special units within the ordinary school. It is also the case that a DES survey in 1972 indicated that 10,200 physically impaired children were educated in ordinary schools in addition to the 12,507 educated in special schools, thus showing that a considerable proportion of physically impaired children were already integrated into the ordinary school system, particularly at the primary school level. What was also notable was the considerably regional variation in practice with many rural local authorities having no special school provision for physically impaired children. It can be argued that some of the integration was as much by default than as a consequence of a positive and well thought out plan for integration. Little is known about the quality of integration and the resources available at this time which makes it hard to compare alongside integration in the 1980s, but does make it clear that integration as a substantial phenomenon predated the Warnock Report.

The Warnock Report suggests that many children with physical disabilities can be integrated into the ordinary school 'if adequately supported'. It goes on to stress the need for teachers and ancillary helpers to have adequate information and in-service training. Like much of the Report, no further details or discussion are given on how this should be arranged or funded. The Report also states that, for children with severe physical and learning difficulties, special school placement will be necessary. It suggests that some of these special schools should be designated resource centres which can offer support and advice to teachers and others working with children with physical disabilities. In addition to this the need for all special schools to form links with ordinary schools and guard against isolation is stressed. Another point of importance is that up until the 1970s a significant proportion (20 per cent) of children with physical disabilities were in residential schooling. The Report considered that this form of schooling would still be necessary for some children where they could not be coped with at home and, for older children, had an important role to play in promoting independence training and leisure skills. No comment is made about the physical and social isolation of many of these schools which are often in country settings, although it is suggested that possibly more short-term residential provision could be offered by them.

Where the influence of the Warnock Report and the subsequent 1981 Act can be more clearly seen in relation to physically impaired children is in the issue of labelling. The Warnock Report, in stressing the importance of children's educational needs, points out that the predominantly medical labels given to many physically impaired children says little about their educational needs. So, for example, a child with cerebral palsy or spina bifida could be of above average or average learning ability or have specific or severe learning disabilities. The Warnock Report also stresses the importance of special needs being seen as a relative concept depending upon the environment that the child interacts with, thus giving an interactive rather than a within child model of disability. To this end the Report recommended the abolition of statutory categories of handicap to be replaced by the concept of special educational needs. Added to this they specified three major types of help likely to be linked to special needs. For physically impaired children they say this mainly in terms of giving them access to the curriculum. The Report does acknowledge that in abolishing statutory categories there is a danger that children with 'severe, complex and long-term disabilities' may not have their particular needs met and that specialist resources may not be safeguarded. The Report comments that there is a dilemma that any form of separate or special pleading for a specific group of children will isolate them and undermine the notion of continuum of special need, but that without a statutory obligation being placed on LEAs for specific groups of children, necessary resources may not be forthcoming. This is a constant dilemma with physically impaired children of how one ensures that their particular needs and particular forms of disability are sufficiently understood without isolating them from the mainstream culture. The danger is that, if too much emphasis is placed on the desirability of treating these children in all cases like all other children, their needs will not always be sufficiently met. In fact, it can be argued that by meeting a child's specific needs, say for independence training and personal counselling, you are enabling them to participate more effectively in mainstream culture. Bill Gillham (1986) has argued that when handicap is seen entirely as a social or environmental concept it can easily minimize the very severe degree of disability that many children have to contend with. Better access may widen the environment a spastic quadriplegic child can utilize, but it doesn't mean that she or he is not severely physically disabled. Gillham suggests that in fact it is the large degree of ignorance about disability that has led to these kinds of glib assumptions, and that children with disabilities are further handicapped if those coming in contact with them do not understand their particular needs, and goes on to say: 'If there is an answer to disability it lies in an informed, adaptive response by the social and physical environment.'

The Warnock Report also points out the importance, particularly with younger physically impaired children, of a multi-disciplinary approach, with effective collaboration of professionals such as physiotherapists, teachers, occupational therapists, speech therapists, paediatricians, etc., but again gives no details on how this collaboration could be improved or even reconceptualized.

The Current State of Education for Physically Impaired Children

As well as the impetus for change promoted by the Warnock Report and the 1981 Act, a major factor bringing about change in the education of physically impaired children has been the change in the nature of this population of children. In the 1940s, 1950s and early 1960s, the major conditions dealt with by schools for the physically handicapped[1] (PH Schools) were polio and then thalidomide. Neither of these conditions involved any additional learning difficulties so that PH schools had a similar if more narrow academic curriculum to ordinary schools with GCEs and subject specialization dominating the secondary curriculum.

But by the end of the 1960s these conditions had virtually disappeared and the dominant disabilities were now cerebral palsy and spina bifida. Both conditions, as well as involving severe physical disability, also often involved neurological impairments leading to additional sensory and learning disabilities. PH schools varied markedly in their ability to respond to the changing needs of their population of children, and it is only in the late 1980s that some of them have started to come to terms sufficiently with the need to provide a curriculum that acknowledges and meets the learning disabilities many of the children have. This change in the needs of physically impaired children attending PH schools has probably been further accelerated by two other factors. The first is the decline in the number of physically impaired children, particularly in conditions like spina bifida and muscular dystrophy, as new screening techniques have become more widely available. The second probable factor is that with the integration of 'brighter' physically impaired children into ordinary schools, PH schools in order to keep up their numbers have in some cases taken physically impaired children with more severe and complex learning difficulties. Expansion of nursery and post-16 education has also taken place.

As the ILEA Report on special education (Fish, 1985) has pointed out, the labels given to schools are still determined by the 'legacy of traditional categorization' and often don't reflect the range and complexity of needs that a school has to meet. This seems very clear in the case of PH schools at present, particularly as some schools, in order to keep up viable numbers, have diversified into taking children who traditionally would have been labelled 'delicate'. The lines drawn between physical impairment (or at least which children are eligible for a place in a PH school) and other descriptions such as severe learning difficulties (SLD) have become more blurred. This is not necessarily a bad thing as it reflects the tenet of the Warnock Report that there is both a continuum and for many children a multiplicity of special needs. It has always been the case that for severe and multiple handicapped children it has been difficult to decide whether they would benefit from placement in a PH or an SLD school. What appears to be happening now is that more PH schools are willing to contemplate taking on 'borderline children' and that the borderline itself is shifting somewhat in degree of severity. These observations are made from talking to heads of a wide number of PH schools and are therefore tentative in nature. There is an urgent need for more systematic research to look at the population of children now attending PH schools and also to look at how PH schools are developing their roles and intend to do so in the future. What is clear is the enormous diversity in the way PH schools have developed in the 1980s. Some still cater largely for children with a physical disability and no other disabilities whereas others, as stated before, are now taking a much wider range of children. Some have specialized in providing nursery or FE provision for a range of special needs, for example. Whereas numbers in many schools are falling, in some schools numbers have been maintained or even increased.

In respect to integration PH schools also differ considerably. A few schools have practised a well thought out scheme of integration, predating the Warnock Report and 1981 Act. Many others, seemingly in response to Warnock and the 1981 Act, have started some integration during the 1980s. But this again can vary widely in terms of the number of children and host schools involved and the degree of integration practised. There are still some PH schools which are dubious of the benefits of integration and have therefore not made development in this direction. Whilst in some cases this can be seen as the inability of a mediocre school to respond to change, in other cases thriving, well directed schools are involved and in these cases vigorous and persuasive arguments are made for the advantages of the form of provision they offer. Allied to the move to integration is also the degree to which PH schools have developed as suggested by Warnock into resource and support centres. Again this is characterized by tremendous variation between schools.

Major Disabilities

As mentioned previously, the two major conditions found in PH schools at present are cerebral palsy and spina bifida. Whereas it seems likely that the number of cerebral palsied children will remain fairly constant, numbers of spina bifida children are beginning to drop. Another group which, as mentioned previously, should be dropping in number is those children with muscular dystrophy. A smaller but possibly increasing group, is children who have had road traffic accidents involving head injury.

There is a wide variety of other rarer conditions such as brittle bone disease and chronic juvenile arthritis encountered as well.

Cerebral Palsy

Cerebral Palsy (CP) is an umbrella term for a group of non-progressive movement disorders characterized by damage to one of the areas of motor control in the brain. This means that the child starts off with undamaged limbs but, as a consequence of the distorted muscle control to the limbs, can gradually develop limb deformities as a secondary characteristic. Cerebral palsy is generally divided by the type of movement disorder and the number of limbs involved. The majority of cases are caused by conditions prior to or during birth, but later onset due to meningitis, head injury, etc., is found in a small percentage of cases.

Spastics

This is the largest and most familiar group. Whilst estimates vary considerably, Bowley and Gardner (1980) suggest that 70 per cent of CPs fall into this group. Movement is characterized by a rigid jerky style with kickback. The degree of severity and number of limbs involved varies considerably.

Athetoid

Movement in this group is characterized by uncontrollable writhing of the limbs, often involving tongue thrusting as well, so that speech may well be impaired. It is also estimated 40 per cent of athetoids have an educationally significant hearing loss. Children in this group are often very severely physically disabled although statistically they are less likely to suffer intellectual impairment compared with the spastic group.

Ataxic

A small group of children who are characterized by an unsteady gait and movement tremors.

Cerebral palsy children can vary from those of above average intellectual ability to those with severe learning difficulties. Many CPs have additional problems with poor visual control, perceptual difficulties, hearing loss, articulation difficulties and epilepsy. So that, for many children, CP is not merely a movement disorder but a constellation of disabilities.

Spina Bifida

Similarly children with spina bifida have a range of disabilities. The degree and nature of these depend on whereabouts and to what extent the spinal cord is damaged. Below the level of damage there is either no sensory control or limited sensory control, leading in many cases to nonambulance and incontinence. In addition to this it is estimated that up to 80 per cent of spina bifida children also have accompanying hydrocephalus which is a build up of cerebro-spinal fluid in the ventricles of the brain. If uncontrolled this leads to extensive brain damage. This condition is either present at birth or soon after is treated by the insertion of a shunt to draw off the excess fluid and relieve pressure. Evidence by Tew and Lawrence (1975) shows that even when hydrocephalus is so treated the IQs of spina bifida children with hydrocephalus are often below average, particularly on performance as opposed to verbal scales, whereas the IQs of spina bifida children without hydrocephalus are around the average. Hospitalization for the insertion of shunts and urinary bypass devices plus further hospitalization for urinary infections, shunt blockages, sores and orthopaedic surgery all mean that considerable time can be lost from school. Other physical factors related to school, apart from the obvious one of access, are the need for adequate toilet facilities with privacy for changing appliances. Teachers, welfare assistants or others responsible for the child need, particularly in the case of younger or less aware children, to know that loss of sensation can lead to pressure sores or damage from excess heat or cold. A shunt blockage may be indicated if a child is sick, dizzy or complains of a headache.

There is evidence (Wedell, 1973) that both cerebral palsy and spina bifida children may have specific learning difficulties, particularly of a perceptual motor nature, which in turn can lead to problems with handwriting, sequencing and number work (Haskell and Barret, 1977).

This brief information is given on these two conditions to illustrate both the complexity and variance in needs that arise. It could be argued that the range of educational needs of physically impaired children is wider than for other groups such as moderate or severe learning difficulties.

Curriculum

This last point about the wide range of educational needs that physically impaired children have has obvious implications for the curriculum. A PH school could be trying to cater for children with severe and complex difficulties who border onto the SLD range and at the same time cater for children of above average learning ability, with a large group in between who have specific or moderate learning difficulties. This mix of children has required PH schools to develop their traditional if restricted curriculum to cater for general and specific learning difficulties, communication difficulties and motor difficulties, and expand teaching and training in areas like independence and social skills and the use of microtechnology. The problem of *time* is obviously paramount if all this is to be fitted in as part of the curriculum, given that many physically impaired children need extra time to perform a range of tasks including simple, taken for granted activities such as moving from one classroom to another or going to the toilet. Extra time is also needed for the completion of work, long journeys to and from school, including arriving late and leaving early, plus time for daily treatment and periods of hospitalization. In fact the head of one PH school whose children integrate into a mainstream school on the same campus has extended the day for the physically impaired children so that they can take full advantage of the mainstream curriculum and still get any necessary treatment or additional support.

The second major problem is in integrating the physical and cognitive goals of education. Traditionally many physically impaired children have had individual physiotherapy sessions within their school day. Sometimes this has been seen as conflicting with or interrupting their 'proper' education. Although there is an increasing tendency for teachers and physiotherapists to work together it is still the case that they often have different priorities in terms of goals and objectives, and that these can still conflict or compete for the available time. One of the arguments in favour of Conductive Education is that physical and cognitive goals are fully integrated. This will be discussed more fully in the section on Conductive Education.

It can be argued that many of the problems for the curriculum in PH schools are exacerbated in the mainstream school setting where the pressures of the mainstream curriculum make it more difficult to make the necessary curriculum adaptations. The assumption is often made that the main issue in an integrated setting in access to the curriculum, although both Brennan (1975) and Wilson (1985) have emphasized that the extra time needed to complete work and for management of the disability do have direct curriculum implications. In looking at the development of the curriculum for physically impaired children in the mainstream school, there seem to be three major factors:

(1) The present state of the school and its curriculum and what this implies in terms of aims, attitudes and ethos, particularly in relation to special needs.
(2) The nature of the disabilities brought by the children.
(3) The resources available and the resources needed both to allow a child to cope with the existing curriculum and to change the curriculum where necessary to meet the child's needs.

At a practical level schools that have a good overall special needs policy with well organized support systems seem best able to identify and attempt to meet the special needs of physically impaired children. Brennan (1985) has emphasized the need to look at the curriculum not just in terms of academic aspects but to see it as covering all aspects of school life including, for example, approaches to learning and social interactions within the school. This is an important point for physically impaired children as there is ample evidence to suggest that they are often excluded from many aspects of the curriculum such as school clubs and visits, and they often suffer social isolation

Figure 10.1. A Model of Curriculum Development in a mainstream school integrating physically impaired children

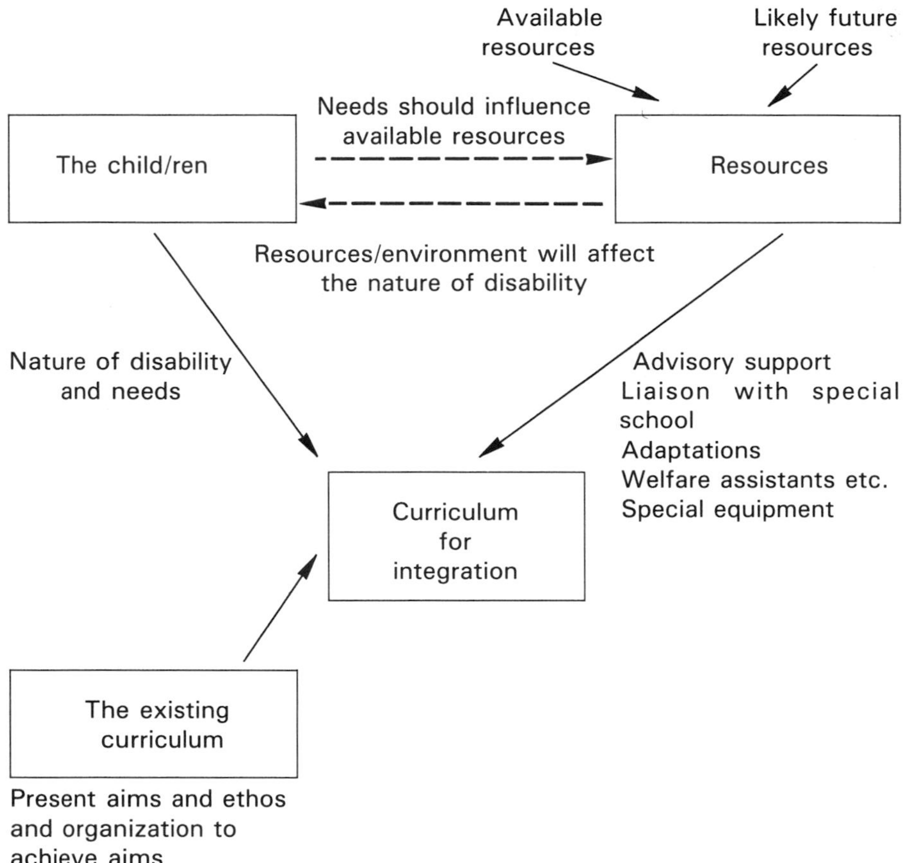

and have fewer than average non-disabled friends. What clearly emerged from research by Anderson and Clarke (1982), and Madge and Fassain (1982) was the need, especially at the secondary school level, for more personal counselling, opportunities to discuss their disability and the implications of being disabled. Swann (1987) even goes so far as to suggest that study of disability could be part of the curriculum at many different levels. It is therefore vital when constructing and evaluating a curriculum for physically impaired children that, as well as obvious questions related to the formal curriculum, plus additional questions such as what learning tasks are needed to manage the disability and additional time needed for doing practical and written work, the following questions are asked in relation to the wider curriculum:

(1) Does the disability preclude the child from any areas of the present

curriculum (e.g. PE, practical aspects of woodwork, home economics, etc.)? If so, can –

(a) access be improved?

(b) the curriculum be adapted?

(2) How will the disability affect involvement in extra curricular activities, e.g. school visits, journeys, lunchtime and after school clubs?

(3) What additional social and emotional needs related to the child's disability may there be?

Integration

It has been suggested that, in relation to physically impaired children, too much attention has been focused on the issue of integration and not enough on curriculum development. Whilst this is a valid point it is difficult to review education in this area without referring to the issue of integration, partly because much of the research and writing has focused on this.

As far back as 1972 a major research study was carried out by Elizabeth Anderson, looking at the integration of physically disabled children in the primary school setting. Her study showed clear differences in the success of integration depending on whether children had purely physical impairments such as congenital limb deficiency or additional neurological impairments as in cerebral palsy. Those children with additional neurological impairments showed on a number of measures looking at behaviour, social interactions, and learning ability, greater difficulties in the integrated setting. What was important, it seemed, was not the degree of physical disability but the degree of learning disability and personal developmental problems associated with the physical disability. So a severely physically disabled but intellectually and socially bright child was more likely to cope successfully in an integrated setting than one with slight physical disability but neurological impairments. Anderson concluded that with the right structural alterations and attitudes it is fairly easy to integrate purely physically impaired children at the primary level but that it is much harder to integrate children with neurological problems. These findings have been confirmed throughout the 1970s and 1980s and emphasize the need to look at the educational needs of each physically impaired child on an individual basis and not lump all physically impaired children into one group. Tomlinson (1982) has pointed out the danger of the notion of the idealized wheelchair child. Even for children without neurological impairments, simple problems of access or inadequate toiletting facilities can in some cases lead to the breakdown of an integrated placement.

Obviously the Warnock Report in 1978 and the 1981 Act have provided impetus to the integration movement in the 1980s with physically impaired children often in the vanguard. Whilst relatively few additional resources have been forthcoming, the pressures to integrate have increased. It has therefore become essential to think clearly about the issues involved in integration and have a coherent picture of what is happening and how to evaluate it. During the 1970s and 1980s many case studies of integration of physically impaired children have been documented, such as those by Hegarty, Pocklington and Lucas (1981) and Booth and Swann (1987). But relatively little research has tried to gain an overview of what is happening.

One attempt to do this is a survey carried out jointly by the NFER and the Schools Council from 1982–1984. This project investigated over seventy primary and secondary schools where children with a range of special needs were integrated into the ordinary classroom. They used interviews, classroom observations and discussions with groups of teachers to collect information. They point out that a distinction can be made between integration as placement (i.e., locational) and integration as education, and that most attention has been focused on the first (i.e., getting children into mainstream schools) rather than on the quality of the education they receive. They reinforced Anderson's findings that being academically able appears to be the most important determinant of success for physically impaired children.

This leads on to the major issue of by what criteria physically impaired children are generally selected for integrated education. The NFER study confirmed the sorts of criteria named by many experienced at integrating physically impaired children. These include:

(1) average or above academic ability;
(2) social and emotional ability;
(3) a desire to be integrated;
(4) support of parents;
(5) ability to communicate effectively;
(6) effective management of continence.

Just as important as selecting children is selecting the right environment. Jones (1983) has pointed out that as important as the concept of the whole child which is central to the Warnock Report, is the concept of the whole school which organizes itself as effectively as possible to meet the needs of all its children. Many heads who have run extensive integration schemes have emphasized the need to have the backing of all the staff in the school. Hodgson (1984) has suggested that schools should think about three levels of preparation when they are getting ready to receive children with special needs. One is preparation of the staff, a second is preparation of parents of pupils already at the school and a third, preparation of the pupils.

What is now needed is much more focus on the quality of integration. Do children, for example, really follow the full curriculum or are they left as onlookers in practical lessons and physical education? What sort of social interactions do they have with their able-bodied peers and what factors appear to influence the nature of these? Is total integration always the ideal solution or is partial integration better able to meet the needs of some physically impaired children? How is the course of integration best monitored and evaluated in specific settings? It is also important that adequate planning for the transference of resources takes place at an LEA level with planning to protect the breadth and balance of the curriculum in PH schools which have falling numbers. Possible solutions to this are the use of partial integration or relocation as a unit or school on a mainstream campus or in concert with other special schools with which there is an overlap of needs. Fish (1984) has suggested that other forms of special school organization should be considered such as providing intermittent specialist help on a short term basis which will enable a child to cope in a mainstream school.

At present most mainstream schools that integrate physically impaired children appear more willing to take on board the problems of physical access than seriously to contemplate curriculum adaptations. Swann (1987) illustrates this with a case study of what at present would generally be considered a good example of an integration scheme at the secondary level. Despite the success of the scheme children are still denied full access to parts of the curriculum such as science, PE and home economics. In addition it is argued that there still isn't a proper assessment of needs in the mainstream school setting. It also raises the difficult question of where expertise is seen to be located, with the special school staff seeing themselves as the specialists and the mainstream school staff arguing that they in fact are the specialists in dealing with children with physical disabilities in an integrated setting.

Conductive Education

Conductive education is a system of education devised by Andros Peto in Hungary. It is argued that in conductive education the physical and cognitive goals are fully integrated and that the child learns to control her movements through active cognitive control and not by passive exercises. Although there is still controversy over the efficacy of conductive education, certainly in the form practised at the Peto Institute, results look impressive and it raises important questions about curriculum organization. In this system children have intensive teaching in basic motor control with well formulated objectives and high motivation and expectation enhanced by group teaching. What is interesting in curriculum terms is that firstly the children undergo a much longer day than children in ordinary schools, with both the conductive education and the ordinary school curriculum to be followed. Hungary has a national curriculum in its schools which all children follow. It also stipulates that physically impaired children will only be admitted to mainstream schools if they can walk, look after their own needs and follow the national curriculum. To this end the Peto Institute aims to make children 'ortho-functional' so they can enter the mainstream school, and also ensures they keep abreast of their national curriculum. Conductive education is therefore seen as a specialized form of education the child follows for a relatively short period of time, ideally about two years, which meets the additional physical learning needs of physically impaired children and enables them to then follow conventional mainstream schooling with little additional support.

Conductive education at the Peto Institute is obviously geared specifically to the needs of the Hungarian education system. What is unclear at present is what are the essential principles underlying conductive education and how successfully they can be applied in other cultural contexts. Whatever the merits of conductive education, what it does raise is the question of whether all the needs of physically impaired children can be adequately met either by existing special schools in this country or in integrated settings without additional time input at some point. Supporters of conductive education would argue that it is essential that this input is given as early as possible so children can learn adequate motor and independence skills. Again, in curriculum terms, this raises the question of the planning and progression of children's learning and how this can be balanced. It also raises the question of whether children's needs can be adequately met within a mainstream curriculum without additional specialist input, either as a preliminary as in Hungary or alongside the mainstream curriculum. As in the UK the quality of integration in Hungary also needs careful evaluation. Another curriculum issue raised by conductive education, which frowns upon the use of aids such as wheelchairs and microcomputers for writing, is how far motor objectives are followed and at what point alternative objectives are formulated. Although views will obviously be diverse, it is important that disabled people are consulted about the aims and objectives of their education.

The Impact of the Education Reform Act

At present it is still only possible to conjecture what effect the Education Reform Act will have on the education of children with special needs and more specifically on children with motor disabilities. Concerns about the setting up of a national core curriculum centre around the point that the curriculum is directly related to the type of society we want children to live in and develop. The proposed core curriculum has a traditional subject basis, which ignores recent educational emphasis on the need to look at skills, personal development and experience in constructing and delivering a curriculum. As Lawton (1988) points out, there is almost no mention of social and personal development or moral, political and economic education and understanding. The whole ethos of the core curriculum seems to militate against an understanding of disability at a personal social level, for both disabled and non-disabled children. At a practical level there may be less time for important areas such as independence skills and social skills within the curriculum.

Many of the points relating to children with motor impairments relate to children with special needs in general and have been made by a number of authors.

Firstly, with the setting of attainment targets linked to the curriculum which will be tested and lead to published results, there will be pressure on schools to produce good test results. The DES (1989) National Curriculum stipulates that modifications can be made to the requirements to publish results for children with special needs so that overall school results will not be depressed and act as a disincentive for admitting children with special needs. Despite amendments to the Act exempting children with statements from some parts of the curriculum, schools may still be reluctant to admit special needs children because they want to focus resources on the main body of children. Physical adaptations to the environment, special transport, auxiliary help, microtechnology, physiotherapy and curriculum adaptations are all needed if mainstream schools are successfully to meet the needs of physically impaired children. It is hard to see how schools which choose to opt out of LEA control can provide the wide ranging and coordinated support needed for successful integration and, given the expense involved, what incentive there would be to do so. If schools opt out, LEAs in turn will be smaller and less well resourced and may find it more difficult to give the specialized support needed for physically impaired children both in special and mainstream schools.

As with other areas of special needs there will be increased pressure for physically impaired children to be statemented, thus promoting the distinction between the handicapped and the non-handicapped that the Warnock Report and the 1981 Act have tried to lessen. The assessment of children with physical disabilities under the national curriculum requires careful consideration of time allowances and response modes and needs to be flexible enough to cater for children's individual needs within a given setting. The kind of microtechnology available to a child could, for example, make a crucial difference to the type of response she could give. It is also important to consider what allowances should be made for time lost through hospitalization and ongoing treatment. Section 19 of the Act allows that children could be given a temporary exemption for six months but, as the 1988 NUT guidelines on the Bill pointed out, this will lead to a cumbersome bureaucratic approach which will be time consuming and confusing and, in many cases, not flexible enough for individual children's needs. If physically impaired children follow the national curriculum and are tested without appropriate allowances, their self-esteem may well suffer. If, on the other hand, they are statemented and excluded from aspects of the curriculum, they will be segregated and excluded from some educational experiences. On the plus side it can be argued that with a national curriculum it will be easier to know exactly what a physically impaired child needs to have learnt in order to integrate successfully into a mainstream school, and that where a special school integrates into several mainstream schools this should not raise problems of diverse expectations about attainments. Another issue is that in some cases PH schools have moved their curriculum closer to that of the mainstream school their children integrate into, in order to facilitate integration. Will they continue to do this even if it makes the curriculum further removed from the needs of their children?

It remains to be seen whether the Education Reform Act will act as a brake to the integration of physically impaired children because it will be harder to meet their needs adequately in the mainstream school. At present integration and curriculum development for physically impaired children is at a crossroads. A start has been made but the quality of what is happening needs careful evaluation and adjustment. As the head of one PH school said, 'I don't want my children to cope in mainstream school; I want them to flourish.' It is hard at present to see how the Act will better enable physically impaired children to flourish in an integrated setting.

Note

1 Schools for the physically impaired are usually referred to as PH schools, and this abbreviation will be used throughout the rest of this chapter.

References

ANDERSON, E.M. (1973) *The Disabled Schoolchild: A Study of Integration in Primary Schools*, Methuen.

ANDERSON, E. and CLARKE, L. (1982) *Disability in Adolescence*, Methuen.

ANDERSON, E.M. and COPE, C. (1977) *Special Units in Ordinary Schools*, University of London Institute of Education.

BOOTH, T. and SWAN, W. (Eds) *Including Pupils with Disabilities: Curricula for All*, Milton Keynes: Open University Press.

BRENNAN, W. (1985) *Curriculum for Special Needs*, Open University Press.
FISH, J. (1984) 'The Future of the Special School', in BOWERS, T. *Management and the Special School*, Croom Helm.
GILLHAM, B. (Ed.) (1986) *Handicapping Conditions in Children*, Croom Helm.
HASKELL, S. and BARRET, E. (1977) *The Education of Motor and Neurologically Handicapped Children*, Croom Helm.
HEGARTY, S. POCKLINGTON, K., and LUCAS, D. (1981) *Educating Pupils with Special Educational Needs in the Ordinary School*, Windsor: NFER-Nelson.
HODGSON, A., ROSS and HEGARTY, S. (1984) *Learning Together*, NFER-Nelson.
JONES, N. (1983) The Management of Integration: the Oxfordshire Experience, in BOOTH, T. and POTTS, P. (Eds) *Integrating Special Education*, Basil Blackwell.
LAWTON, D. (Ed.) (1988) *The National Curriculum*, The Institute of Education, University of London.
MADGE, N. and FASSAM, M. (1982) *Ask the Children: Experiences of Physical Disability in the School Years*, Batsford Ltd, David and Charles.
SWANN, W. (1987) '"Firm links should be established": a case study in conflict and policy making for integration', in BOOTH, T. and SWANN, W. *Including Pupils with Disabilities: Curricula for All*, Open University Press.
TEW, B. and LAWRENCE, K.M. (1975b) 'The effects of hydrocephalus on intelligence, visual perception and school attainment', *Developmental Medicine and Child Neurology 17* Suppl. 35.
TOMLINSON, S. (1982) *A Sociology of Special Education*, Routledge & Kegan Paul.
WEDELL, K. (1973) *Learning and Perceptions — Motor Disabilities in Children*, John Wiley.

Chapter 11

Severe Learning Difficulties and Multiple Handicaps: Curriculum Developments, Integration and Prospects

Jean Ware

Perhaps the single most significant development in the education of children with multiple handicaps in recent years has been the realization of the existence of *multiple* handicap as a problem in its own right. As McInnes and Treffrey so graphically put it: 'the deaf-blind child is *not* a blind child who cannot hear or a deaf child who cannot see . . .' (McInnes and Treffrey, 1982, my italics). Many authors would now agree that this statement could in essence be applied with equal force to any child with two or more severe handicaps; and that consequently work done with children who have only one severe handicap is of limited application to the multiply handicapped child. This is perhaps especially true where one of the handicaps is mental retardation. To take just one example, Bleeker-Wagemakers (1984), writing about visual impairment in the mentally retarded, argues that:

> an educational programme for the visually handicapped mentally retarded cannot be a simple combination of these [the specific programmes for the mentally retarded and the visually handicapped]; on the contrary they mutally exclude each other. On the one hand, for the development of the mentally retarded child concrete and practical situations are important, together with opportunities to learn by imitation. However, this cannot be realized for a child who has a visual handicap as well, who cannot see the concrete situation, nor whom or what has to be imitated.

Arguably, then, multiple handicap presents the greatest challenge to the would-be educator. At the same time there has been a growing awareness of the *extent* of multiple handicap. Any child with severe handicap has a high chance of having additional handicaps, but this is particularly true of children with learning difficulties: and the more severe the learning difficulty, the more likely it is to be accompanied by one or more additional handicaps. The extent of this problem is clearly demonstrated by a number of recent surveys. For example, Kelleher and Mulcahy (1985) in their census of the mentally handicapped in the Republic of Ireland found that even amongst those with moderate and mild learning difficulties (IQs 50–75), 38 per cent had at least one additional disability while amongst the more severely handicapped this percentage rose dramatically to 44 per cent for those with IQs 35–49, 64 per cent for those with IQs 20–35 and 83 per cent for those with IQs below 20. Kelleher and Mulcahy also found that 46.5 per cent of those with IQs below 20 had two or more additional disabilities.

Approaching the problem from another angle, surveys both in Denmark (Hyvarinen and Lindstedt, 1981) and in the UK (Ellis, 1986) have found that children with mental handicaps are 100 times more likely to have a visual impairment than the remainder of the population. Because of this high prevalence of multiple handicap amongst children with severe and profound learning difficulties, this chapter deals mainly with advances made in the education of this group. It is, perhaps, necessary to say at this stage that the word 'advances' is being used in a rather loose way in this context. It is, in fact, extremely difficult to assess the effect of either general changes in educational practice or more specific innovations on the overall achievement of children with multiple handicaps. This difficulty in evaluating the effects of changes in educational practice on the achievements of these pupils stems from at least three sources. First, due to the complexity and number of uncontrolled variables involved, the evaluation of school effectiveness in general represents one of the most difficult problems for educational researchers. Second, there is a paucity of evidence on the achievements of school-leavers with severe learning difficulties over the years. Third, even when there is such evidence, those with multiple handicaps have normally either been actually excluded, or they have not been differentiated from other pupils.

However, innovation has run ahead of evaluation and despite this lack of firm evidence for the effects of different practices in the classroom; there have been a good many changes in the way in which children with multiple handicaps are educated in the past two decades, both in individual curriculum areas (for example, the teaching of language) and more generally across the whole curriculum. In a chapter of this length it is not possible to look at each curriculum area in detail and the discussion which follows therefore focuses mainly on cross-curricular issues, particularly curriculum planning and development, the use of microtechnology, and conductive education. These areas have been selected because they have specific implications for the education of children with multiple handicaps within the mainstream, especially in the context of the 1988 Education Reform Act.

During this time the terminology used to refer to children with intellectual impairments and the schools which provide for them has changed several times. Prior to 1970 the children were generally referred to as severely mentally handicapped (a term which has remained in common use throughout the period), were regarded as unsuitable for education in school and were provided for by the Health Service in Junior Training Centres (JTCs). In 1970 the Department of Education and Science took over responsibility for these children and the JTCs became schools for severely educationally subnormal children (ESN(S) or SSN). In 1983 the implementation of the 1981 Education Act changed the terminology yet again, but this time without any alteration to provision. Currently children in this group are generally referred to as having severe learning difficulties (SLD) and the school which cater for them as SLD schools.

Curriculum Planning and Development

Behavioural Approaches

Almost certainly the single development which has had most impact on the education of children with severe learning difficulties since the 1970 Education (Handicapped Children) Act, which brought them into the school system, has been the development of objectives based approaches to both curriculum planning and programmes for individual children. It is easy, particularly at present when these is a considerable backlash against behavioural methods, to underestimate the contribution these approaches have made, especially in view of the paucity of evidence on the achievements of school-leavers with severe learning difficulties over the years. There was, in fact, a survey by Marshall in 1966 of the attainments of 14- and 15-year-olds in Junior Training Centres (the forerunners of SLD schools) (Marshall, 1967). In this survey 165 children were assessed on the Progress Assessment Charts (Gunzberg, 1966) and the English Picture Vocabulary Test (Brimer and Dunn, 1963) and thus, at first sight, a baseline exists against which more recent developments can be measured. However, not only did Marshall exclude those who were manifestly autistic or had very severe physical handicaps, but by no means all children attended such centres, which makes detailed comparisons difficult. A further, less detailed, survey by Hughes, shortly after the move from Health to Education, also excluded Special Care children and those with severe physical handicaps (Hughes, 1975). Furthermore, no comparable survey has been published on the achievements of the generation of children who have received all their education since 1971.

However, in the current climate it is worth recalling that both Marshall and Hughes suggest that there was little in the way of curriculum planning and development in the late 1960s and early 1970s. Further, both the Junior Training Centres and the 'new' ESN(S) schools were said to lack clear aims and to view the curriculum chiefly in terms of the timetable (Simpson, 1967; Hughes, 1975; Leeming *et al.*, 1979). Thus there was an emphasis on content rather then the interrelationship of the activities to each other or an overall framework within which the content could be conceptualized. Interestingly, however, it was during this period that the idea of social competence as the overall (or most important) aim of education for children with severe learning difficulties became predominant.

Although this aim has a surprisingly modern ring there appears to have been, with a few exceptions, little thought at this time of conceptualizing the curriculum in terms of objectives. Rather, Marshall, Simpson and Hughes all suggest that what was 'missing' from the curricula of the ESN(S) schools/JTCs was sufficient time for free play, especially for the older children. They seem, then, to have been advocating a nursery-type curriculum for all but the oldest children. It is in this context, then, that the introduction and contribution of objectives based approaches should be assessed.

As Wood and Shears (1986) point out in their critique of behavioural approaches, two strands can be identified in their development. On the one hand they are based in research findings concerned with learning in people with severe learning difficulties, especially research in the behavioural tradition, and on the other in the review of the aims of education which was in part at least precipitated by the entry of these children into the education system.

Early research findings indicated that people with severe learning difficulties did not learn things *incidentally* in the way that non-handicapped children did, but that they *could* acquire skills previously thought to be beyond them if the task was broken down into small steps and carefully and specifically taught (e.g. Clarke *et al.*, 1955; Gold, 1973; Horner and Keilitz, 1975). Although much of this early work was carried out with adults, its relevance to teaching skills to individual children in Junior Training Centres was quickly recognized by researchers (e.g. Marshall, 1967). However, there was apparently little impact on practice prior to the move to Education in 1971.

Since 1971 behavioural methods of teaching skills to individual children and objectives approaches to curriculum have become extremely widespread. However, as Kiernan points out, these terms conceal a great diversity of approach and theoretical orientation (Kiernan, 1986) and it is probably more helpful to think of them as a diverse family than as a single unified approach.

The Use of Behaviour Modification to Teach New Skills to Individuals

One of the major contributions of the development of behaviour modification techniques to teach skills to individuals has been the unequivocal demonstration that even those with multiple handicaps can learn new skills when these methods are employed. Both general motor behaviours and self-help skills have been taught by these methods. As several recent and comprehensive reviews are available (e.g. Stainback and Stainback, 1983; Switzsky, Haywood and Rotatori, 1983; and Presland, 1980), only one or two examples will be quoted here. For example, Murphy and Doughty (1977) taught boys with severe learning difficulties and a variety of physical disabilities to reach out and grasp a ring. They report that the boys not only learned to grasp the ring but improved their strategies for performing the task over time. Chandler and Adams (1979) in a piece of work which is particularly interesting because it was carried out by a physiotherapist in a school setting, taught a 10-year-old boy with cerebral palsy to walk using a transistor radio recommended by the parents as one of their son's preferred activities as the reinforcer. Furthermore, it appears that this eventually became a functionally useful behaviour for the boy, maintained without the use of extrinsic reinforcers.

The success of these attempts at using behavioural methods with people with multiple handicaps was particularly important, given the failure of previous approaches to make any significant impact on the complex problems presented by this group. However, comparatively few of the reported studies have been conducted by *teachers* or *therapists* with *children* in *classrooms* and their widespread use owes much to the dissemination efforts of the Hester Adrian Research Centre, particularly throughout the EDY (Education of the Developmentally Young) Programme (Foxen and McBrien, 1981). It is reported that over 2000 people have now been through the EDY programme (Mittler, 1988) and some evaluation has taken place, indicating that the programme is successful in changing staff behaviour and that the new teaching methods continue to be practised at least in the short term (McBrien and Foxen, 1987). A further evaluation which includes the effects on children is in press (Robson *et al.*, 1989) but it is not clear if this will differentiate between children with severe learning difficulties in general and those with multiple handicaps. This is an important issue, since an evaluation of EDY's predecessor by Hogg, Foxen and McBrien (1981) suggested that hospital staff had difficulty in using behaviour modification techniques successfully with the most handicapped children and tended not to continue to do so. Furthermore, a recent study by Hotte *et al.* (1984) also suggested that the most profoundly handicapped did not benefit from intensive programming compared to the slightly less handicapped. Therefore, there are some grounds for suggesting that there may be a small sub-group of the multiply handicapped population who have not yet benefited much from advances in teaching methods in contrast with the majority of the group.

Objectives-based Approaches to Curriculum Design and Organization

While behavioural methods of teaching individual children were taken up by many schools in the 1970s, it was not until somewhat more recently that objectives approaches to curriculum organization became widespread, although these, too, have their theoretical basis in learning theory research. Indeed, in 1981 Wilson reported that many special schools still adopted the 'free play' approach advocated by Marshall and others at the end of the 1960s. (Wilson, 1981).

Objectives approaches to curriculum, although extremely varied, have in common the view that the curriculum can usefully be conceptualized in terms of ordered hierarchies of objectives leading to overall aims. The advantages and disadvantages of this approach to curriculum design have been outlined by a number of authors; for example, Burman *et al.* (1983) quote the following advantages:

(1) Assists teachers in knowing where to start with new children and facilitates smooth progression between classes within the school.
(2) Ongoing assessment of progress.
(3) Structured curriculum removes the need for class teachers to spend time deciding what to teach – hence more time for deciding *how* to teach.
(4) Promotes parent-teacher cooperation.
(5) Positive, optimistic approach.

They also note these problems:

(1) Knowing the order in which sequences should be written.
(2) Deciding the appropriate step-size.
(3) Specification of objectives.
(4) Constraints on individual teacher's freedom.
(5) Need to organize the classroom so the curriculum can be implemented.

The extent to which these problems are seen in practice depends on the way in which an objectives approach is being implemented in a particular school. For example, the sequencing of objectives within hierarchies seems to have proved a particular stumbling block, especially for those with multiple handicaps. Despite warnings in the literature that sequences for the learning of many skills are not known (e.g. Burman *et al.*, 1983), in practice they are often treated as both invariant and as the same for all children: consequently a child with multiple handicaps may become 'stuck' at some stage due to the particular difficulty of performing a specific task. Ware (1986) records one attempt to tackle both this difficulty and that of achieving a suitable step-size for different children by outlining the curriculum in terms of large steps on flow-charts leading to the final aims, so that while most pupils may follow the same sequence, those children with particular difficulties are provided with alternative routes to the eventual aim. A disadvantage of this method, viewed from Burman *et al.*'s perspective, is that individual teachers are not freed from the need to decide what to teach.

A more fundamental criticism of the objectives approach, and one that is particularly relevant in the context of the 1988 Education Reform Act, is that it assumes that the aims of education can and should be pre-specified. Further, the objectives approach is seen as inextricably linked with the view that the aims of education are the same for all children (e.g. Wood and Shears, 1986). During the past decade these aims have come to be seen more and more universally as those stated in the Warnock Report:

> First to enlarge a child's knowledge, experience and imaginative understanding, and thus his awareness of moral values and capacity for enjoyment, and secondly to enable him to enter the world after formal education is over as an active participant in society and a contributor to it, capable of achieving as much independence as possible (Warnock, 1978).

Wood and Shears, Billinge (1988) and others argue that, as far as children with severe learning difficulties are concerned, the acquisition of independence, largely interpreted as competence in dressing, washing and other social skills, has been stressed to the exclusion of all else. Will the Education Reform Act (ERA) change this situation? Superficially, the aims of education as implied in the Act differ little from those of the Warnock report.

The curriculum for a maintained school satisfies the requirements of this section if it is a balanced broadly based curriculum which:

> (a) promotes the spiritual, moral, cultural, mental and physical development of pupils of the school and of society , and
> (b) prepares such pupils for the opportunities. responsibilities and experiences of adult life.

It is likely, however, that the emphasis within these broad aims will change and that the acquisition of subject specific knowledge and becoming a *responsible* contributor to society (interpreted exclusively as being an *economic* contributor) will become ascendant for all children. Potentially, this is even more problematic for those with very severe and multiple handicaps than the current stress on independence. Firstly, although there is provision for modification of the national curriculum for children with severe learning difficulties whose attainments in most subjects for much of their school lives might fall outside the sequence of levels devised for all children, it is much more likely that such children would have the national curriculum disapplied in part or in whole since it is likely to be seen as largely irrelevant to their needs. If this happens there is a distinct chance that they will effectively be excluded from the mainstream of education. Secondly, if the contribution that an individual makes to society is evaluated exclusively in economic terms the great majority of those with multiple handicaps will end up being seen as net debtors, and ironically there may come to be even more stress on the acquisition of skills in eating, dressing, etc., since these will reduce the cost of the support which multiply handicapped people need.

The problem, then I would argue, lies not in the objectives approach, as Wood and Shears suggest, but in the societal values which it reveals. Indeed, as I have suggested elsewhere (Ware, 1986) a major *advantage* of the objectives approach which is frequently ignored is that aims and values which are made explicit are more easily challenged and changed than those which are not. This is particularly important for those with multiple handicaps for whom, for example, the aim of independence may be more realistically attained by acquisition of the ability to express preferences than by partial success in dressing and eating skills.

Of course, education has never been insulated from the social and political climate in which it is embedded; nor is it desirable that it should be. Indeed, as Kiernan has pointed out, although the speed with which the objectives approach to curriculum design spread probably owed something both to the previous disorganized state of provision, and to the fact that it offered both a way of teaching individual pupils and an overall curriculum framework, there were also other, more subtle reasons for this rapid spread (Kiernan, 1985). Kiernan suggests that the optimism about a mental handicap inherent in behavioural theory fitted well with the generally optimisitic mood of the late 1960s and early 1970s. This optimism is apparent in the official publications of the period, for example in the DES pamphlet about the education of children in hospital:

> These children present the greatest challenge to education but at the same time they provide the opportunity to learn a great deal about early stages of learning and effective methods of teaching. By a careful assessment of existing behaviour and response, by imaginative use of familiar things, and by exploiting a wide range of different stimuli, much may be accomplished. Above all, such children, like all others,

> need sustained personal relationships with which to grow and develop as far as they can. There is evidence that all children can acquire some enjoyment and satisfaction through learning if situations are carefully planned and if different professional skills are mobilized to common ends (GB.DES, 1975).

It is particuarly interesting in relation to this that Burman *et al.* quote the optimism of objectives approaches as one of their advantages. Similarly, the current doubts about the long term effectiveness of such techniques may also owe something to the very different social and policital mood of the 1980s (Kiernan, 1985).

This point is an important one, not only in relation to behaviourally based methods of curriculum planning but to all the innovations discussed in this chapter. Indeed, in each case I shall suggest that there are factors other than evidence of effectiveness which have played a crucial role in the adoption of some innovations rather than others at particular points in time. The connection between the prevailing cultural climate and educational practice highlighted by ERA is not, therefore, a new phenomenon, and with the current political emphasis on individual achievement and individual reward it is only to be expected that there will be increased stress on the need for pupils to be educated to *contribute* to society. In this climate, therefore, what is urgently needed, if pupils with severe and multiple handicaps are not to be increasingly marginalized, is a debate about what it means to be a responsible contributor to society.

Programming for Generalization

The influence on curriculum design of the second problem identified by researchers as typically experienced by people with severe learning difficulties, i.e. the great difficulty which they appear to have in transferring learned skills to new problems, is much less easy to discern. Possibly this is because this problem has proved much more intractable. Indeed, it may well be partly this hurdle which has occasioned the current disillusion with behavioural and objectives based approaches. There seems little point in teaching a young person a complex 'independence' skill, such as using a washing machine, if, faced with another machine in a different kitchen, s/he will be unable to apply the skill.

Furthermore, with regard to the group with whom this chapter is chiefly concerned, there seem to have been very few attempts to programme for the generalization of methods used to overcome additional handicaps (for example, the marking of clothes with tactile labels rather than the dial of the washing machine with braille symbols).

In fact, research has made some progress here, too, and it seems to be generally agreed that generalization can be enhanced by varying tasks, trainers and settings *during* the teaching of a new skill (Borkowski and Cavanaugh, 1979; Gow, 1985; Porter, 1986). Colvin and Horner have recently begun to develop a systematic approach called 'General Case Programming' based on these findings. They suggest that six steps are involved in maximizing the possibility of producing generalization. These are:

(1) Define the instructional universe.
(2) Define the range of relevant stimulus and response variation within the instructional universe.
(3) Select examples from the instructional universe for training and probe testing.
(4) Sequence the training examples.
(5) Teach with the training examples.
(6) Test with the probe examples.

Colvin and Horner tested this strategy with eight pupils with severe learning difficulties. The task selected for training was screwdriver use, and the aim was that the pupils would be able to use any type of screwdriver to perform 'any benchwork assembly task that requires screwdriver use'. Unfortunately, Colvin and Horner do not describe their subjects in sufficient detail for it to be clear whether any of them had other handicaps in addition to severe learning difficulties, and this is an important omission since the programme was not equally successful with all the students and there was a considerable IQ range (10–50). However, three of Colvin and Horner's subjects did successfully complete the programme within the space of a school year. Given the length of time required for training (considerably more than Colvin and Horner had anticipated) it is not yet clear to what extent general case programming represents an advance on previous attempts to teach generalization. Additionally, its applicability to those with multiple handicaps needs to be specifically investigated. It is possible, for example, that different sequences might be required for pupils with additional physical impairments; or even that a different strategy might be more effective — for example Brown and Campione (1977) investigating this point in relation to teaching different groups of pupils a metacognitive strategy found that the strategy which proved most effective for pupils with moderate learning difficulties was different from that which was most effective for pupils of average ability.

This work gives rise to two potentially contradictory implications for the education of pupils with multiple handicaps within the mainstream in the context of the national curriculum. On the one hand general case programming might conceivably be a useful tool for enabling pupils with a variety of SEN to approach the same attainment target as all pupils in at least some areas; and on the other the need to use sequences and methods carefully tailored to the individual student might present particular problems in a context where the emphasis is on the proportion of children obtaining each level.

Furthermore, if general case programming does prove to be a particularly useful technique for teaching complex groups of skills to those with severe learning difficulties and multiple handicaps, there are clear implications for the degree of skill and professionalism required by teachers for this group.

Microtechnology

One of the most dramatic changes in schools in general in the past ten years has been the widespread introduction of microtechnology. In SLD schools the microcomputers now so common in mainstream have been accompanied, or often preceded, by reactive toys and a variety of switches and communication aids. These other technological devices are often particularly in evidence in classes for profoundly and multiply handicapped children; while in many schools 'the computer' tends to be more frequently used by the older or more able pupils. Potentially, both microtechnological devices in general and microcomputers in particular represent significant additions to the teachers' armoury. This section looks at the ways in which microtechnology has been used with multiply handicapped children, examines the particular strengths of such devices and discusses the constraints on their use and on future possible developments with particular regard to integration.

The uses to which microtechnology has been put with people with multiple handicaps can be divided into two basic groups: the provision of access to the general curriculum, and as a teaching tool within the curriculum.

Access

Since the publication of the Warnock and Fish reports (Warnock, 1978; Fish, 1985) there has been growing support for the view that not only are the aims of education the same for all children, but that all children have a right to experience the same broad curriculum. The Education Reform Act is likely to increase this trend as, despite the fact that one of the few provisions for children with special needs is a right to receive a curriculum modified from the national one, the national curriculum may well be seen as an entitlement curriculum. In this context micros have provided what are effectively prosthetic devices enabling a good many children with multiple handicaps to participate in the mainstream curriculum, alongside their non-handicapped peers. However, as Sebba (1986) has pointed out, it is ironically possibly that the use of micros may result in the isolation of children with learning difficulties within the mainstream classroom rather than access to a wider curriculum and integration with non-handicapped peers. She cites the example of a child with Down's syndrome working with a teaching machine within a mainstream class on an entirely different topic from the remaining pupils (Sebba, 1986). Nor should it be assumed that microtechnology is always the most appropriate way of providing a prosthesis. Indeed York, Nietupski and Hamre-Nietupski (1985) suggest that 'lower tech' devices are to be preferred whenever possible, since they are both safer and more flexible and enable the pupil to develop what motor abilities s/he has.

Teaching and Assessment Tools

A similar argument can be advanced about the use of microtechnology as a teaching tool: that it should only be used when it is the most appropriate means of achieving particular educational goals, and never simply for its own sake. The integration of micros into the curriculum in this way is still a dream rather than a reality; however, there are two areas in which their particular characteristics seem to hold great promise for people with multiple handicaps, namely the development of contingency awareness and the assessment of reinforcement preferences and the development of choice.

Development of contingency awareness

One of the ways in which reactive toys, switches and microcomputers have all been used with multiply handicapped children is in order to provide consistent consequences to the children's actions. There is general agreement amongst psychologists of differing theoretical persusasions that learning that s/he is able to have an effect on the environment is a critical stage in a child's development and that this process is at risk in handicapped children (see e.g. the reviews by Brinker and Lewis, 1982 and Kysela and Marfo, 1983).

It is particularly at risk in those with multiple handicaps since they may have both a limited response repertoire *and* a limited ability to detect and remember co-occurrences. These problems may well be further compounded by the transactional process, making social responses to the child's behaviour less likely with a probable consequent reduction in the child's motivation.

The use of technological solutions to provide experience of a contingently responsive environment for multiply handicapped children is therefore particularly attractive. Technology should theoretically be able to provide responses which are reliably contingent, allow for an extremely limited range of movements, are individualized in terms of the reinforcement they provide, and are unfailingly patient into the bargain.

Amongst the first reactive toys to be designed specifically for children with multiple handicaps were the Pethna toys (Woods and Parry, 1981). Pethna toys consist of two basic components: an in-box which provides access through any movement which the handicapped child is able to make, and an out-box which provides the consequences. Since these components are interchangeable, Pethna toys provide a reasonably close approximation to both individualized access and individualized reinforcement. Indeed, Woods and Parry stress the need for careful assessment of both manipulative skills and reinforcement preferences, and included a counter in some of their prototype out-boxes to facilitate assessment of reinforcer preferences. In the last half-dozen years the number of devices on the educational market which purport to provide contingency experiences for those with multiple handicaps has mushroomed. For example, Toys for the Handicapped (TFH) produce a wide variety of switches and adapters which can theoretically be combined to operate any battery operated toy or other machinery.

However, if such devices are to fulfil the criterion of providing contingency experiences they need as a basic minimum to operate reliably under classroom conditions, and to be reasonably easy for a busy teacher to set up. I know of no formal published evaluations of the classroom use of such devices, but both anecdotal evidence and student projects evaluating particular switch-toy combinations suggest that in practice a number of factors frequently make these reactive toys unsatisfactory as providers of contingency experiences. For example, leads and connections are frequently insufficiently robust for classroom use and may become broken or disconnected; toys which move become entangled in leads and cease to work; sensitive switches, ideal for children with very limited movement, are triggered by extraneous classroom events: and last, but by no means least, batteries periodically become flat. Additionally, as York *et al.* (1985) point out, it is essential to collect data to monitor progress. Unless these problems are overcome, it seems quite possible that reactive toys, and even microcomputers will, like the touch-tutor and other teaching machines before them, have only a brief life followed by a lingering death in the back of the teacher's cupboard (Hegarty, 1975, 1988).

There has, however, recently been one extremely promising development in the area of data collection and monitoring of progress. This new software development known as performance-contoured programming, collects data on the individual child's performance, adjusts the level of difficulty accordingly and can also provide a record for the teacher (Ager, 1985, 1986).

Assessment of reinforcer preferences

The potential usefulness of automated devices in assessing reinforcer preferences of people with profound and multiple handicaps was early recognized by researchers (e.g. Haskett and Hollar, 1978; Friedlander, McCarthy and Soforenko, 1967; Hogg, Remington and Foxen, 1977); and a good deal has been learnt about developmental trends, both in which reinforcers are preferred and in the context necessary for these preferences to be demonstrated. For example, Glenn and Cunningham (1984) showed that for both 'normal' infants and children with profound and multiple handicaps it is not until a developmental level of more than about 5 months is reached that preference is shown for a rewarded versus a non-rewarded manipulandum and not until nine to ten months that preference for one auditory stimulus over another is demonstrated in a choice situation. However, reinforcer preference can be demonstrated by changes in response rate well before this, and it is with these very young and/or severely handicapped individuals that computer-based assessments could make the most dramatic difference. Theoretically, any voluntary response can be used to activate a suitable switch and software can be designed to change contingencies and record response rates (Brinker and Lewis, 1982; Wallwork, 1986). Indeed it is even possible that physiological changes (e.g. pluse rate) could be used to demonstrate preference (Lloyd, in preparation).

The preferences demonstrated by children in these experiments were sufficiently consistent between individuals to suggest that there are implications for classroom practice, both in the modality of reinforcer which is provided (for example, Sandler and McLain, 1987, found vestibular stimulation was preferred to food) and in its type; (Glenn and Cunningham's subjects preferred the human voice to a simple tone and also preferred that voice to be talking to them).

A number of constraints can be identified which hinder the use of both this assessment methodology in particular, and microtechnology in general, in the classroom. Chief amongst these are probably insufficient staff training (Ager, 1986) and too little attention to the need for devices to be easy for the teacher to set up and operate.

Conductive Education

No review of current developments in the education of children with multiple handicaps would be complete without some discussion of the recent upsurge of interest in Conductive Education in Britain. The topic of what leads to one educational innovation being widely adopted, while another dies a silent death, or how a method which has been available for years suddently becomes popular, has already been briefly discussed, and there is no space here to discuss this issue in greater depth. However, it is worth noting that conductive education was first introduced to this country over twenty years ago (Cotton, 1965) and that the current interest may well be related more to political and social factors than to any new evidence about the efficacy of the methods, particularly perhaps to the current emphasis on parents' rights.

General issues relating to conductive education are discussed more fully in Riddick's chapter and the discussion here therefore concentrates on its applicability to children with severe learning difficulties and multiple handicaps. By contrast with those advocates of microtechnology who chiefly emphasize its ability to give multiply handicapped children *access* to the curriculum, the proponents of conductive education argue that physical disabilities should be regarded primarily as learning problems. As Sutton puts it:

> Thus spasticity, for example, is not regarded from this viewpoint as a reason for a child's being *unable* to walk, dress, etc., but as a reason for the child's finding it *much harder to learn* such motorically dependent skills. For the teacher and the education system, therefore, spasticity is not to be regarded as an immutable impediment, around which education has to be adapted and fitted, but rather as the object or education which, once mastered, should no longer provide a major matter for educational concern. Motorically disabled children are taught to overcome their handicap, after which they can take their place in the normal education process, with no further special allowances than are required to support and maintain mastery of the physical disability (Sutton, 1984).

Perhaps the most well-known of the complex of teaching methods used to achieve this aim is that of rhythmic intention, or the verbal regulation of motor acts. The children are taught to use speech and rhythmic movement to control their motor disabilities. It seems to be widely accepted that this aspect of the method derives from Soviet psychology, particularly that of Luria and Vygotsky, although there is some doubt as to whether this is as a result of a systematic attempt by Peto to base his education method in psychological theory or a more general influence.

Certainly as early as 1969, Burland was suggesting that a system such as conductive educational based on Luria's theory of the verbal regulation of behaviour could accelerate the educational progress of *some* multiply handicapped cerebral-palsied children. Interestingly, Burland did not argue that the method would help all such children, but rather that distinct sub-groups existed within the multiply handicapped cerebral-palsied population who needed different educational treatment. Similarly, Budd and Evans (1975) spoke of a group of cerebral-palsied children who had a certain brightness of response and reaction to people and surroundings which suggested that they were underachieving. This is consistent with Luria's view that only those capable of achieving verbal regulation (Luria, 1961) would be assisted by being taught to control motor actions through speech.

However, this early emphasis on a particular sub-group of the cerebral-palsied population seems to have disappeared in the more recent work. In this country currently conductive education is most frequently being used with the group with whom this chapter is concerned: those children who have both severe learning difficulties and other impairments, including some who are profoundly and multiply handicapped (Sutton, 1984; Cottam, McCartney and Cullen, 1985), who are an extremely heterogeneous group. Indeed, if Sutton's survey is representative, about half the schools in Britain which use conductive education are doing so with children who have severe learning difficulties and some degree of physical disability. In terms of the supposed theoretical basis of rhythmic intention in the psychology of Luria and Vygotsky, however, this group of children would not necessarily be expected to benefit from conductive education, since they are said to be unable to use language in its regulatory function. Indeed, the only published study which attempts to compare the application of conductive education principles with an alternative method (behaviour modification) found no difference in the educational progress made over the course of two years by two matched groups of children with profound and multiple learning difficulties (Cottam, McCartney and Cullen, 1985). These authors additionally quote a paper by Semenova and Mastyukova (1974) which suggests that children with profound and multiple learning difficulties are not considered suitable for conductive education in Hungary.

However, despite the lack of theoretical and research support for the efficacy of conductive education with multiply handicapped children, there are several ways in which the current interest in this method might be instrumental in bringing about a significant advance in their education.

First, the concept of the conductor provides an alternative way of achieving an interdisciplinary approach to multiple handicap without the need for a large number of adults to be involved with one child. For children who are profoundly handicapped and therefore functioning at an extremely early developmental level, being handled consistently by one person may enable them to recognize the adult and begin to develop a reciprocal relationship. This aspect of progress was not measured in the Cottam, McCartney and Cullen study. Furthermore, the length of training given to conductors under the Hungarian system (seven years) may act as a salutory reminder that the expertise needed to educate children who have multiple handicaps cannot be quickly and easily acquired.

Second, although the emphasis on physical disabilities as learning problems underlines both the compound nature of multiple handicap and the enormity of the problem for the teacher in helping a multiply handicapped child to learn, it also offers an alternative perspective to that common in Britain where physical disabilities are often seen as 'barriers' requiring specialized treatment and equipment rather than education (e.g. Ouvry, 1987). There are also strong parallels here between conductive education and functional analysis, since both emphasize the goal rather than following the 'normal' developmental path.

Thirdly, the use not only of group teaching, but of the group as a motivating force within conductive education may provide a useful counter-weight to the stress on individual programmes within traditional behavioural approaches, though it should be noted that the place of group teaching and motivation has also recently been discussed by authors working within a behavioural framework (Brown, Holvoet, Guess and Mulligan, 1980; Sturmey and Crisp, 1986; Ware, 1986). In relation to this group emphasis, the contrast between Eastern and Western European approaches may serve to illuminate the extent to which the way we educate our children, including those with multiple handicaps, reflects the prevailing cultural and social ethos.

Finally, and importantly in terms of this volume, conductive education does not fit easily into either the conceptual framework created by the 1981 Education Act or the legal one enshrined in the 1988 Education Reform Act. In terms of the 1981 Act, conductive education clearly demands that the children who will benefit are separated from their non-handicapped peers at a very early age, and that they receive intensive special education until the point at which they can cope with the mainstream. Furthermore, the judgment as to which children will benefit is made, at least in part, on fairly specific aetiological grounds.

As has already been pointed out, the Education Reform Act enshrines a shift towards individual achievement, and accountability, within a framework of a nationally presented curriculum. Superficially this stress on individual achievement is not dissimilar from some aspects of conductive education, but the philosophy underlying conductive education is very much at variance with that underlying the Education Reform Act. It seems clear that a school working according to conductive education principles would *not* be delivering the national curriculum.

Conclusions

One theme which has emerged throughout this chapter is the need for children with multiple handicaps to receive their education from highly skilled specialist-trained teachers, if they are to benefit fully from the considerable advances in knowledge and techniques which have been made over the past two decades. There is clearly a conflict here between the provision of specialist teaching and the desire to educate children with multiple handicaps in integrated settings, which is highlighted by the current interest in conductive education. While great strides have been made since the passing of the 1970 Education (Handicapped Children) Act, particularly in the area of providing a structured and progressive curriculum, there is still a long way to go, and it is hard to see the momentum being maintained in the current climate. Potentially, both the Education Reform Act and recent government initiatives on teacher training will lead to a neglect of the specific educational needs of this group, and they will neither receive the specialist teachers they desperately need nor be educated alongside their non-handicapped peers.

Teacher Training

The last five years of the 1980s will have seen a radical change in the training of teachers for work with children with multiple handicaps. While there has never been a specific recognized qualification for working with the group, during the 1980s a good many teachers graduated from three or four year specialist initial training courses for those wishing to work with children with severe learning difficulties and some, at least, of those courses included work with multiply handicapped children. However, these courses, together with similar ones for the teaching of visually and hearing impaired children, which were also relevant, are being phased out to be replaced by an expansion of one year post-experience courses funded under the new Grant Related In-service Training arrangements.

Under these arrangements more responsibility for INSET is devolved both on to LEAs and thence on to individual schools. However, the DES sets National Priority Areas on an annual basis which attract a higher rate of grant. There are some positive aspects to this new system. At the school level some schools, identifying their own needs, arrange for all staff to receive training in some aspect of multiple handicap. At national level DES guidelines for one year diploma courses include specific reference to the education of children with profound and multiple learning difficulties, and there is at least one course designed to train teachers of children with multiple handicaps. However, there are also considerable difficulties: *annual* setting of priority areas makes it difficult for either LEAs or course providers to have long-term plans, and with the introduction of the national curriculum, it seems at least possible that priority may go to training teachers for this to the detriment of those children to whom it is not seen as applicable. Furthermore, training via the INSET route exacerbates the problem of providing access to courses for relatively small groups such as teachers of children with multiple handicaps. Unlike initial students, many teachers already in post have family and personal commitments which make it very difficult for them to undertake residential courses, and daily travelling distances may be prohibitive in some areas.

Most recently the Green Paper on Qualified Teacher status with its proposal for the introduction of 'licensed' teachers particularly threatens the quality of education for children with profound and multiple learning difficulties. Classes for these children are especially difficult to staff and already have a disproportionate number of unqualified teachers (Evans and Ware, 1987). Licensing could well exacerbate this situation, as hard-pressed headteachers and LEAs attempt to staff the schools. On the other hand, if the proposed in-service training for licensed teachers is of high quality and carefully planned and monitored, this new initiative may provide a much needed route for able nursery nurses currently employed as assistants to receive the necessary additional training to move from assistant to teacher status. Licensing may also indirectly threaten one year specialist INSET courses, since it will create a potentially anomalous situation where someone with no professional qualifications can be employed in the same post as a highly skilled teacher.

The Education Reform Act

Many of the implications of the Education Reform Act for the education of children with multiple handicaps have already been discussed in previous sections. It has also been suggested above that some of the most profound effects will be mediated through the availability (or rather the potential lack of availability) of resources for training teachers of this group. Arguably the Green Paper on Qualified Teacher status is at least in part a response to the staffing needs created by the introduction of the national curriculum and the recent political history of education.

Other provisions within the Act are also likely to have an effect on children with special needs, with the provisions concerning local financial management, opting out, and the national curriculum with its associated assessment procedures being likely to combine to make real integration within the mainstream more difficult.

In this context, it is hard to be anything other than extremely pessimistic about the future of education for children with multiple handicaps. Indeed it may not be exaggerating to suggest that in the 1990s and 2000s they may once again be both segregated from their peers and catered for by unqualified and untrained staff.

Yet within this bleak scenario there are some rays of hope. We are much less sanguine than once we were about the ability of institution-based training courses to change classroom practice. As a consequence the importance of evaluating such courses in terms of the effects on schools and children is much more widely acknowledged and this is leading to more useful courses. Researchers are also much more aware of the need to disseminate their findings in a form which is usable to practitioners. There are teachers of extremely high quality and commitment in SLD schools, who will continue to demand additional training in educating multiply handicapped children.

Finally, perhaps most encouraging of all, while the heady optimism of the early 1970s may be gone forever, it has been replaced not only by a realization of the complexity and enormity of the task but, as I hope this chapter has demonstrated, by a growing volume of relevant research and good practice which will enable us to proceed, albeit extremely slowly, towards an education system which meets the needs of even the most handicapped children.

References

AGER, A.K. (1985) 'The MICROMATE project: using a microcomputer in teaching people with severe mental handicaps', *Mental Handicap 13*, pp. 62–4.

AGER, A.K. (1986) 'The Role of Microcomputers in Teaching Mentally Retarded Individuals', in BERG, J.M. and DE JONG, J.M. (Eds) *Science and Service in Mental Retardation*, London, Methuen.

BILLINGE, R. (1988) 'The objectives model of curriculum development: a creaking bandwagon?', *Mental Handicap 16(1)*, pp. 26–9.

BLEEKER-WAGEMAKERS (1984) 'Visual Impairment in the Mentally Retarded', in DOBBING, J. *et al.* (Eds) *Scientific Studies in Mental Retardation*, London, RSM-MacMillan.

BORKOWSKI, J.G. and CAVANAUGH, J.C. (1979) 'Maintenance and generalisation of skills and strategies by the retarded', in ELLIS, N.R. (Ed.) *Handbook of Mental Deficiency: Psychological Theory and Research*, Hillsdale, New Jersey, Lawrence Erlbaum Associates, pp. 699–726.

BRIMER, M.A. and DUNN, L.M. (1963) *English Picture Vocabulary Tests*, London, National Foundation for Educational Research.

BROWN, A.L. and CAMPIONE, J.C. (1977) 'Training Strategic Study Time Apportionment in Educable Retarded Children', *Intelligence 1*, pp. 94–107.

BROWN, F., HOLVOET, J., GUESS, D. and MULLIGAN, M. (1980) 'The individualized curriculum sequencing model 111: small group instruction', *Journal of the Association of the Severely Handicapped 5*, pp. 352–67.

BUDD, B. and EVANS, E. (1977) 'What is their future? An Experimental Project in Conductive Education with the Multiply Handicapped', *Apex 4(2)*, pp. 18–22.

BURLAND, R. (1969) 'The Development of Verbal Regulation of Behaviour in Cerebral Palsied Multiply Handicapped Children', *Journal of Mental Subnormality 15*, pp. 85–9.

BURMAN, L., FARRELL, P., FEILER, A., HEFFERNAN, J., MITTLER, H. and REASON, R. (1983) 'Redesigning the School Curriculum', *Special Education: Forward Trends, 10(2)*.

CHANDLER, L.S. and ADAMS, M.A. (1972) 'Multiply Handicapped Child Motivated for Ambulation through Behaviour Modification', *Physical Therapy 52*, pp. 399–401.

CLARKE, A.D.B., HERMELIN-FLIESS, B. (1955) 'Adult imbeciles, their abilities and trainability', *Lancet 2*, pp. 337–9.

COLVIN, G.T. and HORNER, R.H. (1983) 'Experimental analysis of generalisation: an evaluation or a general case programme for teaching motor skills to severely handicapped learners', in HOGG, J. and MITTLER, P. (Eds) *Advances in Mental Handicap Research Vol. 2*, Wiley.

COTTAM, P., MCCARTNEY, E. and CULLEN, C. (1985) 'The effectiveness of conductive education principles with profoundly retarded multiply handicapped children', *British Journal of Disorders of Communication 20*, pp. 45–60.

COTTON, E. (1965) 'The Institute for Movement Therapy and School for Conductors, Budapest, Hungary', *Developmental Medicine and Child Neurology 7*, pp. 437–46.

EDUCATION ACT, 1981, London, HMSO.

EDUCATION (HANDICAPPED CHILDREN) ACT, 1970, London, HMSO.

EDUCATION REFORM ACT, 1988, London, HMSO.

ELLIS, D. (Ed.) (1986) *Sensory Impairments in Mentally Handicapped People*, London, Croom Helm.

ELLIS, D. (1986) 'The Epidemiology of Visual Impairment in People with a Mental Handicap', in ELLIS, D. (Ed.) *Sensory Impairments in Mentally Handicapped People*, London, Croom Helm.

FOXEN, T. and MCBRIEN, J. (1981) *The EDY In-Service Course for Mental Handicap Practitioners: Training Staff in Behavioural Methods*, Manchester, Manchester University Press.

FRIEDLANDER, S.A., MCCARTHY, J.J. and SOFORENKO, A.Z. (1967) 'Automated psychological evaluation with severely retarded institutionalized infants', *American Journal of Mental Deficiency 71*, pp. 909–19.

GLENN, S. and CUNNINGHAM, C. (1984) 'Selective auditory preferences and the use of automated equipment by severely, profoundly and multiply handicapped children', *Journal of Mental Deficiency Research 28*, pp. 281–96.

GOLD, M.W. (1975) 'Factors affecting production by the retarded: base rate', *Mental Retardation*, London, Methuen.

GUNZBERG, H.C. (1966) *The Primary Progress Assessment Chart of Social and Personal Development*, SEFA Publications, Stratford-upon-Avon.

HASKETT, J. and HOLLAR, W.D. (1978) 'Sensory Reinforcement and Contingency Awareness of Profoundly Retarded Children', *American Journal of Mental Deficiency 83*, pp. 60–68.

HEGARTY, J.R. (1975) 'Teaching machines for the severely retarded: A review', *British Journal of Mental Subnormality 21*, pp. 103–14.

HOGG, J., FOXEN, T. and MCBRIEN, J. (1981) 'Issues in training and evaluation of behaviour modification skills for staff working with profoundly retarded multiply-handicapped children', *Behavioural Psychotherapy 9*, pp. 345–57.

HORNER, R.D. and KEILITZ, I. (1975) 'Training mentally retarded adolescents to brush their teeth', *Journal of Applied Behaviour Analysis 8*, pp. 301–9.

HOTTE, R.A., MONROE, H.J., PHILBROOD, D.L. and SCARLATA, R.W. (1984) 'Programming for Persons with Profound Mental Retardation: A Three-Year Retrospective Study', *Mental Retardation 22*, pp. 75–8.

HUGHES, J. (1975) 'The educational needs of the mentally handicapped', *Educational Research 17(3)*, pp. 228–33.

HYVARINEN, L. and LINDSTEDT, E. (1981) *Assessment of Vision of Children*, Stockholm, S.R.F. Tal and Punkt.

KELLEHER, A. and MULCAHY, M. (1986) 'Patterns of Disability in the Mentally Handicapped', in BERG, J.M. and DE JONG, J.M. (Eds) *Science and Service in Mental Retardation*, London, Methuen.

KIERNAN, C. (1985) 'Behaviour modification', in CLARKE, A.M., CLARKE, A.D.B. and BERG, J.M. (Eds) *Mental Deficiency: the Changing Outlook*, 4th ed., London, Methuen.

LEEMING, K., SWANN, W., COUPE, J. and MITTLER, P. (1979) *Teaching Language and Communication to the Mentally Handicapped* (Schools Council Curriculum Bulletin 8), London, Evans/Methuen Educational.

MCBRIEN, J.A. and FOXEN, T.H. (1978) 'A Pyramid Model of Staff Training in Behavioural Methods: The EDY Project', in HOGG, J. and MITTLER, P. (Eds) *Staff Training in Mental Handicap*, London, Croom Helm.

MCBRIEN, J.A. and FOXEN, T.H. (1981) *The EDY In-Service Course for Mental Handicap Practitioners: Instructor's Handbook*, Manchester, Manchester University Press.

MCINNES, J.M. and TREFFREY, J.A. (1982) *Deaf-Blind Infants and Children*, Milton Keynes, Open University Press.

MARSHALL, A. (1967) *The Abilities and Attainments of Children Leaving Junior Training Centres*, London, NAMH.

MURPHY, R.J. and DOUGHTY, N.R. (1977) 'Establishment of controlled arm movements in profoundly retarded students using response contingent vibratory stimulation', *American Journal of Mental Deficiency 82,* pp. 238–45.

OUVRY, C. (1987) *Educating Children with Profound Handicaps*, Kidderminster, BIMH.

PORTER, J. (1986) 'Beyond a Simple Behavioural Approach', in COUPE, J. and PORTER, J. (Eds) *The Education of Children with Severe Learning Difficulties*, London, Croom Helm.

PRESLAND, J. (1980) 'Educating "Special Care" Children: A Review of the Literature', *Educational Research 23* 1, pp. 20–38.

REMINGTON, R., FOXEN, T. and HOGG, J. (1977) 'Auditory Reinforcement in Profoundly Retarded Multiply Handicapped Children', *American Journal of Mental Deficiency 82*, pp. 299–304.

SANDLER, A.G. and MCLAIN, S.C. (1987) 'Sensory Reinforcement: Effects of Response-Contingent Vestibular Stimulation on Multiply Handicapped Children', *American Journal of Mental Deficiency 91*, pp. 373–8.

SEBBA, J. (1986) 'Staff Training to Meet the Future Needs of People with Multiple Impairments', in SEGAL, S. (Ed.) *Severe Mental Handicap: Training in a Changing World*, Bulmershe Publication No. 7, Bulmershe College of Higher Education, Earley, Reading.

SEMENOVA, K. and MASTUKOVA, E. (1974) 'On the Conductive Education of Children with Cerebral Palsy in the Hungarian People's Republic' (translated A. Sutton, 1984), *Defectologia 2*, pp. 93–5.

SIMPSON, P.F. (1967) 'Training Centres — a challenge', *Special Education 56*, p. 338.

STAINBACK, W. and STAINBACK, S. (1983) 'A Review of Research on the Education of Profoundly Retarded Persons', *Education and Training of the Mentally Retarded 18* 2, pp. 90–100.

STOLZ, S.B. (1981) 'Adoption of innovations from applied behavioural research: "Does anybody care?"', *Journal of Applied Behaviour Analysis 14*, pp. 491–505.

STURMEY, F. and CRISP, T. (1986) 'Classroom Management', in COUPE, J. and PORTER, J. (Eds) *The Education of Children with Severe Learning Difficulties: Bridging the Gap between Theory and Practice*, London, Croom Helm.

SUTTON, A. (1984) 'Conductive Education in the Midlands, Summer 1982: progress and problems in the importation of an educational method', *Educational Studies 19*, pp. 121–30.

SWITZSKY, H.N., HAYWOOD, H.C. & ROTATORI, A.F. (1982) 'Who are the severely and profoundly retarded?', *Education and Training of the Mentally Retarded* Vol. 174, pp. 268–72.

WALLWORK, A.S. (1986) *Chance or Choice? — Can students with profound and very severe learning difficulties express preferences by activating switches?*, unpublished M.Ed. Thesis, University of Exeter.

WARNOCK, M. (1978) *Special Educational Needs: Report of the Committee of Enquiry into the Education of Handicapped Children and Young People*, London, HMSO.

WILSON, M. (1981) *The Curriculum in Special Schools*, London, Schools Council.

WOOD, S. and SHEARS, B. (1986) *Teaching Children with Severe Learning Difficulties: A radical reappraisal*, London, Croom Helm.

WOODS, P. and PARRY, R. (1981) 'Pethna: Tailor-made Toys for the severely retarded and multiply handicapped', *Apex 9(2)*, pp. 53–6.

YORK, J., NIETUPSKI, J. and HEMRE-NIETUPSKI, S. (1985) 'A Decision-Making Process for Using Microswitches', *Journal of the Association of Persons with Severe Handicaps 10*, pp. 214–23.

Chapter 12

Children with Speech and Language Difficulties

Jenny Feinmann

Surveys of the prevalance of language disorders in children are reviewed by Webster and McConnell (1987). Estimates vary considerably but these authors conclude about 5 per cent of children enter school with some communication difficulties, with about one in a thousand having severe and persistent difficulties. Several studies have shown that boys outnumber girls in a ratio of almost 3:1 (Robertson, 1987).

There are about ten special schools and over 200 language units for children with speech and language difficulties in England and Wales, the development of this provision representing one of the largest growth areas in special education in recent times. However, the available provision still falls short of estimates of children with needs in this area. This chapter will consider how these children are identified and how pressure on the limited available provision has helped to define the characteristics of this heterogeneous group. Factors affecting how these children's needs are met will be illustrated with case-studies. Some teaching methods will also be described. The assessment of children learning English as a foreign language will be considered and finally some implications of the 1988 Education Reform Act will be raised.

The Classification of Speech and Language Difficulties

As descriptions of normal language development have evolved so our understanding and definition of language disorder has been shaped (see Colmar and Bennett, 1988, for an overview). The main processes of language involve understanding what is said and making oneself understood. Although speech production is centrally involved in making oneself understood it is not a language process as such, but an integral part of communication. These various processes develop in stages and in relation to one another.

Furthermore, a problem in one area is likely to effect not only the expressive and receptive abilities of the child but also most areas of the child's development, so pervasive is the influence of language development (Mogford, 1989).

When the first school opened for children with specific language difficulties in 1946 the terms receptive and expressive aphasia were commonly used because superficially the pupils' difficulty with language resembled some of the abnormalities suffered by people following a stroke or a brain injury. Developmental or congenital aphasia became something of a catch-all category to describe the syndrome in children where the language difficulty could not be attributed to known injury, hearing impairment, mental deficiency, motor deficiency or severe personality disorder.

However, children with language difficulties are a hugely heterogeneous group. Even when the term aphasia was dropped in favour of the less specific 'developmental language disorder' it soon became clear that this term was inadequate. Many children may have needs in the area of language development but provision for children with speech and language disorders is scarce. Because of this there is an increasing demand for a clear understanding as to which children would most benefit from attendance at a language unit. To ensure only those children with a specific language disorder are admitted, units need an admission policy. Statement of need in the area of language development cannot be the only criteria for admission to the highly specialized language units. Most language units are established within infant and junior schools because it is commonly believed that with early attention children's difficulties can be resolved before they are due to begin secondary school. For administrators of language units, often faced with a long waiting list of possible candidates, it would be very helpful to have clear criteria to form the basis of selection. Using these they would hope to be able predict, from the abilities of a child on entry, for how long the place would be needed and to plan appropriate provision for children who would be likely to have continuing difficulties. At present there is sometimes a reluctance to place children in language units who are likely to have persistent difficulties because they will take up a place for too long (ICAN Guidelines, 1988). The alternatives provision for children with less transient difficulties might be one of the few special schools for children with language disabilities, but if such provision is not available locally this may have to be on a residential basis. In these cases the social and emotional needs of the child have to be weighed very carefully against the benefits that might be gained in terms of the child's language development to justify such a drastic and expensive course of action.

A survey of speech and language units carried out by Hutt and Donlon (1987) found considerable variation in the admission criteria for the units they surveyed. As a result, the Invalid Children's Aid Nationwide (ICAN), a charitable organization responsible for several independent special schools, produced guidelines for units for primary school children with specific speech and language disorders. In setting out the selection criteria they make it clear that certain children with language impairments clearly associated with other disabilities such as hearing loss, learning difficulties, autism, behavioural/ emotional problems and physical disabilities should not be admitted unless they have a primary language disorder. Those whose first language is not English as well as those showing moderate delays caused by lack of early stimulation should also be excluded. ICAN provides a categorization of specific language difficulties. In their scheme specific language disorders are described as being either developmental or acquired. The guidelines suggest four broad, exhaustive although not mutally exclusive categories: phonological/grammatical problems (a distinction is made between receptive disorders and those with both receptive and expressive difficulties to make two separate categories), articulatory disorders, and semantic/pragmatic disorders.

Expressive Phonological/Grammatical Disorders

These are recognized in children who can often imitate individual sounds in isolation but are unable to sequence sounds correctly to produce recognizable words. The difficulty may extend to whole words which are produced in the wrong order or omitted altogether. Often the child's expression is very idiosyncratic, inconsistent and therefore difficult to understand. The more subtle and less information-loaded syntactical structures (such as auxiliary verbs, the plural 's', pronouns, etc.) are often omitted or confused producing telegrammatic sentences such as: 'Me come play swing.' Grammatical rules may be overgeneralized: 'We buyed crisps.' Sometimes these errors are typical of those made by young children but in children with phonological/grammatical problems they tend to persist. The terms deviant and immature have been used to distinguish the language patterns of some children. Frequent attacks of tip-of-the-tongue phenomenon or word-finding difficulty is also a common problem.

Receptive Phonological/Gramatical Disorders

These involve the same processes as above but here the difficulty lies in the child's understanding of individual sounds, words and sentences. To be certain that the problem is not due to a hearing impairment may in practice be difficult. Before the technological advancements in audiological assessments and the introduction of more sophisticated hearing aids many children were placed in special schools for the language-impaired with a diagnosis of receptive aphasia. On later examination many were found to have a significant hearing loss (Rosenburg, 1966). Word deafness, congenital auditory imperception and central deafness are terms which have been used to describe the apparently inconsistent responses children gave in successive audiological examinations and in their everyday reactions to sound. Nevertheless there are some children who do have a specific difficulty in correctly interpreting speech sounds, word order and inflectional endings, for instance, as well as the more subtle messages conveyed by intonation and situation. The child with a receptive/grammatical disorder struggles to make sense of literal interpretations. Metaphor, implied meanings, sarcasm and jokes are rarely appreciated and often misunderstood.

Articulatory Disorders

These may restrict speech production by interfering with the coordination of lips, tongue, palate and breathing necessary to produce clear speech. An impairment may be mild, such as a persistent lisp which would be normal in a younger child, or so severe, as in the case or children with supra-bulbar palsy whose speech apparatus is permanently paralyzed, that they may never achieve intelligibility except to those closest to them and then only within a limited vocabulary. Many children with articulatory defects also have limited expressive ability in that the content of their speech is simple and restricted (Whitacre *et al.*, 1970). It is arguable that the quality of discourse open to the partially intelligible child is so limited that they may not develop higher language skills at all. This view is supported by the evidence of Wells (1981), who shows the importance of successful reciprocal communication in the interactions that take place between the language learner and competent language users. Alternatively, it may be that children with articulatory disorders restrict themselves to the bare essentials of communication, the high information carrying words for instance, knowing that much of what they say will not be understood (Shriner *et al.*, 1969).

Semantic/Pragmatic Difficulties

These make up the final category in the ICAN guidelines. This recently recognized disorder of language use is particularly confusing because, in contrast to the other groups, the children produce a wealth of language, often quite complex in structure (Rapin and Allen, 1983). To enter into a conversation with a child who chatters on with only tangential regard to other contributions to the discourse, can be extremely frustrating. Not only do they hold forth with all sorts of irrelevances, they avoid eye contact and so miss many of the usual cues that indicate when it may be their turn to start or stop talking.

The four categories of language disorder suggested by ICAN are a useful frame of reference when broad descriptions of children with language difficulties are required. However, having so identified a child it does not necessarily follow that they will receive extra attention or even that they will be identified as having special educational needs.

The Development of Special Provision

The 1945 regulations following the 1944 Education Act recognized children with speech and language disorders as one of ten categories of handicap. Two years later the Invalid Children's Aid Association (now Invalid Children's Aid Nationwide: ICAN) opened Moor House School for children aged 5–16 with speech and language difficulties. By 1977 about ten schools had been established, two by local education authorities, with 433 pupils attending language units. Since the 1981 Education Act, provision for children with speech and language difficulties has continued to flourish. Surprisingly this growth has taken place during a period of time when many local authority special education departments were looking to reduce the number of children attending special provision in an effort to follow the spirit of the Act and meet needs within the ordinary schools. Why is it then that new language units were opening at the rate of seven or eight each term between 1983 and 1986? There are several factors which taken together may account for this.

The new procedures for referrring children to special education encourages parents to express their views and many are supported by various voluntary agencies such as AFASIC (the Association for All Speech Impaired Children) which not only increase public awareness of children with language disabilities but also lobby local authorities to provide appropriate facilities. There is also a greater emphasis on multi-disciplinary involvement in the assessment and treatment of children with special needs particularly with very young children. Many health authorities have established child development centres and children with difficulties are being identified at a much earlier stage in their development. The health authorities have a duty to alert the education departments to the possibility of children as young as 2 years old as having special educational needs and parents who are used to attending special centres with the their pre-school children expect this special help to continue when they start school.

Although the medical advice is still coordinated by the clinical medical officers there is greater opportunity for speech therapists to contribute directly by alerting the education authorities to a child's special needs and by writing reports which are then included in the advice gathered for the assessment. For many the concern is that they should continue to receive speech therapy.

The ethos of meeting special needs within the ordinary schools encourages all teachers to take responsibility for those who may have special needs and many education authorities have tried to help through the allocation of some additional resources such as non-teaching assistants to individual children as their needs arise. To some extent this may have encouraged referrals. However, there comes a time when the most economical use of resources is to pool the provision in one school or unit.

Such a practice has led to the establishment of language units within ordinary schools. Such provision carries with it the possibility of the children integrating with their peers at least for some of the time and is also in line with the new thinking. In addition the practice is much more acceptable to many parents than a placement in a special school. Furthermore, housing the new units presents little problem since the decline in pupil numbers across the country has left many empty classrooms. Once established, unit places are always much in demand, although making appropriate staffing arrangements is not always so straightforward; neither is the integration of the unit into the host school always easy. To organize a language unit around the children's linguistic, social educational needs required the skills of both an experienced teacher and a speech therapist. The ideal person has training in both areas but, nationally, training opportunities are very limited with trained teacher-therapists thinly spread throughout the country. New units are opening each year but while there is still only limited provision the child's degree of language disability is rarely the sole factor to be considered in the process of identification and assessment.

Identification and Assessment

The restrictive nature of most tools designed to assess a child's language development is now well recognized (see Webster and McConnell (1987) for a review of tests). Nevertheless it probably is useful to gauge some idea of which grammatical structures a child has mastered, how far their vocabulary extends, whether they have word finding difficulties and which sounds they can produce. This information usually forms the basis of a speech therapist's assessment. Equally, the educational psychologist's assessment will be expected to show that the child's problem with language development is not part of a more generalized development delay. However, observations of children's ability to use language for the purpose of communicating something which is of importance to them are much more significant in assessing the extent of the problem. This applies to both verbal and written language.

As the study of language development has turned to an interest in pragmatics, that is how language is actually used, so practitioners working with language disabled children have become more concerned with what has become known as their communicative competence. To this I would add another dimension – that of confidence. By the age of 7, most children both use and understand all but the most complex grammatical structures in the English language. To this foundation they add vocabulary and as their metalinguistic skills develop they can enjoy playing with language, through puns and jokes, for instance. Young children are less sophisticated in their language use but nevertheless through redundancy in language together with the tolerance of inaccuracy that comes with the general understanding that children are language novices, young children are encouraged to gain a good deal of communicative competence and indeed confidence. In this way they are driven to communicate and thus through experience gradually improve their skills.

Unless the child has an obvious speech impairment, the effects of language disability may be quite subtle. Language disabled children, in spite of their often very poor linguistic skills, may nonetheless have the sort of personality that encourages them to persist in communicative exchanges even though they may not be fully understood. They may use all the non-verbal strategies available to them both to understand and to make their intentions clear. Some children may be such good copers that they do not appear to have any special needs and may well continue without any extra help throughout their early school years. Even very young children can make some adaptations and allowances for their less language competent peers. However, problems may arise when the language disabled child is unable to prolong interactions initiated by others, negotiate terms, and so on. A game of chase, for example, is easy to join in and requires little verbal interaction, but these sort of games with often fairly random beginnings develop rules which are negotiated by the participants. At this stage the language disabled child may be unable to participate and either continues to act fairly randomly, incurring the wrath of his colleagues, or opts out as the situation becomes too confusing.

As children progress through the early years of education, teachers expect pupils to understand increasingly lengthy and complex instructions. However, it may not be until demands are made upon literacy skills that the difficulties encountered by some children are recognized. While the effects of phonological/grammatical problems on the reading process may seem predictable, it is not always appreciated that children with articulatory difficulties also have difficulty in learning to read. The reasons for this are the subject of investigation at present. It may be that phonic disability somehow interferes with the development of fluency skills in the reading process (Stackhouse, 1989). Even so, some children with undetected or partially resolved language difficulties do progress through the early stages of reading relying on a good visual memory to help both with reading and spelling. The term hyperlexia has been used to describe some children who can 'bark' at print with little idea as to the content; much the opposite of those children sometimes referred to as dyslexic. The latter group, through their obvious lack of reading ability, gain much more attention than their hyperlexic classmates who may progress into secondary schooling before their limited ability becomes noticeable.

Let us consider a child who has receptive language difficulties. These may be completely obvious in that the child looks blank, responds inappropriately or, in rare cases, asks for clarification. However, except in the artificial situation of the formal administration of a test specifically designed to tap a child's comprehension difficulties, most communication takes place in a context which is often so familiar to the child that it becomes a routine. Familiarity between the communicating individuals leads to joint expectations and often subconscious adaptations to their communicative needs. Take, for instance, the example of John during his first term in a reception class of an ordinary school. PE lessons are timetabled twice a week. At the end of each lesson the children are asked to sit on the floor before lining up to leave the room. Often the boys are asked to line up first but on this occasion the instruction is 'Girls, line up'. John stands, looks around, then promptly sits down again as he realizes that all the other boys are still sitting. Later, John brings his teacher a daisy-chain he has made. 'That's lovely, John,' she says. 'Put it on the table over there.' John does as he is told and goes to his desk. John's behaviour in class was being observed because there was concern about his expressive language difficulties. He rarely spoke and when he did it was in a whisper and mostly in imitation. There was no concern about his understanding because he fitted well into the classroom routine — the most obvious difficulty was his failure to speak. In fact, John had quite severe comprehension difficulties, but gave the appearance of understanding because he made such good use of context cues while his teacher and the other children had adapted to his needs. His teacher was amazed to see herself on video giving many non-verbal cues. To return to the earlier example, 'Put it on the table *over there*' was accompanied by both hand and eye pointing. The other children had also adapted to John's difficulties so that when their teacher gave the class an instruction they would ensure John carried it out.

From situations such as these it can be seen how the extent of a child's understanding may be misjudged, particularly if, like John, the child is quite, obliging, and good humoured enough to attract helpful attention from both the adults and children around him. To complete the story, there was no language unit provision in the small town where John lived so he was placed for a period of observation in a school primarily for children with physical disabilities. Like so many schools of this genre children were admitted because they were difficult to place elsewhere.

There is obviously an interaction between children's linguistic skills and their communicative competence. While a degree of incompetence may be tolerated in a younger child, a persistent lack of communicative skill together with the increased expectations placed on older children may alter their behaviour to the extent that they become withdrawn or at the other extreme become difficult to manage. The level of a child's maturity may be judged by their language competence and older less proficient users may appear very immature, a quality likely to isolate them from their peers and attract criticism from their teachers.

David, aged 14, was referred to an educational psychologist because of his strange behaviour. His classmates were beginning to ridicule him and his teachers were concerned that he was becoming increasingly unhappy. In class he would flap his hands when he wanted to say something but he had tremendous difficulty contributing to a class discussion. In comparison to his classmates he appeared very immature, often laughing rather hysterically. He would talk endlessly about horse-racing about which he had gathered detailed knowledge. In this way, perhaps, he had managed to fend off the sort of attention which might have revealed his difficulties. The headteacher described the day David had been asked to collect his lunch from the cafeteria. 'I'll have anything except pizza,' the head had said. David produced a tray with baked beans and chips. 'But I want more than that!' the head said, rather surprised, since this meal lacked the main dish. David duly returned with more beans and chips, taking what the head had said quite literally. Because David was such a strange lad who was likely to burst into tears if he felt criticized, he was mainly humoured and interactions such as these would go by without much consideration as to the cause of such odd behaviour. It may seem surprising that David should reach the age of 14 before his difficulties were severe enough to attract attention and investigation. One explanation might be that his academic attainments were adequate enough for him to go unnoticed in the bottom set. His teachers reported he could read and write and that there were many pupils with greater difficulty. David had indeed mastered the art of the simple sentence. His work was neat and well spelt but the content repetitive and very simple. His reading ability was a classic example of hyperlexia discussed above in that he could read quite complicated passages but answer only the most basic questions.

David stayed at his comprehensive school for the remainder of his secondary education where all his teachers were informed of his difficulties and asked to carry out a programme to encourage him to improve his social skills and in a sensitive manner to point out situations where he was obviously not understanding. Demonstration and role play were used to help David practise the appropriate responses.

John and David are but two examples of children who certainly had specific language difficulties but were not placed in special provision catering specifically for this group. As is often the case for all children with special needs, assessment and placement decisions will be influenced by factors such as age, personality, educational setting and parental wishes together with the availability of provision.

Special Schools for Language Disabled Children

What do special schools for language disabled children offer, and are residential placements for very young children really justified? The majority of the schools are run by independent organizations and are therefore free to employ speech therapists who are able to specialize in this area. The potential for teachers and speech therapists to work together is much greater when both are employed full time in the same establishment. As these schools are so specialized and may be recognized as centres of excellence in the education of language disabled children many of their staff are either teacher/therapists or teachers with specialist training in this area. Much of the available literature on the education of language disabled children has been produced by the staff from the longer established schools maintained by ICAN. A description of one school's curriculum is detailed in a book by Hutt (1986). As well as the special schemes developed for literacy and numeracy, some, such as the John Lea Colour Pattern Scheme (1970), have been published separately. Hutt also summarizes their approaches to art and craft, drama, and music and movement. Within such an environment the child is urged to communicate through every medium. For many their non-verbal attempts to express themselves may be augmented through the use of sign language. Paget-Gorman Signed Speech (PGSS, formally The Paget-Gorman Sign System) is chosen in preference to British Sign Language of the hearing impaired because semantically it exactly matches English. Within a limited but constantly growing vocabulary there is a sign for every word. All tenses, plurals, prefixes and suffixes are meticulously indicated although in practice one would rarely find a pupil, or teacher using the system at such a high level of sophistication. For many years The Paget-Gorman Society, now under the auspices of ICAN, has protected the system from the development of local dialects or unauthorized adaptations. There is no doubt that sign language is a very useful tool for encouraging communication not only amongst those whose speech is unintelligible but also for those who have difficulty remembering words they want to use. It is also useful in helping such children in the general organization of their speech. Through this approach children are helped towards fluent reading as they discover that signing acts as a prompt and helps them to 'find' the words as they read aloud. This function of sign language seems to persist even as the children acquire quite good speech. I have observed a group of adolescent severely language disabled children in conversation and noticed that their hand movements often contain roughly produced signs accentuating the main points. Although these youngsters will deny that they still use sign language these remnants of the system on which they were once so dependent do seem to serve the dual purpose of helping others to understand what they are saying and in some way serving as prompts to their own speech.

There is little doubt that sign language does help many language disabled children to make themselves understood often for the first time and there is rarely the concern that it will interfere with the development of speech, a problem which has plagued the pedagogists of the hearing impaired. However, the commitment of the whole school staff, parents and non-teaching assistants, is required if the child is to have the freedom of expression which is so essential for the development of communication skills. Many language units have some staff who can use a system proficiently but for the most part there are so few children who need such a sign-saturated environment that it is unrealistic to expect the adults involved to learn a system which they may rarely practice.

There is no doubt that most pupils attending the special schools for language disabled children have achieved excellent results with many managing to pass several CSEs not only in the more practical subjects but also in maths and even science. The Mode 3 CSE syllabus allowed enough flexibility for these pupils to achieve reasonable grades. There were few demands for original written presentations so the rather stilted language produced by the pupils mattered little when they were able to present thick files of diagrams and drawing together with magazine pictures and articles to illustrate their interest and understanding of the main themes in, for example, the Science At Work course (Addison-Wesley, 1981). Unfortunately, these pupils have more difficulty in following the GCSE courses to the same extent since the adaptations for the less able pupils are not so suitable. Records of Achievement based on unit credit schemes do, however, present other opportunities for pupils to leave school with concise details of the skills they have acquired.

Integration

Teachers of children with specific language disorders are often faced with a dilemma when considering the integration of pupils in an ordinary school. Critics of special schools and language units will point out the poor language models and suggest the children should spend more time with their able communicating peers. Children whose language is impoverished through lack of stimulation and those who have achieved a certain level of communicative competence and confidence may well benefit from exposure to a language rich environment but language development is not always enhanced in this way. Children with a specific language disability will only improve their skills if they are able to communicate. For some this may require the language environment to be limited in such a way as to ensure the child is able both to understand and be understood. Given a free choice children will tend to gather with others at a similar stage of language development. In the playground, for instance, children from a language unit are often found together or with younger children rather than with their age peers from the mainstream classrooms. This applies even when the unit children spend a good deal of time in the mainstream; so teachers need to be alert to the children's level of skill as communicators before recommending a programme of integration.

There are children who enter special schools during their infant years and complete their education within the mainstream. For some whose communicative confidence if not competence has reached a level where they can cope this transition may not take place until the lower secondary school stage. However, in common with other all age special schools, a good many children will spend most of their school years in the same establishment amongst the same rather limited number of pupils. For those who have to board, this can be a very closeted experience. Integration schemes with local schools are perhaps easier to set up when the special school is operating within the same local authority, but most, as I have noted, are privately run. Work experience and link-courses at local colleges have produced successful introductions to the outside world. However, these children often face enormous difficulties when they try to extend the use of skills they have learnt within the limited environment of the special school where people know them so well that they are rarely misunderstood.

The following passage is an extract from a piece written by a 15-year-old girl who had transferred to a special school as a day pupil from a junior school. Her expressive language difficulties could be described within the phonological/grammatical group (ICAN Guidelines, 1988). She left school aged 17 to attend a course for children with learning difficulties at a college of Further Education. She passed CSE in Science, Craft Design and Technology, and Art.

What it is like to have a speech difficulty

when I was little people used to make fun of me,
and I used to cry and get bad. when I meet marie, marie made
fun of me I cry and get mad when I talk to some one new
I talk to them to fast. and people did not understand me.
when I have to ask people for directions I get into a
muddle. when I meet people they think I came from a
different country.
when I go to work experience I never talk to them people
for 3 days. then I talk to them a bit.
when I go on the bus I talk loud chudred laugh at me.
but I don't care any more.
one day I went into a cake shop and the lady said
"what do you want?" I said
I want a bottle of milk.
The lady said
"what do you want" I said
"want bottle of milk". and the lady said
go away I have no time for silly children like you.
so I went home and I tell my mum about it.
my mum said "never mind, The lady is ignorant.

After one year at the college she was much enjoying herself and had gained a good deal of confidence although her language difficulties were far from resolved as illustrated by her comment 'Me talk anyone now!'

Helping Children in the Ordinary School

The whole school approach to teaching children with language disabilities as described by Hutt is practically impossible to effect within an ordinary school. Other authors have written specifically for teachers in the mainstream classes who may have individual pupils with language difficulties although the recommendations would apply equally well to the special school.

Beveridge and Conti-Ramsden (1987) described SCORE – a model for language teaching which they suggest may help teachers meet their pupils' communicative needs. SCORE stands for Situation, Contrasts, Order, Regularity and Encouragement. As the authors point out there is nothing particularly revolutionary about these five principles, which are intended to guide teachers in their programme planning for language disabled pupils. The same principles would hold good for most pupils with learning difficulties of any kind. Thus, the *situation* should be a natural communicative context for the child who should be encouraged to make meaning clear by an appreciation of the *contrasts* within a particular frame of reference. They may, for instance, overgeneralize the use of certain words. 'Dog', for example may be used to refer to most small animals with four legs. This may apply at the level of single sounds, between words themselves or at the phrase level. Thus children are taught to distinguish between 'pin' and 'bin', 'dog' and 'cat' and that you may 'pat a dog' or 'stroke a cat'.

Two considerations may help the teacher decide the *order* in which new language skills are taught. Taking a functional approach, the selection would be on the basis of what the child needs to know. Alternatively, they may adopt a developmental approach so children are introduced to new concepts in roughly the order that follows normal language development.

Regularity refers to the organization of the language environment so the adults are all aware of the child's abilities. Because they all have similar expectations of the child's performance, consistent feedback is given during the communicative exchanges that take place. To achieve this, adequate liaison between parents, teachers, therapists and assistants is very important.

The final principle of *encouragement* is self-explanatory. Language disordered children who have had many experiences of failing to make themselves understood or who have been embarrassed by misunderstandings often feel very vulnerable. A great deal of tact and sensitivity is required to encourage and prompt the child to communicate effectively.

Further advice on good practice for helping communication in the ordinary school is given by Webster and McConnell (1987). They also stress the importance of natural contexts and advise against the direct teaching of language skills, arguing that using published language schemes and contrived situations can lead the child into stereotyped responses which may be more correct in their form but less meaningful in their content. Language taught in this way is unlikely to be incorporated into a child's general language use.

The development of literacy skills is also discussed in both books. Some children, as we have already seen, do manage to decode text quite accurately albeit with little understanding. Others find it quite impossible to make any sense of the written word. For both groups the recommended approach is to encourage children to extract the meaning from text without necessarily decoding every word. This technique is similar to that adopted by confident, fluent readers and for this reason it is sometimes described as a 'top down' method. The process applies both to the beginner reader and to more advanced pupils. First, they are encouraged through shared reading to understand the structure of text and then to develop guesswork strategies using picture cues and story content, for instance, to augment any decoding strategies they may have such as initial letter recognition. Later they may be taught that text can be used to analyze, argue, describe, expose, instruct and express. An appreciation of these functions of written language may be helpful not only to encourage children to understand more complex text but also in the planning of their own communicative exchanges both written and verbal (Beveridge and Conti-Ramsden, 1987).

Children Learning English as a Second Language

A relatively recent consideration in the history of children with speech and language difficulties concerns children whose first language is not English. The issues surrounding the language development of children learning more than one language are too numerous and complex to discuss here in any detail.

There are many factors which must be taken into account in order to establish whether the multilingual child has a specific language difficulty in contrast to a more generalized learning difficulty, a hearing impairment, or is showing the effects of interference between the developing languages. The child's ability, personality, contact with English speakers outside school, school attendance and age at which English was introduced are but a few factors which must be considered when a child fails to develop English language skills in the expected way. For many, time will tell and experienced teachers of children learning English as a foreign language are familiar with normal rates of progress taking these factors into account. However, there are certain pointers which can help to establish if the difficulty is likely to be a specific problem with language development. Difficulties in the mother tongue are a major cause for concern, as is a family history of language difficulties, both of which indicate a need for early intervention. In almost every case if it can be established that the child appears to be developing normally in the first language then specific language impairment is highly unlikely. Such assessment is not always straightforward. The services of professionals with some proficiency in the child's mother tongue are invaluable but rarely available. Without such first hand assessment where necessary interviews with parents and children should involve interpreters to establish whether the child does have difficulty in the mother tongue. There is a great demand for interpreters in schools and they are involved in many and varied activities with little opportunity to develop a specialism. Their central role in the assessment of children with language impairments and other special needs calls for special training.

Implications of the 1988 Education Reform Act

The history of the education of children with language disabilities is relatively short but in the main has followed the path set by other groups. The concerns with identification, assessment and special school or unit placement are shared but unlike other disabilities the main effect on the child's development is mostly confined to the early years. For many children full integration will be achieved during or towards the end of their primary school years. However, while children return from language units to mainstream schools with their early language difficulties resolved to some extent, residual problems of memory and sequencing often remain which can severely effect their ability to develop numeracy and literacy skills beyond a very basic level. Their general personal organizational abilities may also be effected such that they may appear chaotic and unsettled. With the advent of the 1988 Education Reform Act what may the future hold for these children and their peers with even more severe and persisting difficulties in the special schools?

The difficulties presented by the English curriculum alone would take another chapter. A few illustrations from attainment target 1 (speaking and listening) will have to suffice. At the simplest level it is expected that pupils will be able to 'participate as speakers and listeners in group activities, including imaginative play . . . listen attentively and respond, to stories and poems . . . respond appropriately to simple instructions given by a teacher'. The examples include re-telling a story, role-play, and asking questions. These tasks not only make demands on expressive language skills but also require children to have a degree of confidence to perform in front of their peers. Given a small group and carefully controlled language input it may be possible for young language impaired children to meet these requirements in some form. The examples do suggest the children might draw a picture to illustrate a story or poem but they obviously need first to have understood the story or poem. Signing, symbols or lip-reading are acknowledged as *alternatives* to speaking and listening but the *augmentative* role of these systems is not mentioned.

The new regulations are optimistic in their expectations that all children including those with special needs should be included in the national curriculum. Within the attainment targets and programmes of study that have been produced to date there is certainly scope for teachers to make the necessary adaptation for language impaired children at least in the early stages. However the demands on children's language skills increase quite rapidly so that even at level 2 (average 7 years) the pupils are expected to cope with complex instructions involving three consecutive actions, for example: 'Write down the place in the classroom where you think your plant will grow best, find out what the others on your table think and try to agree on which is likely to be the best place.'

Clearly the task for teachers is not straightforward and there will be an increasing need for teachers to understand language development. This issue is highlighted by the national curriculum. In order to help pupils with language difficulties to achieve their full potential teachers themselves will need to devise the appropriate teacher based assessments both to monitor progress and develop method and content. Thus there are likely to be many calls for in-service training in this area.

Concluding Comment

This chapter has outlined the complex issues that children with speech and language difficulties present and has addressed some of the educational implications. The assessment of children with English as a second language and concerns brought about by the introduction of the national curriculum are also noted. If the needs of these children are to be met it will be necessary for much more speech therapy to be available preferably from qualified speech therapists, although substantial improvements could be made through the appropriate training of interested teachers. At the time of writing there are plans to establish a distance learning course based at Birmingham University to enable teachers to qualify as teachers of the language impaired. This move is to be welcomed and may herald the establishment of new peripatetic services such as those already maintained by most LEAs for children with hearing and visual impairments.

The issue of speech therapy provision and its role in the education service is currently being considered in the case of R. v. Lancashire County Council. There is potentially good news here since the Court of Appeal has agreed that speech therapy is an educational (as opposed to a medical) requirement. This decision is important since it has significant implications for provision that might be made under the 1981 Act's 'statementing' arrangements with all of the additional resources that would follow.

This case has been brought about largely as a result of parental pressure. The outcome represents a ray of hope for other parents who feel that their children's needs, in spite of the good intentions of teachers, are not being matched in terms of additional funding from the Government for resources and adequate in-service training for what are very complex teaching challenges. There is a parallel here to the pressure of the dyslexia lobby which has also made large gains in provision for their children many of whom will have had speech and language difficulties of a more general kind. There is a lesson here for all parents. What will be the next test case?

References

BEVERIDGE, M. and CONTI-RAMSDEN, G. (1987) *Children with Language Disabilities*, Open University Press.

COLMAR, S. and BENNETT, E. (1988) 'From Language to Languaging — An Historical Perspective of Language Research and Theory Relevant to EP Assessment Strategies', *Educational Psychology in Practice, 3*, pp. 4–10.

HUTT, E. and DONLAN, C. (1987) *Adequate Provision? A Survey of Language Units*, Invalid Children's Aid Association Nationwide.

ICAN (1988) *Units for Primary School Children With Speech and Language Disorders — Suggested guidelines*, Invalid Children's Aid Association Nationwide.

LEA, J. (1970) *Colour Pattern Scheme*, Oxted, Surrey: Moor House School.

RAPIN, I. and ALLEN, D. (1983) 'Developmental Language Disorders: Nostologic considerations', in KIRK, U. (Ed.) *Neuropsychology of Language, Reading and Spelling*, New York, Academic Press.

ROBERTSON, R.J. (1987) 'The Causes of Language Disorder: Introduction and Overview', in *Proceedings of the First International Symposium on Specific Speech and Language Disorders in Children*, Association For All Speech Impaired Children.

ROSENBURG, P.E. (1966) 'Misdiagnosis of children with auditory problems', *Journal of Speech and Hearing Disorders, 31*, pp. 279–83.

Science at Work (1981) London: Addison Wesley.

SHRINER, T.H., HOLLOWAY, M.S. and DANILOFF, R.G. (1969) 'The relationship between articulatory deficits and syntax in speech defective children', *Journal of Speech and Hearing Research, 12*, pp. 319–25.

STACKHOUSE, J. (1989) 'Relationship between spoken and written language disorders' in MOGFORD, K. and SADLER, S. (Eds) *Child Language Disability*, Multi-Lingual Matters Ltd. Clevedon. Philadelphia.

WEBSTER, A. and MCCONNELL, C. (1987) *Children With Speech and Language Disorders*, London, Cassell.

WELLS, G. (1891) *Language, Learning, and Education*, Windsor, NFER-Nelson.

WHITACRE, J.D., LUPER, H.C. and POLLIO, H.R. (1979) 'General language deficits in children with articulation problems', *Language and Speech*, **13**, pp. 231–9.

Chapter 13

Curriculum Support and the Continuum of Emotional and Behavioural Difficulties

Irene Bowman

Introduction

These are both exciting and dangerous times for schools. They are exciting because we are beginning to understand something about schools as social systems, about enabling the children and adults who comprise school communities to commit themselves to working towards working together, and about the importance of social and affective processes in the functioning of schools. They are dangerous times because the Education Reform Act 1988, fiscal policy and lack of support in the management of change, may pressure schools to give up the positive struggle to educate all pupils.

In particular, these are troubled times for those schools where pupils' personal and social needs are not being met and their potential for satisfactory involvement in learning remains unrecognized. For despite the apparently integrationist philosophy of the 1981 Education Act, its labelling of pupils as having emotional and behavioural difficulties seems to have legitimated emphasizing pupil defect rather than curriculum change. The intention apparently was to focus on difficulties which arise in the interaction between what the school requires of and provides for the pupil and what the pupil brings to and demands of the school. However, teachers are still mostly not sufficiently supported to enable them to do this as a consistent and positive problem management strategy within the curriculum. Now we find that the 1988 Education Reform Act does not even address the philosophy of integration. Rather, the Act implicitly demands that schools decide whether to be socially and educationally inclusive or exclusive.

There is no encouragement to adopt an inclusive policy. For example, neither extra finance nor staff seem about to be introduced to enable schools to support those pupils whose personal and social needs may make it very hard for them to engage with the demands made by their post-1988 curriculum entitlement. (I am not referring to temporary funds which are the result of a moral panic, as in the outcome of the Elton enquiry, but to permanent recognition of the need to fund inclusive policies.) On the contrary, it seems that the possibility of 'temporary' or more permanent disapplication from national curriculum requirements for such pupils, may tempt both schools and LEAs to provide segregated settings which (unintentionally?) deprive pupils of a broad and balanced curriculum.

So perhaps more than ever, schools require constructive curriculum encouragement. We need to affirm the positive discoveries made in the last ten years — for example, in the area of personal and social education, a mainstream curriculum development with tremendous potential across the continuum of emotional and behavioural difficulties. We need to say where we stand in relation to inclusive and exclusive education policies.

This chapter is meant simply as a contribution to the current debate about the implementation of the Education Reform Act, in particular the national curriculum. It shows my present thinking, rather than a finished product. The discussion focuses upon the issues raised above, and argues for a socially and educationally inclusive commitment. It attempts to indicate certain school-level hard decisions which have to be made explicitly rather than implicitly. But, especially, the chapter considers implications for building on what we know about positive social structure and emotional climate and personal and social education for all pupils, including the continuum of pupils considered to have special social and emotional needs. The question is raised: Is disapplication from national curriculum requirements really likely to help pupils — even in or especially in special schools for pupils labelled EBD (emotional and behavioural difficulties)?

Pro-social School Structure, Social Climate and the Education Reform Act

It is usually assumed that pupils labelled, formally or informally, EBD have unmet affective and social needs which unfavourably mediate learning experiences. In order to meet these needs, both Warnock and the 1981 Education Act recommend modifications to the social structure and emotional climate in which education takes place. The terms social structure, and emotional climate, were originally interpreted as those features of the school which conveyed hidden messages to pupils about their acceptability. These features included the rule and sanction system and the school's social norms, together with arrangements for pastoral care, and the school's relations with parents. Reviewing his and others' research on the effects of these features of school systems upon pupils, Galloway (1985) suggested that if social structure and emotional climate were unsuitable for the 20 per cent we could not assume that they were suitable for the other 80 per cent. How the whole school interacted with its pupils required examination and possibly restructuring in order to improve the educational experience of all pupils and to prevent school generated emotional and behavioural difficulties. Others were drawing attention to the same need to review the impact of school systems upon the wider school population. For example, in its report Improving Secondary Schools, the Hargreaves Committee (ILEA, 1984) argued that attention to hidden curricular messages had to be accompanied by a review of the formally offered curriculum — its content, phasing, methods and assessment. So in the mid-1980s the social organization of the curriculum, teaching methods, arrangements to meet personal and social educational needs and to recognize achievement, emerged as key factors in improving the educational experience of all pupils.

The importance of social structure and social climate, in the senses discussed above, has taken on new significance now that the Eduction Reform Act 1988 is being implemented. We have to asked whether its constraints and possibilities can be managed in such a way as to improve the personal and social education of all children and young persons, with the intention to prevent school-created emotional and behavioural difficulties and to help pupils whose difficulties are brought with them into school.

This is obviously a vast topic and the extent to which it is explored in the next few years depends upon whether LEA, school governors, headteacher, staff and parents commit the school to that intention and whether government contributes adequate funding and the conditions of service which might increase teacher morale and the supply of teachers. Much of our present understanding and hard data here come from school effectiveness studies and in particular the work of theorists in the area of disruption and alienation, such as Reynolds (1976) and Galloway (1983).

In addition, especially in some LEAS, a great expansion of curriculum innovation has been taking place in relation to personal and social education, both as timetabled curricula and as cross-curricular principles and methods. These two broad sources of information suggest that especially where there is rapid organizational change, and where there are multiple cultural and social class groups contributing to the school community, it may not be enough for a school to adopt a somewhat liberal or *laissez-faire* attitude to its social policy. Rather, the school may need to be positively *pro-social*; that is, to implement planned attempts to consider actively the social and political complexity of the school community, to recognize the positive aspects of diversity, and to work towards collaborative, negotiated social structures. In other words, the school decides whether it will be inclusive or exclusive in its educational and social philosophy, policy and practice.

The movement towards whole school policy-making, school focused curriculum and staff development, demonstrates this in relation to the largely unfunded 1981 Education Act. Schools have introduced shared management of change, learning from research in organization development (Pountney, 1985). This has led to the use of staff-focused decision-making processes and organizational structures in curriculum review and development (McMahon, 1984). School-focused INSET programmes and external consultants have offered support to schools both to make externally imposed change their own, and to innovate their own policy and practices.

Where a school has been able to establish such whole schools pro-social structures, it has often become concerned with re-thinking its pupil-focused processes and organizational structures. It is clear that what happens to pupils in schools does influence educational outcomes as much as or more than their lives outside school. This has become known through school effectiveness research: from the early work of Reynolds (1976) on delinquency prone schools to more recent primary school surveys (Mortimore *et al.*, 1986).

We now know some of the ways in which schools generate disaffection, disruption and alienation and how they may become positively social and inclusive, rather than negatively exclusive. High rates of disruption have tended to be associated with a rigorously imposed discipline and rule system which is constituted by traditional values, norms and forms of communication. For example, Reynolds (1975) noted schools which had no 'truce' areas, so that punishment followed smoking even in the toilets (claimed by pupils as an unofficial 'truce' area), or in the local community. Such schools dis-valued local pupil subcultures, engaging in a constant battle to impose the narrow mono-cultural values of the school and suspending pupils who persistently resisted. On the other hand, whole staff involvement and consultation with pupils and parents in planning a positive system, an emphasis on positive expectations, together with positive reports to parents, are pro-social strategies which reduce behaviour difficulties (Watkins and Wagner, 1987). With this in mind the National Association for Pastoral Care in Education suggested in its evidence to the Elton enquiry that 'schools should promote structured occasions for pupils to reflect upon patterns of behaviour and discipline in schools' (NAPCE, 1989).

Further, Galloway (1983) has shown that the division of academic and pastoral systems and the negative net function of the latter are associated with high rates of suspension, whereas a policy and practice of shared responsibility for care and socially positive behaviour are associated with lower rates.

We have also begun to understand how sexist and racist practices exclude and alienate pupils from a broad and balanced curriculum. And there is a growing realization that the culturally exclusive practices observed by earlier researchers also contain elements of social class exclusiveness. Thus whilst Reynolds (1976) some years ago was asking how the school might 'tie in' the local youth subcultures in order to reduce disaffection, Coulby (1987) now asks how can urban schools in particular become inclusive in terms of the diversity of local cultures and social classes.

The work referred to above focuses mostly upon the secondary age phase largely because changes demanded of schools during comprehensivization and the raising of the school leaving age in 1973, threw up immense teaching and social control problems, understood by teachers at the time in terms of pupil deviance from social norms due to individual defect.

Primary schools have not been exposed to organizational and social change of the same kind as secondary schools. But educational researchers such as Galton *et al.* (1984), and theorists such as Alexander (1984) have investigated the influence on teachers of Plowden (DES, 1967). In particular, Alexander asks whether a strongly child-centred primary school ideology often effectively 'cocoons' teachers and prevents them from reflection and curriculum development. Teaching and behaviour difficulties have tended to be explained in Plowden's terminology of developmental defect or social and emotional 'deprivation'. These almost 'horticultural' perspectives may incline teachers to understand the social as naturally constituted, and thus to wait for 'growth' (Walkerdine, 1983). One of the consequences of this is that pupils whose social learning needs are not being met become crisis management referrals to outside agencies.

Galton *et al.* (1980) and Mortimore *et al.* (1986) have indicated that there is a contradiction between such child-centred ideologies and the didactic whole class teaching methods often found in classrooms. Whilst employing didactic methods, teachers often also group pupils, with the intention rather vaguely formulated of encouraging communication skills and social development. But pupils in these groups are given individualized tasks in literacy or numeracy or the creative arts. This confusion of goals and methods can generate difficulties which teachers then tend to explain in terms of within child socialization problems. The tendency to proceed as though the social is naturally constituted, also shows in sexist assumptions, confusing biologically given sexual characteristics with socially constructed gender (Walkerdine, 1983). This difficulty is not confined to primary schools, but may have particular significance at that age phase in producing early constraint upon pupils' self concept as learners, through whether and how they are given access to equal curriculum opportunities.

On the other hand, more recently there have appeared many accounts of primary school innovations in structuring social curricula (Lang, 1988), and improving the emotional climate by helping pupils to record their social and learning progress and to choose new targets (Richardson, 1988). Coulby's (1987) brief vignette of one inner city primary school, indicates what is involved in taking seriously the diversity of cultural contributions to curriculum, the diversity of ways pupils learn and the active promotion of equal opportunities in preventing alienation and stereotyping. The importance of clear, positive expectations of pupils and the statement of the school's inclusive philosophy which parents, staff and pupils are expected to respect, is noted by Coulby as an important contribution to the reduction of disaffection in the school.

So both in secondary and primary age phases we have indications of ideological and historical constraints on how schools and their teachers structure social experience: whether the social is given enough attention in relation to the cognitive dimensions of learning experiences, and whether the school as a social institution is inclusive or exclusive in its philosophy and organization. But we also note that headteachers and their staff can have choices, can make philosophical and ethical decisions such as those they have already made in relation to the principle of integration and equal opportunities (Dessent, 1987). Governing bodies can and do help schools to make these decisions.

As schools interpret the requirements and possibilities of the Education Reform Act 1988, will they choose commitment to working towards inclusive social structures? Or will some feel constrained to adopt/extend a largely exclusive philosophy and traditional imposed value and rule system? This decision will affect the extent to which the school generates behavioural and emotional difficulties, not only through the way the philosophy permeates the rule system but through its permeation of curriculum content, method and assessment. It will affect the extent to which pupils' personal and social needs and their contribution to learning needs, are seen as part of the school's curricular and pastoral responsibilities. It will also affect the extent to which difficult, socially incompetent, or merely different pupils are moved out into special classes, units and schools either more or less permanently through section 18 statementing procedures, or 'temporarily' through section 19. We know how 'temporary' procedures have functioned during the 1980s to exclude disproportionate numbers of black working-class boys from secondary schools (Topping, 1983; Ford, Mongon and Whelan, 1982; Lloyd-Smith, 1987; Tattum, 1989).

The 1988 Education Act sections on disapplication of national curriculum requirements can be interpreted so as to continue to offer schools such options, rather than helping schools to take the difficult path of working towards socially inclusive curriculum practices. Nevertheless, the inclusion of personal and social education and health education as cross-curricular themes in the *whole* curriculum, has considerable potential for meeting personal and social needs and so improving both the social structure and social climate. The pressure which schools may experience to concentrate on national curriculum attainment targets in core and foundation subjects, and to achieve a high rating in standard assessment tasks, may mean that the importance of personal and social education may be overlooked.

Cross-curricular Social and Personal Demands in the National and Whole Curriculum

The requirement that schools must see that the broad and balanced curriculum is 'fully taken up', also imposes demands on pupils to fully take up their curriculum entitlement. They are therefore asked to engage with the school's selection from programmes of study in three core subjects, seven other foundation subjects including a foreign language, together with religious education, certain cross-curricular themes, formative methods of assessment and the experience of standard assessment tasks in national curriculum components.

In addition, by implication, pupils are asked to engage through and with the methods selected by the school. Methods are not merely social contexts, they constitute the social processes through which learning is mediated; they also make social and personal demands on pupils. The 1980s have produced an increase in active participant methods which involve pupils in pairs, groups or whole class based projects. Some secondary age-phase schools have adopted complex organizations of resource-based learning. These have emerged as schools broaden in their philosophy of learning and try to find ways to motivate, to maintain pupils' locus of control in relation to their learning, to extend their study skills and their social and personal development. Traditional pedagogy, with its focus on teacher led content — the selective 'what' of learning — is found alongside progressive pedagogy, with its focus on pupil led process — the 'how' of learning (Ryder and Campbell, 1989). Arguably, both are necessary to a broad and balanced curricular experience, but together they make considerable demands on the social competence of pupils and on personal resources such as self-confidence.

Where pupils are unable to meet those demands social interaction may become inappropriate and escalate into classroom crises. Unfortunately, when teachers are confronted by these curriculum-situated difficulties, there is still a tendency to overemphasize individual negative behaviours, as it were in a curriculum vacuum. In this respect, the use of behaviour check lists by schools to gather information about trouble in classrooms may not help teachers to understand that pupils' social competence and self-image may need attention in relation to specific curricular situations. Behaviour check lists contain largely negative individual attributions, and we have to turn these around in order to perceive the positive requirements of pupils related to the curriculum situations in which difficulties are generated and sustained. So, for example, 'lacks concentration' becomes a socially situated requirement: 'concentrates upon a task whilst in a distracting situation'.

Other positive requirements which appear when negative attributes are turned around and socially situated, are: cooperating on task with individuals, groups and the whole class; finding, sharing and using resources appropriately; queuing up and waiting; communication skills including decoding nonverbal messages; managing without an adult; allowing an adult to be in authority; social problem solving; generating appropriate alternative responses and making choices; learning from social mistakes; appropriate self assertion; coping with provocation; establishing socially constructive friendships; taking responsibility.

Put in this way, we have a list which includes social and personal goals, towards which pupils are working or need to be helped to work towards across the curriculum. These include skills and personal qualities and attitudes nominated by the DES in an earlier attempt to identify the key elements of a common curriculum to which all pupils were entitled (DES, 1983). They could reasonably be included as elements in the cross-curricular theme of PSE (personal and social education), referred to by DES (1989) in relation to giving coherence and continuity to the whole curriculum. They also relate to the five skills enumerated by Ryder and Campbell (1989) in their discussion of PSHE (personal, social and health education). The five skills are:

communication: especially interpersonal skills such as listening, discussing, summarizing and reporting back from group work;
decision-making: cooperative choosing e.g. of project;
problem-solving: critical evaluation of alternative strategies, knowing and using problem-solving procedures especially in relation to recognizing and dealing with interpersonal and socially situated problems;
reflection: considering the implications for other of one's actions, or the group's actions;
transfer: recognizing connections between situations, the relevance of responses and actions common to both, and differences which require adaptive responses.

The point I am making is that, at least during some phases of their school career, whole years or classes may require particular attention to acquiring such skills and working towards those social and personal goals. Might a cross-curricular approach to PSE be sufficient? Specific help may be required, in the form of PSE timetabled sessions targeted on particular needs. It is this specific help which may enable difficulties which emerge from the interaction of pupil and curriculum to be investigated and managed early.

Meeting Personal and Social Needs in the National and Whole Curriculum

According to Lang (1988) and a number of other PSE theorists and practitioners, the key principles of PSE seem to be that pupils should have time to be listened to in non-judgmental ways, to reflect upon their social and personal learning experiences, to record their learning and to set themselves new goals. At the individual level, this can be made available through the teacher-pupil consultation and curriculum based processes involved in Records of Achievement, which may shortly be extended to younger pupils (DES, 1989). In discussing the affective curriculum and profiling, Broadfoot (1986) notes the importance of these teacher–pupil consultations. However, at the level of group or class social skills and personal qualities involved in curriculum in action, individual teacher–pupil consultation is inadequate. Where pupils are unable to be cooperative, to work in group-based tasks, what options are open? For example, at secondary school level, can science teachers be expected to focus upon group social learning and group processes when a particular class is demonstrating unsocial skills? Is the solution to exclude classes or pupils from certain curriculum methods such as problem-solving tasks in groups? The answer to both questions must be NO. In the first case because as a general rule subject specialist teachers cannot be expected to explore group social process, except in terms of building in group self evaluation of how the task was managed. Where the group is persistently incapable of carrying out the task, this seems not very helpful. In the second case, if the aims of education are to extend, not narrow, pupils' learning experiences and competencies, then one does not exclude them from such methods.

Consequently, if the school is to maintain a pro-social inclusive policy, there may be a good case to be made for timetabled PSE curricula in the secondary school. This is clearly a difficult area, for the aim of PSE is not to further the divide between pastoral and academic but to see them as part of a continuum of provision for meeting pupils' needs (Ryder and Campbell, 1989).

Many forms of PSE curricula have been developed within the form tutor period. A framework of activities is often adopted, such as those in Developmental Groupwork (Button, 1987) or Active Tutorials (Baldwin and Wells, 1979, 1980, 1981). These provide themes related to adolescent developmental phases, school situated sensitive periods such as transfer in or out, option choices, examinations and study skills. These are added to by the relevances brought by the young people themselves. Methods include a mixture of games, simulations, role plays and opportunities to reflect upon, learn from and record learning both as individuals and as a group. When well conducted, PSE can improve the emotional climate, pupils learn to trust one another and the teacher, individuals are listened to and learn to express their feelings in a non-judgmental climate; pupils learn to be constructively critical.

The attention to group process is important and involves acknowledging and working with both the affective and cognitive aspects of situations. Several contributors to the written debate about social process in schools have stressed that teachers and pupils need to understand the difference between sitting in groups, working in groups and learning about groups (Ryder and Campbell, 1989). Learning about how individuals function in groups and discovering how to improve teamwork and resolve hidden personal and political issues which emerge, may be necessary to improving the social competencies of classes or sections of classes. But these discoveries have to be made in relation to real or simulated situations: discussion at the hypothetical level or cognitive counselling on its own, have been found ineffective. On the other hand, much criticism has been directed at the middle-class, liberal and white mono-cultural character of 'pastoral' curricula. The unreality of trying to develop an inclusive, open and enabling personal and social curriculum in a conflicted school has also been pointed out. Where the rest of the hidden curriculum, the rule and sanction system and the other pedagogic experiences are didactic and hierarchical, or when programmes are used to dictate moral and social values, then pupils may perceive PSE as another form of exclusive social control — directed at deviants — and reject it. However, when related to an inclusive whole school policy and practice, with adequate staff training and support, with communication between those who currently do, and do not, provide this curriculum input, PSE programmes do seem to have considerable potential to offer help to all pupils, extending and supplementing the cross-curricular provision.

In primary schools, where classes may have their own class or home base teacher for a good deal of time, and where integrated curricula are quite common, it does seem logical and possible to train class teachers and to give them time to work with their classes on social competencies. It may be assumed, sometimes probably erroneously according to Lang (1988), that social and personal needs are met as it were naturally, through the continuity of class teacher–pupil interaction. But we noted earlier that there is quite a good deal of evidence that social goals and social structure may be more implicit than explicit, and made problematic by particular versions of child-centred ideology. Teachers may respond by labelling individuals rather than by examining social situations and social needs, and goals. However, there are now published studies of the development of PSE principles and practices in primary schools, and these tend to show both that a whole school approach is necessary and that schools need help to clarify their goals and strategies (Lang, 1988).

Quite central to PSE in both primary and secondary schools is the concept of social and personal problem-solving, and it is this which provides what seems to me to offer a clear if not self sufficient contribution to structuring help for most pupils. Problem-solving is given earlier in this chapter as one of five PSHE skills which appear to be interrelated and should be worked upon together. For example, one may be a competent problem solver at a purely pragmatic selfish level, but not care much about the consequences for others; so empathy and ethical issues also need to be addressed. However, the importance of making such a basic process available to pupils within a pro-social school policy and practice, show very clearly in two primary school examples given below.

Each school took the leap from negatively labelling pupils to setting out to meet positively identified social needs and targets for and with all pupils. In the first example, the introduction of problem-solving is approached as part of a school wide but classroom based, cooperative learning programme (Wagner, 1988). Teachers targeted cooperative social skills, communication competencies and study skills. Pupils were consulted about their existing repertoire of responses to potentially difficult social situations. Cooperative learning tasks were designed by teachers, and the class-generated repertoire of social responses was made available to the pupils in problem-solving sessions. The aim was to enable pupils to become aware of their own and others' usual responses, to consider their usefulness and to develop extensions or alternatives in relation to the cooperative tasks given to them. Cooperative tasks were given in drama, numeracy and language development.

One of the consequences of this intervention, was that the curriculum-based social interaction of the pupils changed towards the positive. During the evaluation period, extensive periods of self-directed, collaborative group work were observed, including periods of one hour by a class of 6- to 8-year-olds, who previously were unable to interact socially in a positive way. The school SEN school coordinator is overseeing the maintenance and development of the project, with monthly consultations for the whole staff from the educational psychologist. We need a longer term follow up report on this project.

Problem-solving skills are also central to the second example. Brier (1988) records that frequent crisis management and staff stress, together with evidence tht the school had always suffered similar difficulties, led her to draw upon the support of INSET to work with her staff on producing a social curriculum. This was based upon the principles of Interpersonal Cognitive Problem-solving (Shure and Spivack, 1979). The staff aimed to produce guided practice in personal and social problem-solving based on real life situations. A four phase structure was chosen linked with two year age phases:

(1) identification of feeling (4-6 yrs);
(2) cause and effect (6-8 yrs);
(3) generating alternative solutions (8-10 yrs);
(4) evaluating solutions (10-12 yrs).

Staff recognized that pupils did not learn step by step in the given sequence and that all phases were involved in any problem-solving session. However, staff used the sequence as a guide for themselves as to how the learning progression might go in terms of emphasis at any period. Three teacher teams specializing in social skills curricula for early years, transition, and upper school, are now developing the project across schools. Brier has not yet reported on the outcomes of this initiative in relation to her own school's original difficulties. We need longer term follow up evaluations of both the single school and the cross-schools initiatives.

Both of these examples show that child-centredness can be linked with planned social learning for pupils and INSET to support such developments.

Neither of these schools were willing to go on waiting for pro-social competencies to emerge or develop. They considered that it is better to show children how to be pro-social and to organize socially constructive curricula. In addition they recognized the importance of staff support in the management of change. It is interesting to note that in both examples, the teachers themselves were using problem-solving strategies — in one case supported by the educational psychologist and in the other by college-based but school-focused INSET.

Cross-curricular Support for Special Personal and Social Needs: Is Disapplication Necessary?

However supportive and positive the school at whole school and class levels, there will be pupils whose severity of need will require special help. The needs may not always present themselves in the form of unacceptable antisocial or disruptive behaviour. Some pupils are impaired in their social interaction skills through shyness, low self esteem and fear of failure. Some may have a long history of failure and rejection, but the failure to proceed successfully through the curriculum may have more to do with their inadequate social skills in relation to curriculum demands, than any intrinsic cognitive impairment. In these cases, modifications to the social demands made and to the emotional climate of the classroom, can be achieved by an in-class support teacher, who will make a curriculum-based assessment of social and personal needs, and provide strategies designed to meet those needs.

On the other hand, some pupils may also have been identified as having learning difficulties in relation to cognitive tasks and may be receiving in-class support from the learning support or SEN department or SEN coordinator. Curriculum based assessment of cognitive learning needs should also include assessment of social learning needs. Support teachers will thus be working to both. Whilst cognitive learning goals may be largely individual and perhaps related to literacy or numeracy skills, social skills by definition will involve planned strategies to increase cooperative working skills.

Opportunities for pupils to make their own assessment, to reflect on their own achievements and to set new targets which are recorded, would be part of this and some aspects would constitute part of their individual records of achievement for communication with parents. In other words, although most national curriculum targets do not include social targets, for these pupils teachers will have to write a programme with the pupil's collaboration, which shows progression through social targets. This probably means that for at least some time the selection from programmes of study will have to be adapted to allow for social target priority.

Such modifications may not have to be accompanied by temporary disapplication (section 19) of any national curriculum requirements. Indeed the whole aim is to enable the pupil to manage the social elements involved in participating in programmes of study. Possibly the only justification for disapplication could be to gain support teacher time. Whether and how support staff are made available will no doubt affect the school's policy on disapplications.

However, the pro-social school will want to avoid deliberately invoking disapplication *instead* of providing support to manage the social aspects of curricular tasks. The crucial principle is to maintain as much of the entitlement curriculum base as possible for the modified tasks and targets. It is important for this to be recognized by LEA, headteachers, governors, classteachers and parents as positive curriculum based rather than negative individual pupil based identification and intervention.

Richardson (1988) has recently discussed the advantages of having a whole school policy and practice at the primary level which enables all pupils to maintain their own records of social achievements. If this was part of PSE cross-curricular provision, special social and personal targets and achievements could be inserted very easily by the pupil.

Small group support teaching to social targets can also take place within the class's usual curriculum. In secondary schools subject-based group problem-solving or other teaching methods can be supported in this way. Whether in primary or secondary settings, such in-class support might usefully be followed up by group tutorials in which the reflection, review and targeting take place. It may be necessary to devise support strategies for groups of pupils in PSE whole class sessions. In this respect co-working by form tutor or class teacher plus special needs or learning support teacher has been tried successfully by teachers on placement from an INSET course at the Institute of Education University of London. This enables pupils to be maintained in the sessions, whose personal and social needs are otherwise likely to dominate the group. It is still rare to find recorded collaboration of this kind between pastoral and SEN departments in secondary schools. Lowe's (1989) recent discussion in relation to the work of both, and to TVEI, offers a stimulating contribution. Further, Lowe also discusses the necessity to find curriculum based ways to support the personal and social needs of students in FE, especially where students are already designated and statemented SEN.

Peripatetic school support teaching services presently offer interventions at the level of individual pupil and teacher, but some also provide relevant group and whole class interventions in social and personal difficulties, helping the class to target and work together on improving specific aspects (Coulby and Harper, 1985). However, the aim of such services has to be the eventual self-sufficiency of the school in this respect. That is, the school moves from calling on crisis management services to structuring positive social and personal help in the curriculum.

All of these support and social education programmes require staff. Will LEAs and schools be funded to try these integrative measures? The funding basis of Local Management of Schools is not encouraging; some schools will almost certainly not have money for support teachers unless they statement pupils; and even this is no cast-iron guarantee. Further, might the lack of teachers in inner urban areas mean that difficult pupils are excluded and placed together so that they lack role development models and the possibility of being supported in learning how to work within a more socially balanced group?

Alternative Personal and Social Curricular Provision: a Possible Case for Section 19 Disapplication?

The argument in this chapter is that all pupils require maintaining in broadly balanced age-related peer groups, in order to make cross-curricular social and personal progression. Where they need help to manage this, a number of organizational strategies exist which enable most social and many personal needs to be met both cross-curricula and in specific targeted curricula. Within this overall commitment, there is a case to be made for partial, temporary small group work either on or off site. Pupils may need a partial or complete respite from having to face the hury-burly and pace of the average noisy and busy school. Education Reform Act guidelines recognize this in relation to temporary disapplications (section 19) where bereavement and similar extreme stresses exist (DES, 1989). But the alternative curriculum and its goals will need careful thought, for the aim will be to enable the pupils to have very special social and personal attention, and return to mainstream curriculum, where they are likely to remain in need for some time. This suggests that PSE principles and relevant curricula, and PSE training, may be the most appropriate for such specialist teachers. They can maintain close links with the mainstream school and perhaps contribute to its PSE work on-site, including supporting pupils within the school whom they help outside the school. They may also act as consultants in relation to modifying the social and emotional climate there, thus sustaining their own professional skills and knowledge of the on-site social conditions. It might also be important that these teachers have their own additional national curriculum area speciality so that they can maintain subject based curriculum skills and updated knowledge. In addition, they clearly will need to maintain a breadth of knowledge in relation to curriculum developments and their implications for social needs.

Specialist Curricula in Special Schools: Is Disapplication Really Necessary?

Although the Fish Report (ILEA, 1985) doubted that any justification could be found for placing pupils labelled EBD in special schools, these schools still exist for children who have been processed out of mainstream. In theory, these small special schools offer the ultimate modifications to meet the personal, social and cognitive needs of 'EBD pupils'. But in practice they can present the most difficult, anti-social conditions for both staff and pupils. As HMI (1989) point out, groups are frequently so small and so scattered in age range, so often composed mostly of overtly hostile and disillusioned children and young people whose basic social and personal needs have not been met for a long time, that staff face an almost impossible task. In addition, the scattered age range and small size of roll, and consequently of staff, makes curriculum coverage and development extremely difficult. In such conditions disapplication of national curriculum requirements (section 18) may have more to do with the impossibility of staffing the full curriculum, than with any intrinsic pupil needs.

The point at issue is that pupils labelled informally as disturbed, disruptive or maladjusted or formally as having emotional and behavioural difficulties, require both special personal/social education curricula and support to manage cross-curricula methods. Removing them from a broad and balanced curriculum will probably not enable them to progress either socially or personally, especially in relation to curriculum requirements, thus producing a self-fulfilling prophecy.

HMI (1989) observe that in most of the nineteen units and fifty-seven special schools (emotional and behavioural difficulties) they have surveyed since 1983, learning tasks were observed to be narrow and highly individualized. Such limited individualized learning tasks and seating arrangements can be used to try to control social interaction, to prevent escalations of conflict which teachers may not be trained to prevent or to reduce by more positive educational methods. One of the consequences of this curricular and social organization seems to be that many social interaction difficulties in relation to peers, are not tackled in classroom-based learning situations. Yet these difficulties must have been major factors in the removal of pupils from the ordinary school. So not only are pupils in danger of being deprived of increasing those social competencies relevant to curriculum progression, they are also in longer term danger of being deprived of eventual access to their entitlement curriculum.

This is the key problem for teachers in specialist provision – how to design, implement, monitor, record and maintain both the personal and social curriculum and the broad, balanced curriculum based upon selections from programmes of study in subjects or areas of experience. In residential schools this key problem is shared by residential social workers and teachers and perhaps they need supportive INSET on such collaborative tasks.

Individual staff–pupil relationships are commented upon by HMI as of very good, caring quality. However, these individual relationships seem to exist in a curricular vacuum, for many of the schools did not appear to understand curriculum as a means to meet personal or social needs. There was no planned progression of social achievements; schools seemed not to know how to provide such progression, or how to structure it.

This apparent difficulty in conceptualizing an alternative curriculum, may be contributed to by two factors. One is the pre-Warnock preference for medical model perspectives which suggest that these pupils are incapable of curricular progress, as opposed to individual participation, until their emotional deprivation has been compensated for (Wilson, 1984). The emphasis upon caring individual relationships is a positive part of this. However, the negative part is that teachers may become anti-curricular or rather anti-school subjects. We are already seeing responses to the Education Reform Act curriculum requirements, in advertised posts for EBD schools in which references are made to putting the child before 'imposed' curriculum. The other factor may be that special schools are often cut off from mainstream, and staff may be de-skilled by the absence of curricular stimulation and support. For example, an enquiry at a local teacher's centre for personal, social and health education before the 1988 Education Act, showed that only individual teacher initiatives were known. We know that such individual initiatives tend to fall on stony ground in the teacher's school. This does not imply that the PSHE curricula and methods available for mainstream are directly transferable into special schools, but they can at least open up alternative sources of support for developing and structuring personal and social education. However, this would involve whole school decision making and practice, including school-focused INSET, rather than individual initiative, which tends to be absorbed into the inertia of closed systems such as small special schools.

The five PSHE skill areas referred to earlier, and including social and personal problem-solving, will be recognized by EBD special school staff as skills they would wish to enable their pupils to achieve and indeed to help some pupils to achieve. On the other hand, whilst the philosophy of PSHE may be congruent with that of special school staff, its group-based methods may be thought to be too difficult, where pupils offer such extreme social difficulties. But does the realistic need to impose limits to pupil behaviour necessarily preclude a more carefully structured group approach to tackling social interaction difficulties? The curriculum in leavers' groups in special schools already does some of this in relation to work experience: HMI note this as an area of observed progression but fail to tell us the positive aspects.

Another obvious source of support for special school staff, may be outreach collaboration with schools which have successful PSE policies and practices. The interpersonal skills of special school teachers and their pupil management knowledge, could be a strength to be welcomed by the mainstream school. Where special school pupils join the mainstream, the importance of preparation to manage the social requirements of curriculum methods in new social situations needs recognition. But this presupposes that special school staff are in touch with mainstream curriculum developments and know how to prepare their pupils. Such support from special school staff needs providing for in the staffing of special schools or of outreach staff working with ordinary schools. Flexibility of staffing, with work at any point along the continuum of provision, becomes important. Where LEAs have cluster organizations (Fish, 1985), this kind of collaboration and extension might be most easily facilitated.

One of the irritating aspects of the HMI report, is that though HMI found some instances of special schools and units which did seem able to extend the pupils through the curriculum, they do not show how the schools did this. This raises even more concern when one considers that staff appear to have little access to sharing more widely based curriculum developments, whether mainstream or special. HMI have followed up their survey with dissemination conferences for certain special school staff, but perhaps the DES might also consider funding a publication contributed to jointly by the schools?

Throughout this chapter reference has been made to the necessity for staff training and for continuous support to recognize *their* positive achievements. Management of change for either pupils or staff requires whole school and often also external decision-making backed up by action in relation to improving the social structure and emotional climate of the school for *both*. Perhaps taking seriously a commitment to working towards an inclusive educational practice, implies inter-disciplinary collaboration on curriculum development? This could mean that special and mainstream school staff and whatever multi-disciplinary support services remain in the 1990s, could be developing social and personal curricula and cross-curricular methods *together*, especially for vulnerable children and young people.

References

ALEXANDER, R. (1984) *Primary Teaching*, Holt Education.

BALDWIN, J. and WELLS, H. (1979, 1980, 1981) *Active Tutorial Work*, Books 1–5, Oxford, Basil Blackwell.

BOOTH, I. and COULBY, D. (Eds) (1987) *Producing and Reducing Disaffection*, Milton Keynes, Open University Press.

BRIER, J. (1988) 'Developing a Structural Social Development Programme in an Inner City School', in LANG, P., Oxford, Blackwell.

BROADFOOT, P. (1986) 'Profiling and the affective curriculum', *Journal of Curriculum Studies* Vol. 19, 1, pp. 25–34.

BUTTON, L. (1987) 'Development Group Work as an Approach to Personal, Social and Moral Education', in THACKER, J. *et al.* (Eds) *Personal, Social and Moral Education in a Changing World*, Windsor, NFER.

COULBY, D. (1987) 'Changing Urban Schools', in BOOTH, I. and COULBY, D.

COULBY, D. and HARPER, I. (1988) *Preventing Classroom Disruption: Policy, Practice and Evaluation in Urban Schools*, London, Croom Helm.

DEPARTMENT OF EDUCATION AND SCIENCE (1967) *Children and Their Primary Schools* (The Plowden Report), London, HMSO.

DEPARTMENT OF EDUCATION AND SCIENCE (1978) *Special Educational Needs* (The Warnock Report), London, HMSO.

DEPARTMENT OF EDUCATION AND SCIENCE (1981) *Education Act 1981*, London, HMSO.

DEPARTMENT OF EDUCATION AND SCIENCE (1988) *Educaton Reform Act*, London, HMSO.

DEPARTMENT OF EDUCATION AND SCIENCE (1989) *National Curriculum from Policy to Practice*, London, DES.

DEPARTMENT OF EDUCATION AND SCIENCE (1989) *HMI Report: A Survey of Provision for Pupils with Emotional/Behavioral Difficulties in Maintained Special Schools and Units*, London, DES.

DESSENT, I. (1987) *Making the Ordinary School Special*, Lewes, Falmer Press.

FORD MONGON, D. and WHELAN, M. (1982) *Special Education and Social Control*, London, Routledge & Kegan Paul.

GALLOWAY, D.M. (1983) 'Disruptive Pupils and Effective Pastoral Care', *School Organisation* 3, pp. 245–54.

GALLOWAY, D.M. (1985) *Schools, Pupils and Special Educational Needs*, London, Croom Helm.

GALTON, M., SIMONS, B. and CROLL, P. (1980) *Inside the Primary Classroom*, London, Routledge & Kegan Paul.

HARGREAVES, D. (1982) *The Challenge for the Comprehensive School: Culture, Curriculum, Community*, London, Routledge & Kegan Paul.

INNER LONDON EDUCATION AUTHORITY (1984) *Improving Secondary Schools* (The Hargreaves Report), London, ILEA.

INNER LONDON EDUCATION AUTHORITY (1985) *Educational Opportunities for All?* (The Fish Report), London, ILEA.

LANG, P. (Ed.) (1988) *Thinking About ... Personal and Social Education in the Primary School*, Oxford, Basil Blackwell.

LLOYD-SMITH, M. (1987) 'Sorting Them Out: Provision for Young Deviants', in BOOTH, T. and COULBY, D.

LOWE, P. (1988) *Responding to Adolescent Needs — A Pastoral Care Approach*, London, Cassell.

MCMAHON, A. (1984) 'Reviewing and Developing the Curriculum: the GRIDS Project', in SKILBECK, M. (Ed.) *Readings in School-Based Curriculum Development*, London, Harper.

MORTIMER, P. *et al.* (1986) *The Junior School Project*, Research and Statistics Branch, ILEA.

POUTNEY, G. (1985) *Management in Action*, York, Longman.

REYNOLDS, D. (1975) 'When Teachers and Pupils Refuse a Truce — the Secondary School and the Generation of Delinquency', in MUNGHAM, G. and PEARSON, G. (Eds) *British Working Class Youth Culture*, London, Routledge & Kegan Paul.

REYNOLDS, D. (1976) 'The Delinquent School', in HAMMERSLEY, M. and WOODS, P. (Eds) *The Process of Schooling*, London, Routledge & Kegan Paul.

REYNOLDS, D. (1976) *The Process of Schooling*, London, Routledge & Kegan Paul/Open University.

RICHARDSON, T. (1988) *Education for Personal Development: A Whole School Approach*, in LANG, P.

RYDER, J. and CAMPBELL, L. (1989) *Balancing Acts — In Personal, Social and Health Education*, London, Routledge & Kegan Paul.

SHURE, M.B. and SPIVACK, G. (1979) 'Inter-personal Cognitive Problem Solving and Primary Prevention', *Journal of Clinical Child Psychology* 2, pp. 89–94.

TATTUM, D. (1989) 'Violent, Aggressive and Disruptive Behaviour', in JONES, N. (1989) *Special Educational Needs Review*, Vol. 1, Lewes, Falmer Press.

TOPPING, K. (1983) *Education Systems for Disruptive Adolescents*, Beckenham, Croom Helm.

WAGNER, R. (1988) 'Developing Co-operative Learning in the Primary School', in LANG, P.

WALKERDINE, V. (1983) 'Its Only Natural: Rethinking Child-Centred Pedagogy' in WOLPE, A.M. and DONALD, J. (Eds) *Is There Anyone Here From Education?*, London, Pluto.

WATKINS, C. and WAGNER, P. (1987) *School Discipline: A Whole School Approach*, Oxford, Blackwell.

WILSON, M. (1984) 'Why Don't They Learn? Some Thoughts on the Relationship Between Maladjustment and Learning Difficulties', *Maladjustment and Therpaeutic Education* 2, No. 2, Autumn.

Chapter 14

Sensitivity to Special Educational Needs: Trends and Prospects

John Fish

Introduction

During the 1960s the education system became increasingly responsive to individual differences and to the nurturing factors which affected them. Comprehensive primary and secondary schools were seen to be the most appropriate settings for an education sensitive to the wide range of abilities, aptitudes and learning styles to be found among children.

At the end of that decade the right to education was extended to all children by the 1970 Education Act. This abolished the concept of ineducability. All children, regardless of the nature and degree of any disabilities they might have, are now entitled to be educated. The local education authority has to make appropriate opportunities available. Since that time provision for children with severe and complex learning difficulties has been among the most progressive and innovative in the field of special education.

In the early 1970s concern about special education resulted in the setting up of the Warnock Committee in 1974. The Committee was asked to review the whole field of provision and services. Its Report *Special Educational Needs*, published in 1978, represented a high tide in constructive thought about special education.

The influence of the report on thinking and practice continues to be widespread. The 1981 Education Act incorporated some of its recommendations. However, since its implementation in 1983, official interest, guidance and action have been limited and appear to have been reluctant. It was unfortunate that the proposed changes coincided with a decrease in the school population and a more rigorous control of educational spending by the government. Local education authorities were expected to implement the 1981 Act within existing reduced budgets.

More recently, political thinking about education, together with that of some special interest groups, has turned attention to raising academic standards, to standardizing the curriculum and to giving parents and school governors more powers to manage schools. These trends, exemplified in the Education Reform Act 1988, need not necessarily inhibit concern for children who are less successful or who have special educational needs but recent reform proposals appear to pay little attention to the effects of the changes in responsibility and financial management on provision to meet special educational needs.

Sensitivity to individual needs seems to be ebbing. Market forces, cost effectiveness and achieving national standards tend to decrease attention to this area of education, to limit resources for it and to reduce the value placed on it. Before turning to the possible consequences of the 1988 Act it may be helpful to establish and defend what has been gained since 1970 and to identify what is now at risk.

Major Developments in Perception

The Nature of Special Education

The Warnock Report and subsequent legislation endorsed a number of major changes which had been slowly occurring in theory and practice since 1944. Some of these changes are particularly significant and are not yet fully appreciated within the education system. The most important are:

(1) the change from medical diagnosis to multi-professional assessment;
(2) the change from treatment to education;
(3) the change from meeting categorical needs to meeting individual needs;
(4) the change from category specific curricula and methods to appropriate variations of the curriculum for all.

1. Assessment. Although other elements of assessment were recognized in the 1944 Education Act, until 1983 a medical opinion was all that was legally necessary to determine the need for special educational treatment. In the years following the 1944 Act, educational and psychological assessment techniques became more widely known and a broader basis for assessment was recognized as necessary. The Warnock Report endorsed the trend and the 1981 Act now requires educational, psychological and health service contributions as a minimum and recognizes the importance of other professional contributions.
2. Education. The original medical model was also evident in the description of provision in the 1944 Act. The phrase 'special educational treatment' was

used to describe what was to be provided in special schools and elsewhere for children ascertained to require it.

We do not now consider that children with disabilities and significant difficulties are different kinds of children. They have many of the same needs as other children and should be educated and not treated. The 1981 Act refers to educational and other provision that is additional to or otherwise different from that provided for children of the same age.

3. Categories of Handicap. In 1944 it was thought that children could be categorized and that there would be a curriculum and methodology appropriate to each category of handicap. Categories were based on 'disabilities of mind or body' and ten were defined. Experience has shown that most children requiring special education have a mixture of disabilities and difficulties and do not fall neatly into categories.

Although different methods and techniques are required within special education there has been no evidence that complete and separate curricula are appropriate for definable categories of disability. The 1981 Act abolished categories and recognized special education as a variation of the education provided for children of the same age.

4. Categories of Children. The same trend which led to the abolition of categories led to the belief that children should be assessed as individuals and that their special educational needs were in some senses unique. The objective of assessment is no longer to attempt to place children in separate homogeneous groups based on category of need. The 1981 Act requires needs to be individually assessed and met. This is a clear move to get away from disability stereotypes and the potentially adverse effects on a child of assuming that his or her needs can be summarized by a group label.

In retrospect these four profound changes in thinking and practice have not yet been generally recognized and accepted. There have been new labels for special schools and units and by implication for the children who attend them. Administration finds individuality difficult to manage. We need to think of types and groups of needs *not* types and groups of children but old habits die hard.

The Extent of Special Educational Needs

Even in the 1940s it was recognized that special educational needs might be extensive in the school population. The figure of 15 per cent appeared in the Ministry of Education Pamphlet Number 5 published in 1946. What developed in the next few years was, however, an administrative division, which distinguished the commoner needs which existed in primary and secondary school from the more severe needs met in special schools.

The fiction was maintained that the needs in primary and secondary school were remediable. Hence a division arose between 'remedial' education and 'special' education in administrative, inspectorate and professional staffing and responsibility.

Many authorities considered special educational provision to be confined to special schools which although increased in number never catered for more than 2 to 3 per cent of the school population at the most. Many authorities provided special school places for less than 1 per cent of their school population.

Concern about the effects of separation in special schools led to the setting up of recognized special education units in primary and secondary schools. Those for children with hearing impairments were among the first. This led to a slow breakdown of the artificial barrier between 'remedial' and 'special' education.

The Warnock Report wished to see the division abolished. That report suggested that up to 1 in 5 of all children of school age might have special educational needs for some period in their school life. There was a continuum of needs for which a range of provision was necessary.

It could be argued that the 1981 Act's procedures for assessment and making statements have perpetuated a division between 'proper' special educational provision, when a Statement is made, and less important provision for the wide range of special educational needs commonly met within primary and secondary schools. Certainly the emphasis on children who are the subject of statements in recent consultation documents and reports and the officially admitted ignorance of the extent of the wider range of needs, or of appropriate provision to meet them, would seem to support this view.

Major Developments in Practice

Since 1978 there have been significant developments in pre-school, school and post-school arrangements largely on the initiative of voluntary organizations and local authorities. Department of Education and Science initiatives have largely been confined to home-teaching schemes and teacher training through the educational support grant programme.

1. Age Range

The Warnock Report extended the range overwhich provision to meet special educational needs should be made. It stressed pre-school programmes, and appropriate arrangements after the end of the compulsory school period. As a result of the report the age range over which provision is being made has almost doubled.

2. Pre-school Developments

There has been no real increase in nursery school and class provision for this age group, as a whole, or in places for children with special educational needs. The voluntary sector has made some additional arrangements. The most obvious advance has been in making available Portage-type home teaching programmes.

3. School Years Developments

Many significant developments have occurred in the compulsory school years. Most of them have been the result of local education authority initiatives, although the Department of Education and Science has made a major contribution to teacher education in this field. Among these are:

(a) the recognition of special educational needs in primary and secondary schools and of the need for provision for them;
(b) the training and appointment of special educational needs coordinators in primary and secondary schools;
(c) the reorganization of peripatetic and remedial teaching services;
(d) the setting up of more special education units in primary and secondary schools;
(e) the support, in terms of non-special teaching and non-teaching time, of more children who are the subject of statements in regular classes in primary and secondary schools;
(f) the development of much closer relationships between the staff and pupils of special schools and their local primary and secondary schools.

In recent years priority has been given to developments of these kinds in many areas. What is now uncertain is their future within an educational system where more powers are delegated to schools.

4. Post-school Provision

On their own, and later with the support of the Further Education Unit, many further education colleges and adult education centres have made a significant contribution to the continued education of young people with special educational needs. The report *Catching Up* provides a review of what has been accomplished in terms of courses and places and other Further Education Unit publications show how much thinking has been devoted to curriculum development in this field.

Major Ideas and Aspirations

Two ideas have dominated much of the thinking about special education, parental partnership and integration. Both are enshrined in some form in the 1981 Act. While the former is very consistent with the additional responsibilities on offer to all parents in new legislation the latter runs counter to the possible fragmentation of the education system embodied in the same legislation.

1. Parental Partnership

Since 1978 parental views on their children's education have received more consideration. There has been an increase in the recognition of the contribution they can make to meeting special educational needs. The 1981 Act gave parents greater powers to receive information and to contribute to decision making. Subsequent research has shown that many professonals are still reluctant to give genuine weight to parental concerns and that many parents require help to make their contribution.

2. Integration

The topic of integration is a complex one. At its simplest it concerns the recognition of equal rights to consideration and to participation in the same range of choices as other children and young people. Without looking at the issue in detail it is possible to see that trends in 1978 were integrative. Schools were to be comprehensive, special education was to be an integral, not marginal, part of the school system and individuals were to be given the opportunity, wherever possible, to be educated with their contemporaries.

Much progress has been made to these ends. However, the potential fragmentation of the secondary school system, together with the increased powers of governors given by the Education Reform Act (1988), may create new barriers to equal opportunity. Integration may now become a question of access to the same range of schools as others rather than to a 'school for all'.

What is Special Education?

Before turning to the possible effects of new legislation on special education it may be important to consider the nature of special educational provision. It could be argued that most progress has been made in assessment, methodology and individual programming and that little attention has been given to the systems by which what is required to meet speical needs is delivered.

There are at least four implicit assumptions about the nature of special education which need to be questioned before a framework for providing special education under the 1988 Act can be developed. They are that:

(a) any work by teachers with special educational qualifications or experience is by definition special education;
(b) what goes on in special education classrooms is necessarily special education;
(c) grouping children by disabilities and by special educational needs itself defines special education; and
(d) any additional teaching or non-teaching time given to children with special educational needs, in primary and secondary schools, is special education.

By making the first assumption we make no distinction between 'good' teaching and the special educational skills and knowledge necessary to supplement such teaching that some children require. The second assumes that location defines the nature of special education.

By making the third assumption special educators may be colluding with administrators in the belief that a group of pupils necessarily defines the education they receive. Finally, the fourth assumption implies that special education is simply a matter of anybody's time.

There now appears to be an overwhelming case for attention to the nature of special education, the degree to which primary and secondary education has to be varied to meet individual needs and the different levels of skill and knowledge that are necessary to meet those needs. An approach to these topics is set out in a recent Open University Press publication (Fish, 1989).

The absence of such an agreed framework makes it difficult to ensure and monitor special educational provision in primary and secondary schools, to define and cost the services of peripatetic and advisory teachers and to develop sensible criteria for determing when a statement might be made.

Indeed, although the intentions of the Department of Education and Science in respect to special education in the new free-for-all education system are far from clear, there is equally no evidence that special education interests are at all certain what it is they want to see maintained and developed.

Present and Future Trends

Until guidance about the implementation of the 1988 Education Act is complete, and there has been practical experience of its requirements, future trends in the field of special education are uncertain. However, there are a number of aspects of special education where there may be adverse effects. They are grouped under different spheres of interest.

Parents

Parents have a duty to see that their children are educated. The local authority has the duty to provide education and governors of schools now have major responsibilities for admission to their schools. A major question, which may have to be answered, is how these conflicting interests will be resolved where a child with special educational needs, not the subject of a statement, is refused admission to schools chosen by his or her parents.

Special Educational Provision in Primary and Secondary Schools

There are few generally agreed national or local guidelines about the nature of provision in primary and secondary schools for children whose needs are not thought to require a statement. Although some local education authorities recognize this aspect of school's work by the allocation of staff and resources within school budgets (House of Commons Education, Science and Arts Committee, 1987), much provision is relatively *ad hoc*, being made 'when circumstances permit'.

Current provisional guidance is not particularly clear about the children for whom the national curriculum should be modified or disapplied. Nor is it clear how much priority will be given to studies outside the national curriculum, such as personal and social education, which are so vital to pupils who are less successful or who have special educational needs.

A number of questions arise from the delegation of more responsibilities, including financial management, to school governors both within the local authority system and outside it in grant maintained schools financed by the Secretary of State. Among these are:

(a) What kinds of arrangement to meet the special educational needs of pupils, not the subject of statements, will be recognized and required in primary, secondary and grant maintained schools? How will these arrangements be monitored and evaluated?
(b) Will grant maintained and voluntary aided schools be required to make the same kinds of provision to meet special educational needs as maintained schools?
(c) What elements for special educational provision will be included in arrangements for grants and for local management?

It seems likely that restricted resources and delegated management will make it increasingly difficult for local education authorities to develop and maintain a coherent policy for meeting special educational needs and a comprehensive range of special educational provision. This will be more evident in authorities which have not had such a policy and which have responded to such needs in an *ad hoc* way.

As schools strive to raise standards they may give less priority to meeting special educational needs. The more uncertain the answers to these questions the more likely it is that there will be increased pressure on maintained schools to make more provision as grant maintained schools opt out. As a consequence there will be increased pressure from maintained schools, as they attempt to raised standards, for more separate provision in special schools.

Support Services

The practices of school psychological, educational welfare, peripatetic and support teaching services have changed as a result of the Warnock Report and the 1981 Act. They have become less fragmented and given more time to working with other teachers to create more favourable classroom conditions. Separate work with individuals and small groups has decreased and more time has been devoted to support teaching in the classroom.

Services have been active in negotiating their contributions to individual schools. If such services are now to be costed, and have to be paid for out of school budgets, their relationships to schools will be radically changed. Schools may be more dominant in negotiations with professionals. While professionals may define a tariff of services, which they can and wish to provide, schools will determine the kind of services they think they need. This may lead to considerable changes in the way such services operate.

Another pressure will result from the increased demand, under the Act, to inspect, monitor evaluate and otherwise spend time looking at what schools are doing as an important aspect of quality control. Advisory and support services will have very conflicting demands: on the one hand, to support children with special needs and create the right conditions for them in schools and, on the other, to act as judges of the effectiveness of those conditions.

The education authority is expected to maintain the same level of service to maintained and grant maintained schools. Will the grants to the latter contain an element to buy such services? If not, how much can authorities withhold from delegated local finance to their own schools for such services? Will not their services to grant maintained schools impoverish those to maintained schools?

Children who are the Subject of Statements

When resources and supporting arrangements are adequate teachers in primary and secondary schools are sympathetic to meeting more complex special educational needs in their schools. Limited resources and restricted staffing ratios have led to increasing numbers of children being referred for formal assessment in the hope that a statement will secure more resources.

The Act's provision that statements may be used to exempt children from all or parts of the national curriculum, and from attainment targets, may further increase pressure on assessment services. These services are already stretched and are taking too long to complete statement procedures.

Separate Special Educational Provision

It has already been suggested that primary and secondary schools may have to become less sympathetic to children with special educational needs, particularly those who are the subject of statements.

In the 1944 Act the trend was 'outward' in the sense that separate provision was considered optimum and primary and secondary schools were encouraged to believe that they could not meet special educational needs. Later the trends was 'inward' as peripatetic and support teaching services, together with special schools, began to support primary and secondary schools in making provision to meet a wider range of special educational needs.

Now the limitations of all kinds placed on schools, together with increased expectations, may be expected to reverse the trend again. It seems likely that there will be a change back to an 'outward' movement of children from primary and secondary schools.

Special Schools may be expected to face a number of problems. To provide the national curriculum in small schools is going to prove almost impossible with existing resources. However, they will be faced with attempting to provide such a curriculum while many of the pupils admitted to the school have statements which modify or disapply that curriculum.

It is also likely that the links many have forged with primary and secondary schools will be increasingly difficult to maintain.

If primary and secondary schools become increasingly reluctant to admit pupils with statements, or to act as hosts to special education units, pressure on special school places will increase. In rural areas this may lead to increased pressure to provide, at least weekly, boarding provision.

The Local Education Authority

A number of comments have already been made about the implications of new legislation for special educational provision for local authorities. There is one other issue which requires thought. It is becoming evident that the Department of Education and Science is reluctant to recognize any special educational need which is not the subject of a statement. It is becoming more difficult for local authorities to provide resources to meet needs in the absence of statements.

Is the trend going to be towards a special education system entirely confined to pupils with statements? This is the position in the United States where the Individual Education Plan is the criterion by which special educational needs are defined. If this is to be the direction in which things move it is as well to recognize that the percentage of the school population with individual Education Plans, in that country, is between 9 and 12 per cent.

Conclusion

Although many of the questions raised in looking at future trends are adminstrative and financial they are fundamental to the delivery of special educational services to children who need them.

First, they influence the extent to which special education is seen to be an integral part of the school and college system for all children and young people. Having become a more central element in educational provision as a whole is special education to be forced back to the periphery?

Second, an increase in separate provision will lead to special education being reidentified with failure to meet standards just when it is becoming recognized as providing success for individuals who have difficulties.

Finally, curricular and other links between special schools and units, now becoming effective and valued, may become more difficult with the result that such schools and units may become more isolated from the main current of curriculum development.

If these trends become evident one of the reasons will be that the field of special education has not defined what it offers. It has become too identified, over the years, with location and professional qualification. One positive outcome of the current reforms could be a much clearer definition of what special education is and how it is to be delivered.

References

DES (1944) *Education Act*, London, HMSO.

DES (1970) *Education (Handicapped Children) Act*, London, HMSO.

DES (1978) *Special Educational Needs: Report of the Committee of Enquiry into the Education of Handicapped Children and Young People*, (The Warnock Report) London, HMSO.

(DES (1981) *Education Act,* London, HMSO.

(DES (1988) *Education Reform Act,* London, HMSO.

FISH, J. (1989) *What is Special Education?*, Milton Keynes, Open University Press.

Further Education Unit Publications, FEU Information Section, 2, Orange Street, London WC2H 7WE.

House of Commons Education, Science and Arts Committee, Third Report (1987) *Special Educational Needs: Implementation of the Education Act (1981)*, London, HMSO.

Ministry of Education Pamphlet No. 5 (1946) *Special Educational Treatment*, London, HMSO.

STOWELL, R. (1987) *Catching Up*, London, National Bureau for Handicapped Students.

Index